BUSINESS AND LEGAL 500 LETTER TEMPLATES

A BOOK FOR BUSY PROFESSIONALS

A. M. FRITH

Copyright © 2019 A. M. FRITH

All rights reserved. No part of this publication may be reproduced, distributed, or transmitted in any form or by any means, including photocopying, recording, or other electronic or mechanical methods, without the prior written permission of the publisher, except in the case of brief quotations embodied in critical reviews and certain other noncommercial uses permitted by copyright law. For permission requests, write to the publisher.

BUSINESS AND LEGAL 500 LETTER TEMPLATES

DRAFTING MADE EASY

**HARVARD BUSINESS
CAMBRIDGE ISSUE**

A BOOK FOR BUSY PROFESSIONALS

PUBLISHED IN ASSOCIATION WITH THE COUNSEL OF
DIRECTORS AND SOLICITORS

A. M. FRITH

BUSINESS AND LEGAL 500 LETTER TEMPLATES

A BOOK FOR BUSSY PROFESSIONALS

PUBLISHED IN ASSOCIATION WITH THE COUNSEL OF DIRECTORS AND SOLICITORS

**BUSINESS & LEGAL
500 LETTER TEMPLATES**

An essential guide for professionals

A. M. FRITH

Published
2020
© A M. FRITH 2020
Conditions of sale

All rights reserved. No part of this publication may be reproduced, stored in a retrieval system or transmitted, in any form or by any means, electronic a retrieval system or transmitted, in any form or by any means, electronic, of the publisher, except the individual LETTER.

THE VIEWS OF THE AUTHOR DO NOT REPRESENT THOSE OF THE COUNCIL OF THE DIRECTORS OR SOLICITORS.

ALL NAMES IN THIS BOOK ARE FICTITIOUS. ANY RESEMBLANCE TO THE NAME OF ANY EXISTING PERSON, BUSINESS OR COMPANY IS PURELY BY CHANCE' AND IS QUITE UNINTENTIONAL.

EXCLUSION OF LIABILITY AND DISCLAIMER

Whilst every effort has been made to ensure that this book provides and expert guidance in draft templates, it is impossible to predict all the circumstances in which it may be used. Accordingly, the publisher, authors and retailer shall not be liable to any person or entity with respect to any loss or damage caused or alleged to be caused directly or I indirectly by the information or any mistake contained in this BUSINESS & LEGAL 500 LETTER TEMPLATES publication.

BUSINESS & LEGAL 500 LETTER TEMPLATES

Designed by Ana Maria Sava
in England, Sydney Street, Chelsea,
South Kensington, London, SW36PS

Table of Contents

Preface 1

About The Author 2

An Introduction 3

To Business And Legal Letter Writing 3

Chapter 1: Business Letter Templates 14

    General Format Business Letter 14

        To Request Information Or Routine 17

        Follow Up Letter 18

        To Demand Action 19

        Apologizing In Difficult Times 20

        Communicating A Decrease In Earnings 21

        Layoffs (Personal Version) 22

        Layoffs (Less Personal) 24

        Merger 25

        Invitations And Community Actions 27

        To Provide Information Or Describe An Event 28

        To Acknowledge Information Or An Event 29

        To Convey Bad News Or Decline A Request 30

        Memorandum | Memo 31

        Complaint Replay 33

        Email Communication Message 34

        Email 36

A Slightly More Formal Email 37

E-Mail Following A Meeting 38

E-Mail Where Tone Is Important 39

Email Potentially Large Business Enquiry And Reply 40

Requests For Advice Enquiry And Reply 41

General Enquiry Recommendation Enquiries And Replies 42

An Enquiry With Numbered Points... 44

Request For Goods On Approval 46

Visits By Representative... 49

Supplier's Offer Of Visit... 50

Request For Concessions X 6 51

Quotations, Estimates Tenders.. 55

Inquiry And Requests For Information X 13.......................... 60

Replies To Letter Of Inquiry X12 66

Follow-Up Letter X5 73

Letter Of Complaint X8 76

Responding To Letter Of Complaint X8 81

Letter Of Apology X3 86

Letter Of Congratulation X5.. 88

Letter Of Appreciation X5 93

Thank-You Letter X2 95

Announcing The Acquisition Of A New Distribution Company X8 97

Informal And Formal Invitations X13 105

Asking For Or Making An Appointment X8........................ 114

 Letter Requesting, Acknowledging, Or Refusing Donations X6 117

 Reservations Of Meeting Room And Other X2 121

 Dealing With Club Membership X8 123

 Business Offer And Requests X10 131

 Placing And Acknowledging Orders X13 139

 Urgent Collection Payment Reminder X11 151

Letter For Banking And Credit Concerns Letter 159

 Requesting A Credit Report 160

  Adding Or Removing Someone From A Credit Account 161

  Requesting Information On Available Services 162

  Requesting Status Of A Loan Application 163

  Instructing That An Overpayment Be Applied To A Mortgage Principal 164

  Requesting Investigation Of A Possible Bank Error 165

  Disputing Denial Of A Loan Or Credit Card 166

  Disputing Fee Increase Or New Fee 167

  Disputing A Charge 168

  Requesting A Credit Card Limit Increase 169

  Negotiating A Payment Schedule With A Creditor 170

  Demanding Action 171

  Closing An Account 172

  Recognizing Good Service 173

  Closing A Long-Standing Account 174

Medical And Insurance Concerns Letter 175

Authorizing Release Of Medical Records 176

Requesting Medical Information For An Employer 177

Requesting Information On A Pending Claim 178

Requesting A Change In Beneficiary...................................... 179

Requesting Information About A Disease 180

Disputing A Straightforward Billing Error 181

Disputing A Less-Than-Straightforward Billing Error 182

Disputing Denial On Insurance Coverage Or A Claim......... 183

Arranging For Monthly Payments 184

Complaining About Medical Services Or Staff..................... 185

Terminating Poor Medical Care.. 186

Showing Appreciation For Good Care Or Service 187

Terminating A Long-Standing Healthcare Relationship 188

Consumer Letter Samples 189

Making A Reservation 191

Requesting Information From A Merchant......................... 192

Requesting Information On A Rent Increase Or Maintenance Problem 193

Cancelling An Order For Merchandise Or Service 194

Returning Merchandise 195

Requesting Return Of A Deposit 196

Requesting Repair Or Replacement (Under Warranty)......... 197

Requesting Repair Or Replacement (No Longer Under Warranty) 198

Requesting A Refund... 199

Informing Utility Of A Billing Error 200

Breaking A Service Contract 201

Breaking A Lease; Request Security Deposit Return 202

Another Alternative To Complaining: Requesting Help 203

Informing Of Hazardous Product 205

If Previous Requests Fail 206

Declaring Your Intention To Go To A Third Party.............. 207

Reporting To A Third Party 208

Recognizing Good Service... 209

Ending A Long-Standing Business Relationship 210

Requesting Information On Placing A Classified Ad 211

Requesting A Correction Or Retraction............................. 212

Voicing An Opinion 213

Demanding A Correction Or Retraction 214

Announce The Event... 216

Thanking A Reporter For Fair Coverage............................ 217

Cancelling A Long-Held Subscription 218

Sales Reply 219

Sales Enquiry 220

Response To Sales Enquiry 221

Template For A Cold E-Mail 222

Professional Email For Salary Negotiation 223

Salary Negotiation 224

Letter Of Reference/Reference 225

Sales Orders And Their Fulfilment 226

Placing Orders 228

Confirmation Of Telephone Order 229

Tabulated Order 230

Order Based On Quotation 231

Covering Letter With Order Form 232

Formal Acknowledgement Of Routine Order (By Email Communication) 233

Acknowledgement Of A First Order 234

Acknowledgement Of Order Pointing Out Delayed Delivery 235

Acknowledgement Of A First Order 236

Acknowledgement Of Order Pointing Out Delayed Delivery 237

Supplier Refuses Price Reduction 238

Supplier Rejects Buyer's Delivery Terms 239

Refuses To Extend Credit 240

Supplier Sends A Substitute Article 241

Supplier Makes A Counter-Offer 242

Request For Forwarding Instructions 243

Advice Of Goods Ready For Despatch 244

Notification Of Goods Despatched 245

Report Of Damage In Transit 246

Report Of Non-Delivery Of Goods 247

Complaint To Carrier Concerning Non-Delivery 248

Covering Letter With Invoice 249

Supplier Sends Direct Debit Note 250

Buyer Requests Credit 251

Supplier Refuses Request For Credit Note 253
Supplier Reports Underpaid 255
Buyer Reports Errors In Statement 257
Customer Requests Time To Pay (Granted) 258
Customer Requests Time To Pay (Not Granted) 260
Supplier Questions Partial Payment 262
Supplier Asks Customer To Select Terms Of Payment 263
Late Payments Explains Inability To Pay 264
Customer Explains Late Payment 265
Personalised Collection Letter 266
Specimen Final Collection Letter 269
Customer Requests Open-Account Terms 270
Customer Requests Credit Extension Due To Bankruptcy 272
Supplier Requests References 273
Supplier Asks For Completion Of Credit Application Form . 274
Customer Supplies A Banker's Reference 275

Reports And Proposals 276

"Brevity" Memo To The War Cabinet From Sir Winston Churchill 277
Memorandum 279
Report 281
A Longer Proposal 284
Sale Letter Appeal To Economy 289
Sale Appeal To Economy 291
Sales Appeal To Efficiency 293

Sales Appeal To Security 294
Sales Appeal To Comfort 295
Sales Appeal To Leisure 296
Appeal To Sympathy 297
Appeal To Comfort 298
Sales Appeal To Heat 299
Offer To A Newly Established Trader 301
To A Regular Customer 302
Offer To New Homeowners 303
Offer Of A Demonstration 304
Press Release Announcing New Hotel Wing 305
Article In Staff Newsletter 307
Announcing Dinner And Dance 308
Manufacturer's Confirmation Of Agency Terms 309

Announcing Changes In Business 311

Change Of Company Name 312
Opening Of A New Store 313
Expansion Of Existing Business 314
Opening Of A New Business 315
Establishment Of A New Branch 316
Removal To New Premises 317
Reorganisation Of A Store's Departments 318
Death Of A Colleague 319
Retirement Of A Partner 320
Appointment Of A New Partner 321

Conversion Of Partnership To Private Company 322

Dismissal Of Firm's Representative 323

Appointment Of New Representative 324

Announcement About New Working 325

Letter Regarding Outstanding Holiday Entitlement 326

Chapter 2: Legal Letter 327

Legal Templates Letter 333

Legal Research Letter 338

Share Purchase Agreement Sample Advise 342

Dispute Advice Sample 345

Consumer Sale Of Goods Certificate Of Guarantee 349

Unsolicited Goods 350

Goods Sent On Approval 351

Confirming Contract Ended 352

Claim Payment For Work Done Under Contract And For Extra Work Requested 353

Claiming For Work Done Over And Above The Contract ... 354

Claiming To Have Completed The Contract 355

Ending A Contra Which Has Been Frustrated 356

Accepting A Breach Of Contract As Repudiation 357

Giving Notice To End A Contract 358

Contract Entered Into Under A Mistake Of Fact And Requesting Return Of Moneys Paid 359

Request For Repayment 360

Recording A Rectification Of A Mistake 361

Comfort Letter	362
Request For Time	363
Referring To Lapse Of An Offer	364
An Offer Not Accepted In Time	365
Deferred Acceptance	366
Accepting Subject To Conditions	367
Accepting Subject To Conditions	368
Correcting A Quotation	369
Accepting An Offer	370
Following An Acknowledgement Of Order	371
An Offer	372
An Option To Purchase	373
Contractual Letter Of Offer To Buy Property	375
Negotiating To Sell Property	376
Negotiating A Contract	377
Giving A Trade Reference	379
Declining To Give A Reference	380
Reference For An Employee	381
Claiming Payment For A Secret Profit	382
Holding Agent Liable As Principal	383
To Undisclosed Principal	384
Claiming Commission	385
Recording Agency	386
Agent Claiming Indemnity	387
Warning Agent That He Is Exceeding His Authority	388

Notifying A Customer That An Agent Has Exceeded His Authority 389

Agent Confirming Sale 390

Appointing A Sales Agent 391

Answering A Claim For An Alleged Debt 392

Making An Offer Of Payment 393

Statutory Demand For Debt From An Individual 394

To A Company Making Statutory Demand For A Debt....... 395

Before Action Is Brought 396

Stopping Further Work 397

Retaining Goods For Non-Payment 398

Second Application For Debt.. 399

Reminder Of Outstanding Account 400

Claiming Damages For Failure To Take Delivery 401

Claiming Liquidated Damages 402

Claim For Damages... 403

Claim For Damages... 404

Agreeing To Arbitrate.. 405

Rejecting A Claim 406

Settling A Claim 'Without Prejudice"................................... 407

Answering A Claim In A Conciliatory Manner 408

A Claim In A Conciliatory Manner 409

Complaining Of Breach And Keeping Open All Rights......... 410

To Insurers Notifying A Claim 411

Reserving Title On A Sale... 412

Making Interest Payable	413
Suspending Services	414
Notifying Delivery Of Service	415
Accepting Goods And Notifying Claim For Damages	416
Where Carrier Left T Goods	417
Rejecting Goods Because Of Late Delivery	418
Rejection Of Goods Reply To Claim By Liquidator	419
To Receiver Claiming Goods	420
Complaining Of A Slander Of Goods	421
Complaining Of A Passing Off	422
Complaining Of An Induced Breach Of Contract	423
To Ex-Employee In Breach Of Contract Against Competition	424
An Employee Leaving For Pregnancy	425
To The Court Notifying Ending Of Employment	426
To Employees Following Take Over	427
Appointing An Independent Contractor	428
Giving Discharge From A Guarantee	431
Claiming Discharge By Operation Of Law	432
Release Of A Guarantee	433
Request Payment Made Under A Guarantee	434
Agreeing To Give A Guarantee	435
Protective Form Of Guarantee	437
Letter Of Guarantee	438
Declining To Give A Trade Reference	439

Making A Claim Under An Insurance Policy 440
Auditors Appointment 441
To Solicitors Asking For A Quotation 442
To Solicitors Making A Complaint 443
Authorizing A Bank To Disclose Information 444
To A Bank Following Agreement For A Facility 445
Creating A Service Tenancy 446
Requesting Permission To Change Use 447
Requesting Permission To Carry Out Improvements 449
Real-Estate Opening Negotiations For A New Lease 450

Legal Documents Templates 451

Legal Research Letter 453
Share Purchase Agreement Sample Advise 457
Draft Advice Dispute 460
Letter Before Claim 464
Draft Particulars Of Claim 468
Draft Defence From 472
Draft Email Instruction 475
Points To Note Advise On Expert 478
Attendance Note 480
Real Estate Contract Purchase Propriety 482
Bank Bonds Investment Draft Advise 491
Experts' Without Prejudice Meeting Statement 494
Claimant's Part 36 Offer Letter 497
Defendant's Brief To Counsel 498

Meeting Documentation Minutes Of A Meeting Of The Board Of Directors.. 504

Notice Of The General Meeting 511

Consent Of The Short Notice.. 513

Procedure For Conversion Of A Shelf Company On Full Notice (15 Days).. 514

Agreement For The Sale Of Goods 520

Drafting A Will... 521

Draft A Valid Will... 522

Sample Codicil Or The Last Will And Testament................ 526

Company Situation Advise Letter... 529

Memorandum Purchase Plant 534

Dispute Letter Answer... 545

Reply's To Client Share Purchase Agreement....................... 549

Banking And Finance 552

Legal Research Landlord Tenant Dispute Memorandum...... 558

Chapter 3: Social Letter 561

Event Invitation Social Letter... 563

Event Invitation 564

Making Other Straightforward Requests.............................. 565

Making Other Straightforward Requests.............................. 566

Making Not-So-Straightforward Requests 567

Making Not-So-Straightforward Requests 568

An Alternative To Complaining: Requesting Information 569

Announcing A Graduation... 570

Announcing A Move	571
Announcing An Engagement	572
Announcing A Marriage	573
Announcing A Birth	574
Announcing An Adoption	575
Announcing A Divorce	576
Sending Holiday Greetings	577
Accepting An Invitation	579
Accepting An Invitation	580
Congratulating On A Graduation	581
Congratulating On A Graduation	582
Congratulating On A Promotion, Award, Or Other Achievement	583
Congratulating On A Promotion, Award, Or Other Achievement	584
Congratulating On An Engagement Or A Marriage	585
Congratulating On An Engagement Or A Marriage	586
Thanking For A Gift Or Other Kindness	587
Thanking For A Gift Or Other Kindness	588
Sending Get-Well Wishes For An Illness Or Accident	589
Sending Get-Well Wishes For An Illness Or Accident	590
Declining An Invitation	591
Declining An Invitation	592
Delivering Bad News With Apology	593
Event Conference Invitation	594

Requesting Information 596
Soliciting Participation In An Activity 597
Persuading Someone To Accept A Leadership Position 598
Confirming Others' Participation In An Activity 600
Agreeing To Participate In An Activity 601
Refusing A Request To Serve Or Contribute 602
Thanking Others For Their Contributions Or Time 603
Acknowledging A Refusal To Serve Or Contribute 604
Refusing A Leadership Role 605
Resigning A Leadership Role.. 606
Personal Greeting 607
Explaining Delayed Reply... 608
A Visitor From Abroad 609
Apology For Poor Service... 610
Apology For Cancelling An Appointment........................... 611
Regretting An Oversight 612
Conveying Unwelcome News 613
Letter Of Thanks... 614
Formal Letter Of Congratulation On A Promotion............. 615

Perfect Lines, To Establish Mission 618
Professional English Writing 623
Appendix.. 631
Legal Implications Of Letter 633

PREFACE

Business is taken through many of the problems that it may face. From the first exchange of LETTER, to sales and reporting, to when a business, shareholder purchases into the company, through the acquisition of property, the setting up of the conditions of sale and the making of contracts, to the problems of employment and dealing with agents and the various professionals (directors, bankers, solicitors, accountants) that will be involved in the company's activities.

BUSINESS AND LEGAL 500 LETTER TEMPLATES publication it is designed to help you drafting the subject matter covered. If legal advice or other expert assistance is required, the services of a competent professional should be sought.

As with any business and legal matter, common sense should determine whether you need the of a banker or solicitor rather than relying on the information and forms in this BUSINESS AND LEGAL 500 LETTER TEMPLATES book.

ABOUT THE AUTHOR

A. M. Frith the author of a multitude of books. Qualified in Business and later in Law from Cambridge and London with a GDL, LLM and Solicitor Vocational Course specialised in Real Estate, Merges and Acquisitions, Finance and Capital Markets. Also holds a BA (Hons) Business Studies.

Over time held positions as Director of various ventures, Real Estate Investor, Marketing Manager, EA to CEO and Directors, Legal Secretary to Solicitors and Law Society President. Legal CAE in PWC Corporation, FTSE 100 Division focused on Risk and Client Finance in Tax, Compliance and Legal. Legal Aid volunteer to London Court and Charities in Social Poverty Alleviation. Devotes time to Business Management as the founder of various businesses.

A. M. FRITH

AN INTRODUCTION TO BUSINESS AND LEGAL LETTER WRITING

It seems we are writing more than ever. With hundreds of template will help you send out professional LETTER. BUSINESS AND LEGAL 500 LETTER TEMPLATES book will help you write perfect LETTER, save time and embracement. We figure that if you're taking the time to pull a letter together (or just to right ready-made letter), you want it to be effective. E-mail has promised us a future of minimum effort and maximum communication. Effective communication gives a professional impression of you and of your organisation. Effective communication helps to get things done.

Whether you are an administrative assistant or a senior this book will help you to get message across and make your best impression in any situation. Beyond that, if writing is a task you find challenging or don't enjoy, you picked the right book. Many, if not most, of the LETTER that a business professional has to write are routine commercial LETTER or maybe, social LETTER of greeting. The LETTER that give rise to difficulty are those that create some form of legal liability or are written with one eye on the possibility of trouble ahead. Writing a letter that may possibly end up by being read in front of a judge or public requires careful thought and a good deal of expert knowledge. When professionals writes such LETTER will have in the front of their minds the legal consequences of what she is saying. She will use words and expressions that knows will be familiar to the audience and they may well have in their mind a case or an Act of Parliament from which they can make quotations, just as the quote from Shakespeare or other poet.

When people read a letter from a professional or organisation they frequently complain that it is too complicated, or that it uses language that they do not understand. The first and overriding rule is not to use any expression u are 100 per cent sure that you understand its meaning. Be especially careful to avoid legalisms and jargons.

Do not think that you can write anything like simply by putting 'Without prejudice' on the top of your letter, or that the words 'Private and confidential' automatically mean what they say. They do not. Even those businesses that have their own legal departments, or have a solicitor on the staff, cannot expect them to see everything. The template LETTER that are set out here are an attempt to suggest the way in which professionals would draft the letter.

Do bear this in mind. Although this is a book about LETTER, a word must be said about telephone convert scenarios. The point is made that in English law there are very few contracts that need to be in writing. You can commit yourself to a legal obligation just as effectively by a telephone call as you can in one of those beautiful legal documents all sewn up in green silk with heavy seals at the end. The trouble is that both parties to the telephone call may think that they agreed different things. Half of the conversation was taken up by greetings and commentary on the Test Match or the weather. When it comes to the real business of the call, two or three years later neither will have a very clear memory. Both honestly believe that her is the true memory of what was said and will be convinced that the other is trying to cheat.

A wise businessperson records their telephone calls with a confirming letter. As well as writing a letter, even wiser businesswoman keeps his telephone pad beside him when he phones and he notes down immediately what has been said. Lawyers always do this. They call them 'attendance notes'. Those notes do more than as a memory, they are evidence that can be referred to if there is any dispute in court. So, be careful with your telephone calls and try to see that one way or another, what was said is recorded in writing. That way, if you have to prove that it is not your memory that was at fault, you have something to help you.

In the pages that follow are to be found hundreds of specimen LETTER dealing with a comprehensive range of transactions of the kind handled in business every day. They are represented, not as models to be copied, for no two business situations are ever quite alike, but rather as examples written in the modern English style to illustrate the accepted principles of good business writing. Every business letter is written to a purpose; each has its own special aim, and one of the features of this book is its use of explanation to show how the various LETTER set out to achieve their aims.

The speed of sound is old hat today. People want speed of thought and to write effectively is perhaps the most demanding work we do. Writing imagination, creativity, organisation, careful planning and many other skills if a message is to be effective and get results. In today's fast-paced business world, there should be no room for yesterday's old-fashioned, long-winded jargon. Today's business language should be proactive, stimulating, interesting, and most of all it should reflect your personality. Instead of using boring clichés that have been around for decades, the key is to write in a natural style, as if you were having a conversation. The golden rule of all communications is mentioned regularly throughout Model Business LETTER, E-mails and Other Business formats.

Rules to Professional Writing
Business and Legal

If I could write a note of advice about emails and business communication to the 22 years old EA, Director or even to 30 years old Professional Ana, I would probably send her this checklist. I just wish someone had told me these simple rules.

1. Forget your ego. Never write with the objective of impressing someone, even if that someone is you! Sometimes we write and then re-read what we have written a few times, then we give ourselves a mental round of applause before sending it. The problem is, our priority wasn't communication in this scenario, it was to feed our ego. Trying to impress people with long over-complicated sentences and words has the opposite effect. Always keep clear communication and context in mind in every exchange.

2. Focus and aim to explain difficult concepts or problems in a simple understanding way. This shows intelligence, because it means you have digested the concepts and are skilful enough to explain them. When you make concepts sound more complicated than they are, it gives people the impression that you don't understand, because you probably don't.

3. If it's not relevant to the situation or the decision being made, don't mention it, it will clutter your communication and cause confusion.

4. When you need to write important or sensitive emails, stick to the facts. Your emotions or opinions are not important or relevant in most .

5. Context always remember that the same email can have a different effect depending on the context it's sent in. Emails are not separate things outside of real Life. As you don't have the benefit of facial expressions and body language, they ate very susceptible to the state of mind of the reader, If your reader is in a bad mood, they may interpret your message differently. Be aware of this when you write.

6. Use emails as a way to keep written records of your meetings and important communications with colleagues. This is particularly important in difficult situations or conflicts. Don't fall for the age-old trick of "oh let's talk about it on the phone, or face to face, there's no need to email about this." When there is potential conflict speak to the person face-to-face or on the phone after you have outlined everything in writing. This would save loads of hassle from others and management.

7. Tone of voice is everything! It can make an innocent email sound malicious and vice-versa, Remember this always.

8. If an email annoys you, don't reply immediately! Re-read it your head has cleared up. Try not to introduce your own tone of 'voice as you read it.

9. Unless you know someone relatively well, avoid contractions like we're; use we are in formal writing.

10. Use correct spellings.

11. Use formal English words, such as 'discuss' rather than 'chat if you're writing a format document or if you wish to distance yourself from the person, '

12. Never ever use 'slang' spellings like 'going to', even if you we're; use we are in formal writing.

13. Use correct punctuation: avoid very long sentences absolutely needed.

14. Use your own words, or give a dear reference to the source if appropriate.

15. Connect your ideas clearly (e.g. Finally/In conclusion/However)

16. Use correct grammar that makes your meaning clear.

17. Attractive and consistent presentation of your business documents is vital if they are to make a good impression.

18. The fully blocked layout is now the most widely used method of display for all business documents. This style is thought to have a business like appearance. This layout reduces typing time as there are no indentations for new paragraphs or the closing sections.

19. Some companies have printed continuation sheets that are used for second or subsequent pages of business LETTER. Such printed continuation sheets usually show just the company's name and logo. If printed continuation sheets are not available,

the second or subsequent page should be typed on plain paper of a similar quality to that of the letterhead.

20. The date should always be shown in full. In the UK it is usual to show the date in the order day/month/year. No commas are used. Example 10 March 2025 In some other countries the date is typed in the order month/day/year, often with a comma after the month.

21. Inside address the name and address of the recipient should be typed on separate lines a would appear on an envelope. Care should be taken to address the recipient exactly as they sign their LETTER. For example, a person signing as 'Mike Johns' should be addressed as such in the inside address, preceded with the courtesy title 'Mr'. To address him as 'Mr D Johns' would not be appropriate. Again note that the appropriate courtesy title (Mr/Mrs/Miss/Ms) should always be shown: Example AIRMAIL Mr Mike Allen Moon Press Inc 24 South Bank Sydney Australia M4J 7LK .

22. Special markings: If a letter is confidential it is usual to include this as part of the inside one clear line space above it. This may be typed in upper case or in initial capitals with underscore. Example CONFIDENTIAL name and address or FOR THE ATTENTION OF MR LISA TAYLER, SALES MANAGER

23. Salutation , If the recipient's name has been used in the inside address, it is personal salutation. Example Dear Mr Johnson, Dear Frith,   Dear Miss Smith, Dear Lisa . If your letter is

addressed to a head of department or the head of organisation whose name is not known, then it would be more appropriate use a salutation as shown here. Example Dear Sir or Madam

24. Name of sender and designation after the complimentary close 4 or 5 clear spaces should be left so that the letter can be signed. The name of the sender should then be inserted in whatever style is preferred – upper case, or initial capitals only. The sender's designation or department should be shown directly beneath his/her name. In these examples note that the title 'Mr' is never shown when the writer is male. However, it is usual to add a courtesy title for a female; this is shown in brackets after her name.

25. Enclosures, There are many different methods of indicating that an enclosure is being sent along with a letter's coloured 'enclosure' sticker usually in the bottom left-hand corner of the letter , Type 'Enc' or 'Encs' at the foot of the letter, leaving one clear line after the sender's designation. This is the most common form of indicating enclosures. Type three dots in the left-hand margin on the line where the enclosure is mentioned in the body of the letter. Example, Yours sincerely LISA FRITH (Mrs) Marketing Director Enc .

26. Copies, When a copy of a letter is to be sent to a third party (usually someone in sender's organisation) this may be indicated by typing 'cc' (copy circulated or courtesy copy) or 'Copy' followed by the name and designation of the recipient. If there are two or more copy recipients, it is usual to show these in

alphabetical order. Copy Perry Moon, General Manager Ana Yong, Company Secretary Christina Sava, Accountant. If the writer does not wish the recipient of the letter to know that a third person is receiving a copy of the letter, then 'bcc' (blind courtesy copy)is used. This should not be shown on the top of the letter, only on the file copy and bcc copy. Example, bcc Mr Larisa Clark, Chief Executive. (TIP) Don't send a cc to everyone you know –just send them to people who need to know.

27. OPEN PUNCTUATION, Open punctuation is commonly used with fully blocked layout. Only punctuation marks that are essential to ensure good grammatical sense are included. Within the main body of the message itself. AU other commas and full stops are omitted, especially in the presentational aspects like the date, inside address, year etc. Date 21 September 2025 10 July 2024 and NOT 25th September or 2022 July 14[th]2034

28. Names and addresses Mr G P Ashe no full stops Ashe Publications Pte Ltd no commas at the end of lines.

29. A memo is a written message from one person to another (or within the same organisation. Memos or memorandum serve a several purposes: to provide information to request information to inform of actions, decisions to request actions, decisions. Some companies have pre-printed forms for internal memos but very templates are saved on word processing systems. The typist then only bas to insert the relevant details alongside the given headings.

30. Format to Professional looking Memo/Letter. See examples to inside.

31. Compose CLEAR communications.

    1. Leave no doubt in your reader's mind.

    2. Logical Structure your messages logically. Start with an introduction, develop your logically in the central section, and come to a natural conclusion in which you state the action you need from the reader. Finish an appropriate one-liner.

    3. Empathetic Put yourself in your reader's place and ask yourself how t reader will feel when he/she reads your message. If anything is unclear, or if anything is worded badly, then change it before you send it.

    4. Accurate Make sure all the relevant details are included – times, dates, names, facts and figures.

    5. Right proofread carefully (not just spell check!) to make sure every thing is 100% right before you send the message. One error is too many.

    32. WORKING WITH E-MAIL What you put in your subject line can often mean the difference between whether your message is read right now, today, tomorrow, next week or never! The Internet has made it possible tor us to communicate with people from all over the work. The only way those people can form an opinion of us is by looking at

the way we write. Your credibility could be ruined with one swift check of the 'send' button.

33. Enquiries and replays, A clear style projects an efficient image, so choose your words carefully.

USEFUL EXPRESSIONS REQUESTS:

1. We are interested in ... as advertised recently in ..
2. We have received an enquiry for your ..
3. I was interested to see your advertisement for ...
4. I understand you are manufacturers of (dealers in) ... and should like to receive your current collection. When replying please also include delivery details.
5. Please also state whether you can supply the goods from stock as we need them urgently
6. If you can supply suitable goods, we may place regular orders for large quantities.
7. Thank you for your letter of ... As requested we enclose ...
8. I was pleased to learn ,.. that you are interested in our
9. Thank you for your enquiry dated ... regarding ...
10. We look forward to receiving a trial order from you soon.
11. We shall be pleased to send you any further information you may need.
12. Any orders you place with us will have our prompt attention.
13. Please let me know if you need any further details.

CHAPTER 1

BUSINESS LETTER TEMPLATES

General Format Business Letter

1. To request information or routine

2. Follow up LETTER

3. To demand action

4. Apologizing in Difficult Times

5. Communicating a Decrease in Earnings

6. Layoffs (Personal Version)

7. Layoffs (Less Personal)

8. Merger

9. Invitations and Community Actions

10. To acknowledge information or an event

11. To convey bad news or decline a request

12. Memorandum

13. Complaint Replay

14. Email communication Message

15. Email

16. A slightly more formal email

17. E-mail following a meeting

18. E-mail where tone is important

19. Email Potentially large business Enquiry and Reply

20. Requests for advice Enquiry and Reply

21. General enquiries and reply's

22. An enquiry with numbered points

23. Request for goods on approval

24. Visits by representative

25. Request for concessions x 6

26. Quotations, estimates tenders

27. Inquiry and Requests for Information x 13

28. Replies to LETTER of Inquiry x12

29. Follow-up LETTER x5

30. LETTER of Complaint x8

31. Responding to LETTER of Complaint x8

32. LETTER of Apology x3

33. LETTER of Congratulation x5

34. LETTER of Appreciation x5

35. Thank-You LETTER x2

36. Letter announcing the acquisition of a new distribution company x8

37. Informal and formal invitations x13

38. Asking for or Making an Appointment x8

39. LETTER Requesting, Acknowledging, or Refusing Donations x6

40. Reservations of Meeting Room and Other x2

41. LETTER Dealing with Club Membership x8

42. Business offer and requests x10

43. Placing and acknowledging orders x13

44. Cancelling an Order

45. Collection payment reminders x12

46. Urgent collection payment Reminder x11

Template 1

To Request Information Or Routine

Dear

Your Master Gardener Software, featured in this past Sunday's Star newspaper, really interests mc. Could you please send me information about how I can get involved?

The article explained the cost for classes; I now need more information on where and when classes are being held, whether I can jump into a series already in progress, and what happens if I must miss a class or two. (Must I pass a test at the end of a series?)

Please send me any information you feel I would find valuable, by phone or email communication information if is easier for you.

Thank you for your time, and I look forward to receiving more information on the Master Gardener Software!

Sincerely yours

Template 2

Follow Up Letter

Dear

As we have not heard from you since we sent you our collection of filing we wonder whether you require further information before deciding to place an order.

The modem system of lateral filing has important space-saving advantages wherever economy of space is important. However if space is not one of your problems, our flat-top suspended system may suit you better. The neat and tidy appearance it gives to the filing drawers and the ease and speed with which files are located are just two of its features which many users find attractive.

Would you like us to send our representative to call and discuss your needs with Merry Robinson has advised on equipment for many large, modern offices and would be able to recommend the system most suited to your own There would of course be no obligation of any kind. Perhaps you would prefer to pay a visit to our showroom and see for yourself how the different filing systems work.

You may be sure that whichever of these opportunities you decide to accept, you would receive personal attention and the best possible advice.

If you have any further questions please call me 076 989889.

Yours Sincerely

Template 3

To Demand Action

Dear

I am concerned that I have not received a response to either my (dated May 3, 2004) or telephone calls (June 6, 15, and 18) watch I sent back to you for further repair. I would greatly prompt attention to this situation.

My watch was losing time just two months after its repair in your shop in early March. On May 3, I sent the watch back to you to have the resolved. I expected the repair to be done within just a few weeks; nearly two months have passed, and I now must insist on my watch back from you as soon as possible.

In fact, if I don't receive either my watch or a telephone call from you explaining the delay by July 10, I will be forced to take my concern to the management of Northbrook Mall and the local Better Business Bureau.

Thank you, and I look forward to receiving either your call or my repaired watch no later than July 10.

Sincerely

Template 4

Apologizing In Difficult Times

INTEROFFICE MEMORANDUM

Dear

The past several days certainly have been challenging for all of us and I understand that getting the contracts signed within the time-frame provided has not been possible.

I appreciate your efforts in getting them signed when feasible.

Please keep me informed on the progress you are making.

Thank you for your good efforts.

Regards

Template 5

Communicating A Decrease In Earnings

Dear all

This has been a particularly challenging year. We have lost a number of strong accounts to competitors and [endured the flooding in our warehouse in March]. As a result of all this, earnings have dropped by %.

Despite being a serious drop in performance, with everyone's help And support, it can definitely be turned around next year. {As you know, we implemented a hiring freeze in October. Which we will continue through at least the first quarter. In addition, we have decided we have no choice but to forgo year-end bonuses

These steps will enable us to allocate more resources to and customer service, in order to increase the number of new If we attract new customers and retain long-time customer relationship, we will see a rise in earnings in the coming months.

Yours truly

Template 6

Layoffs (Personal Version)

INTEROFFICE MEMO

Dear

As you all know, our company is currently engaged in a struggle for survival. Lower than expected sales in several of our main product lines have damaged our pursuit of new markets with greater potential. Knowing that customers in [Switzerland and Austria] need our products but that we are unable to reach them is frustrating and discouraging.

Even more discouraging is the knowledge that the only way to fully engage in out fight for survival, is to drastically cut costs as well as reallocate and refocus our limited resources. We simply cannot take every skilled and experienced employee with us on this journey toward a turnaround. As much as we dislike having to give up some of our most valued members of staff, 8 positions, including your position, have been eliminated this week.

We will do everything our limited resources permit to make this layoff more bearable. You will receive [eight months' severance pay in addition to any holiday pay you are entitled to. William Strunk Jr.j, assistant HR director, will be available to you for career counselling. He also has a wealth of information on training courses, placement agencies, and other resources.

If our turnaround plans are on target, there may be several in [procurement management in nine to twelve months.] . I would like to assure you that whenever there are any suitable vacancies, your mane will be at the top of our list. We would like to be able to recall all laid off employees within a year if everything goes as planned.

Template 7

Layoffs (Less Personal)

INTEROFFICE MEMO

To

FROM

DATE

SUBJECT

The market has changed a lot over the last ten years or s, and our strategy as a business must adapt to these changes. Your main product used to be [TV remotes]. Of course, [TV components have comprised 85] percent of our business for the past [five years now]. At the last board meeting, our directors voted to close our [assembly line] and focus all our resources on our growing [components service plant.]

The [assembly line] will close on [April 12m 1   Each of the [22]members of staff will receive a generous severance package, including counselling, twelve months' salary, and added benefits. Any employees desiring to transfer here to [our growing service plant} will be considered for openings as they occur.

Department heads who expect to have position openings in the next eight to ten months may send job descriptions to the human resources department to match with potential candidates.

Template 8

Merger

INTEROFFICE MEMORANDUM

TO

DATE

Blink and the world of financial institutions has changed radically irrevocably. During the past decade we have witnessed d tremendous changes, with insurance companies and other interests increasing their financial services. Competition for customers has grown fierce. To ensure our success and survival, our board has decided to merge this corporation with [Statewise Savings Bank].

The merged bank will retain our current [COMPANY] name. The merger will be a pooling of interest, with each of our receiving [7.62 shares of Statewide common stock] for each share for each share they own in [COMPANY] , regulatory approval and is expected to be finalized in November.

[Statewide] provides access to additional markets, especially in the North where our market share is small. It also offers the latest in technological and support services, including one of the best data processing centers in the region.

Since we operate in some of the same cities where [Statewide] has branch offices-and .in some cases on the same street-[between 11 and

15 branch 15 branch offices eventually will close. We do not expect any layoffs due to these closings. Employees will be transferred to other positions become available.

In fact, the merger will enable us to grow further and faster than either of the two individual corporations could do on their own.

Template 9

Invitations And Community Actions

Dear all,

This year, the annual Digi-World Conference will be held November 2nd -5th. The conference provides excellent information on industry trends, new financial products, and professional development opportunities. (Please find the current agenda attached to this this message.)

If you are interested in attending all or part of the Software, please reply to this email directly. I will coordinate our schedule at the conference and do my best to ensure that any employee who wants to participate can do so, even if only for a half day.

The conference will be held on the third floor of the RM Hotel, in the conference centre. Gary More, Smith and Lisa will organize several car pools.

Regards

Template 10

To Provide Information Or Describe An Event

Dear

In our conversation last week, you asked me to send you information about Bobby's performance at his last school. Here is that information.

Bobby is an outstanding student academically. Here are his grade point averages for (out of a possible 4.0) grades 3, 4, and 5. A detailed transcript of his grades for these years is attached.

Grade 3   3.72
Grade 4   3.66
Grade 5   3.80

In addition to doing well academically, Bobby sang in his school choir for two years, played soccer for three, and has recently developed an interest in school plays.

If you need further information about my son's performance at his last school, please call me xxxx (days) or 867-2345 (evenings). You may also send an e-mail to Email@xxxx.com

Thank you for taking such an active 'interest in my son's school performance. I'm sure you'll find he's dedicated to doing his very best at New Ridge County Day School.

Kind regards

Attached: London Southfield school transcripts (1 pages)

Template 11

To Acknowledge Information Or An Event

Dear Grace

I received, with regret, your letter of resignation from our neighbourhood Crime Watch committee.

Thank you for two years of constant dedication to the cause of increased safety on our block. You've been a dedicated member of the committee, and your actions have greatly contributed to our neighbourhood's safety.

The entire committee will be sad to see you go.

Yours truly

Harry Todd

Template 12

To Convey Bad News Or Decline A Request

Dear Harry

As you know, Crime Watch requires a lot of time and energy to make it work for our neighbourhood.

And time really comes at a premium for me these days. My two children are in school full-time (which means soccer practices, band practices, you know the routine), and I've recently taken on more responsibilities at New Ridge County Day School, where I previously taught and now serve as acting principal. In my "time off," I'm also busy helping my husband get his new home-based business off the ground.

In short, I'm afraid I find it necessary to resign from the Crime committee, effective immediately. I simply no longer have the time to of benefit to the committee.

I'm sure the committee will continue to make a difference to our neighbourhood. I, for one, really appreciate the committee's continued to our cause.

Cordiall

Template 13

Memorandum | Memo

To

From

Ref

Date

INHOUSE DOCUMENT FORMATS

Many congratulations on recently joining the staff in the Chairman's office.

I hope you will be very happy here.

I am enclosing a booklet explaining the company's general rules regarding document formats. However, I thought it would be helpful if I summarised the rules for ease of reference.

1. DOCUMENT FORMATS

All documents should be presented in the fully blocked format using open punctuation. Specimen LETTER, Email communication messages, memoranda and other documents are included in the booklet. These examples should guide you in our requirements.

2. SIGNATURE BLOCK (LETTER)

In outgoing LETTER it is usual practice to display the sender's name in capitals and the title directly underneath in lower case with initial capitals.

3. NUMBEREDITEMS

In reports and other documents it is often necessary to number items. In such cases the numbers should be displayed alone with no full stops or Subsequent numbering should be decimal, ie 3.1, 3.2, etc.

I hope these guidelines will be useful and that you will study the layouts shown in your booklet. If you have any questions please do not hesitate to ask me.

Enc

Copy   Personnel Department

Template 14

Complaint Replay

Dear

YOUR ORDER NUMBER TH 2457

Thank you for your letter of 27 March.

I am very sorry to hear about the mistake made with your order. I have looked into this and found that the mistake happened in the packing section. Unfortunately it was not discovered before the goods were sent to you.

I have arranged for a repeat order to be sent to you today, and I hope this meets your requirements.

Once again, please accept my apologies for the inconvenience caused.

I enclose a copy of our new collection and I hope you find it interesting.

Please give me a call soon on 2358272 if you have any questions.

Yours sincerely

Template 15

Email Communication Message

Tele Communications   Mobile
Phone specialists

21 Ashton Drive

London   Tel +44
114 2871122

SW10MP   Email

Email TeleComm@admin

EMAIL COMMUNICATION MESSAGE

To

Company

Email communication Number

From

Ref

Date

Number of Pages

(including this page)   1

VISIT TO TOKIO

Thank you for calling this morning regarding my trip to Singapore next month. I am very grateful to you for offering to meet me at the airport and drive me to my hotel.

I will be arriving on flight SQ101 on Monday 8 July at 1830 hours. Accommodation has been arranged for me at the Supreme International Hotel, More Road.

I will be travelling up to Kuala Yan on Sunday 14 July on MH989 which departs from Singapore Airport Terminal 1 at 1545 hours.

Look forward to meeting you.

Sincerely

Template 16

Email

Hello

I hope things are with you.

I was pleased to hear that you will be back in Malaysia again in November to hold your seminar on Effective Business Writing.

Some bookstores are interested in asking you to do a talk and signing event. I hope you will agree to take part. If so, please let me have some free dates while you are over here.

See you soon.

Template 17

A Slightly More Formal Email

Dear

We are considering sending some of our staff on a training course on Customer.

Do you have a suitable course available within the next few months?

If so please let me have the dates and times plus costs.

There isn't a regular Pioneer course scheduled, can you tailor-make a specially for our staff? We could hold it in our conference room.

Perhaps we can arrange to meet to discuss this are you free next Friday 20 August at 11 am? I could come over to you, or you could come over to my office. Please let me know.

Project Manager

Training and Consultancy

Template 18

E-Mail Following A Meeting

Dear

It was good to meet you again last week. As discussed, I would like to invite you – to give the opening speech at the launch of our Healthy Eating Campaign.

This will be held at our Leeds superstore on Monday 8 August.

Richard and I are very excited about this campaign. We are hoping it will make the public more aware of the importance of choosing a variety of fresh fruit and as part of their daily diet.

l am attaching a provisional Software, from which you will see that 10 minutes been allocated for the opening speech at 9.30 am. We will be happy to your transport to and from our superstore on launch day.

l know that your high profile in this industry would bring the crowds flocking to this launch. We hope you will decide to join us.

Best wishes

Marketing Manager

Name Ltd

Telephone +44 0000000

www.name.com

Template 19

E-Mail Where Tone Is Important

Hi

Some of the staff from your department are still bringing their petty cash vouchers to me. However this responsibility was taken over by Martin in Accounts last month.

Please inform your staff that they should deal with Martin in the future.

Thanks for your help Anna.

Yours truly

Template 20

Email Potentially Large Business Enquiry And Reply

Enquiry

Dear Sir/Madam

Please send me a copy of your collection and price list of Email communication machines, with copies of any descriptive leaflets that I could pass to prospective customers.

Yours faithfully

Reply

Dear Sir/Madam

I have seen one of your safes in the office of a local firm and they passed on your address to me.

Please send me a copy of your current collection. I am particularly interested in safes suitable for a small office.

Yours faithfully

Template 21

Requests For Advice Enquiry And Reply

Enquiry

Dear Sir/Madam

I have a large hardware store in Southampton and am interested in the electric heaters you are advertising in the West Country Gazette.

Please send me your illustrated collection and a price list.

Yours faithfully

Replay

Dear Mrs/Mr

Thank you for your letter enquiring about electric heaters. I am pleased to enclose a copy of our latest illustrated collection.

You may be particularly interested in our newest heater, the FX21 model. Without any increase in fuel consumption, it gives out 15% more heat than earlier models. You will find details of our terms in the price list printed on the inside front cover of the collection.

Perhaps you would consider placing a trial order to provide you with an opportunity to test its efficiency. At the same time this would enable you to see for yourself the high quality of material and finish put into this model.

If you have any questions please contact me on 62000007.

Yours sincerely

Template 22

General Enquiry recommendation enquiries and replies

Enquiry

Dear Sir/Madam

My neighbour, Mr W Stevens of 98 High Street, Derby, recently bought an electric lawnmower from you. He is delighted with the machine and has recommended that I contact you.

I need a similar machine, but smaller, and should be glad if you would send me a   I copy of your collection and any other information that will help me to make the best choice for my purpose.

Yours faithfully

Reply

Dear Mrs

I enclose a collection and price list of our lawnmowers, as requested in your letter of 18 May.

The machine bought by your friend was a 38 cm RANSOME' which is an excellent machine. You will find details of the smaller size of 30 cm shown on page 15 of the collection .

Have both these models in stock and should be glad to show them to you if you would care to call at our showroom.

Please contact me on 2314679 if I can provide any further help.

Yours sincerely

Template 23

An enquiry with numbered points

Enquiry

Dear

During a recent visit to the Ideal Home Exhibition I saw a sample of your plastic tile flooring. I think this type of flooring would be suitable for the ground floor of tile flooring. I think this type of flooring would be suitable for the ground floor of my house, but I have not been able to find anyone who is familiar with such thing.

Would you please give me the following information:

1. What special preparation would be necessary for the under flooring?
2. In what colours and designs can the tiles be supplied?
3. Are the tiles likely to be affected by rising damp?
4. Would it be necessary to employ a specialist to lay the floor'? If s, can you recommend one in my area?

I should appreciate your advice on these matters.

Yours faithfully

Replay

Dear

Many thank for your enquiry of 18 August regarding our plastic tile flooring. A copy of our brochure is enclosed showing the designs and range of colours in which the tiles are supplied.

London Tiles, 22 The Square, Rugby, is a very reliable firm which carries out all in your area. I have asked the company to get in touch with you to inspect floors. Their consultant will be able to advise you on what preparation is necessary and whether dampness is likely to cause a problem.

Our plastic tile flooring is hardwearing and if the tiles are laid professionally. I am sure the work will give you lasting satisfaction.

Please let me know if I can provide any further help.

Yours sincerely

Template 24

Request for goods on approval

Request

Dear

Several of my customers have recently expressed an interest in your waterproof garments, and have enquired about their quality.

If quality and price are satisfactory there are prospects of good sales here.

However before placing a firm order I should be glad if you would send moon 14 days' approval a selection of men's and children's waterproof raincoats and leggings. Any of the items unsold at the end of this period and which I decide not to keep as stock would be returned at my expense.

I hope to hear from you soon.

Yours faithfully

Reply

Dear

I was very pleased to receive your request of 12 March for waterproof garments on approval.

As we have not previously done business together, you will appreciate that I must request either the usual reference or the name of a bank to which we may refer. As soon as these enquiries are satisfactorily settled we shall be happy to send you a good selection of the items mentioned in your letter.

I sincerely hope that our first transaction together will be the beginning of a long and pleasant business association.

Yours sincerely

Despatch of goods

Dear

I have now received satisfactory references and am pleased to be able to send you a generous selection of our waterproof garments as requested in your letter of 12 March.

This selection includes several new and attractive models in which the water-resistant qualities have been improved by a special process. Due to economies in our methods of manufacture, it has also been possible to reduce our prices, which are now lower than those for imported waterproof garments of similar quality.

When you have had an opportunity to inspect the garments, please let us know which you have decided to keep and arrange to return the remainder as early as possible.

I hope this first selection will meet your requirements. If you would like a further selection, please do not hesitate to let me know.

Yours sincerely

Template 25

Visits by representative

Dear Sir/Madam

I read with interest your advertisement for plastic kitchenware in the current issue of the House Furnishina Review.

I hope you can arrange for your representative to call when next ki this district. It would be helpful if he could bring with him a good selection of items from your product range.

This is a rapidly developing district and if prices are right your goods should find a ready sale.

I look forward to hearing from you soon,

Yours faithfully

Template26

Supplier's offer of visit

Dear

Thank you for your enquiry dated 1 November.

Our representative, Ms Jane Whitelaw, will be in your area next week and she will be calling on you. Mean white I am enclosing an illustrated collection of our plastic goods and details of our terms and conditions of sale.

Plastic kitchenware has long been a popular feature of the modem kitchen. Its bright and attractive colours have strong appeal, and wherever dealers have arranged them in special window displays good sales are reported.

When you have inspected the samples Ms White will bring with her, you will why we have a large demand for these products. Therefore if you wish to have a stock of these goods before Christmas we advise you to place your order by the end of this month.

We look forward to working with you.

Yours sincerely

Template 27

Request for concessions x 6

Request for sole distribution

Dear

We have recently extended our radio and television department and are thinking of adding new ranges to our present stocks. We are particularly interested in your Home radio and television models and should be glad if you would send us your trade collection and terms of sate and payment.

Your products are not yet offered by any other dealer in this town, and if we decide to introduce them we should like to request sole distribution rights to this area.

I hope to hear from you soon.

Yours faithfully

Request tor special terms

Enquiry

Dear

Please send us your current collection and price list for bicycles. We are interested in models for both men and women, and also for children.

We are the leading bicycle dealers in this city where cycling is popular, and have branches in five neighbouring towns. If the quality of your products is the prices are reasonable, we expect to place regular orders for fairly large numbers.

In the circumstances please indicate whether you will allow us a special discount. This would enable us to maintain the low selling prices which have been an important reason for the growth of our business. In return we would be prepared to place orders for a guaranteed annual minimum number of bicycles, the figure to be mutually agreed.

If you wish to discuss this please contact me on 6920001.

Yours sincerely

Reply

Dear

I was glad to learn from your letter of 18 July of your interest in our products. As requested our collection and price list are enclosed, together with details of our conditions of sale and terms of payment.

We have considered your proposal to place orders for a guaranteed minimum number of machines in return for a special allowance. However after careful consideration we feel it would be better to offer you a special allowance on the following sliding scale basis.

On purchases exceeding an annual total of:

1,000 but not exceeding 3,000	3%
3,000 but not exceeding 7,500	4%
3,000 but not exceeding 7,500	4%

No special allowance could be given on annual total purchases below 10,000.

I feel that an arrangement on these lines would be more satisfactory to both our

Companies.

I look forward to working with you and hope to hear from you soon.

Yours sincerely

Letter declining special terms

Dear

We have carefully considered your letter of 18 December.

As our companies have done business with each other for many years, we would, like to grant your request to lower the prices of our sportswear. However our Overheads'2 have risen sharply in the past 12 months. And to reduce prices by 15% you mention could not be done without considerably lowering our standards, of quality. This is something we are not prepared to do.

Instead of a 15% reduction on sportswear, we suggest a reduction of 5% on all our products for orders of 800 or more. On orders of this size we could make such a reduction without lowering our standards.

I hope that you will agree to this suggestion and look forward to continuing to receive regular orders from you.

Yours sincerely

Template 28

Quotations, estimates tenders

Dear Sir

We will soon be requiring 200 reams of good quality white poster paper suitable for auction bills and poster work generally. We require paper which will retain its white appearance after pasting on walls and hoardings.

Please let us have some samples and a quotation, including delivery at our works within 4 weeks of our order.

Yours faithfully

Quotation

Dear

Thank you for your enquiry dated 21 June.

As requested we enclose samples of different qualities of paper suitable for poster work.

We are pleased to quote as follows:

A1 quality Printing Paper white 2.21 per kg
A2 quality Printing Paper white 2.15 per kg
A3 quality Printing Paper white 2.10 per kg
A3 quality Printing Paper white 2.10 per kg

These prices include delivery at your works.

All these papers are of good quality and quite suitable for poster work. We guarantee that they will not discolour when pasted.

We can promise delivery within one week from receiving your order, and hope you will find both samples and prices satisfactory.

Please give me a call on 2634917 if you have any questions.

Yours sincerely

Foreign buyer's request for quotation Enquire and Reply

Enquire

Dear

We have recently received a number of requests for your lightweight raincoats and believe that we could place regular orders with you, as long as your prices are competitive.

From the description in your collection we feel that your AQUATITE range would be most suitable for this region. Please let me have a quotation for men's and women's coats in both small and medium sizes, delivered to London.

If your prices are right, we will place a first order for 400 raincoats, namely 100 of each of the 4 qualities. Shipment would be required within 4 weeks of order.

I look forward to a prompt reply.

Yours faithfully

Replay

Dear

Thank you for your letter of 15 June. I was pleased to learn about the enquiries you have received for our raincoats.

Our fashion AQUATITEM range is particularly suitable for warm climates. During the past year we have supplied this range to dealers in several tropical countries. We have received repeat Orders from many of those dealers. This range is popular

Not only because of its light weight but also because the material used has been specially treated to prevent excessive condensation on the inside surface.

We are pleased to quote as follows:

100 AQUATITEM coats men's medium 17.50 ea 1750.00
100 AQUATITEM coats men's small 16.80 ea 1680
100 AQUATITEM coats women's medium 16.00 ea 1600.00
100 AQUATITEM coats women's small 15.40 each 1540.00

less 33'h% trade discount

Net price   4382.19

Freight (London to Alexandria)   186

Insurance   170

TOTAL   4690.69

Terms: 2% one month from date of invoice

Shipment: Within 3-4 weeks of receiving order

For acceptance within one month.

We feel you may be interested in some of our other products, and enclose descriptive booklets and a supply of sales literature for issue to your

We hope to receive your order soon.

Yours sincerely

Template 29

Inquiry and Requests for Information x 13

Dear

Could you please send us your current collection and price list of the office chairs advertised in this month's issue of Professional Office chairs We are operating a store facility/and are particularly interested in Models AA5 and AA8.

Please, reply as soon as possible as we would like to make a purchasing decision early next month.

Yours sincerely

Dear

Send us two copies of the colour brochure on your new Samson Colour Copier 33H advertised on page 15 in your "Office Supplies" collection No. 93.

Prompt reply would be appreciated.

Yours sincerely

Dear

We have seen your advertisement in the March issue of Business Catering Management be grateful if you could send us details about your catering services for medium-sized companies.

A prompt reply would be appreciated.

Yours sincerely

Dear

Could you please e-mail me information about the international sales training Software as advertised in the April issue of International Sales Training Magazine? Thank you very much.

Yours sincerely

Dear

We are interested in having a stand in next year's Consumer Electronics Exhibition in Boston and would be grateful if you could mail us a copy of your detailed Exhibition Folder via email.

Yours sincerely

Dear

Your company has been highly recommended to us by the Alex Thallier Company in Paris,   p France. We are a small company specializing in cellular telephone equipment and numerous inquiries from our business customers for a cell phone that delivers sound to that of a landline telephone. We want to expand our range of equipment and would like you to send us full details of your mobile phone models as well as the latest collection and your most competitive dealer prices. Please, also include information packing and shipping (CIF Boston) and the minimum quantity for a trial order.

We look forward to hearing from you soon.

Yours sincerely

Dear

When we attended the International Electronics Trade Fair in London last month, we visited your stand and saw a very interesting demonstration of your automatic high-security garage doors. The ability to drive straight in and out of your garage from the comfort of your car, as well as your emphasis on theft protection, appealed to us. We believe that there is a ready I market for this in the Tokyo.

Our company is a wholly owned subsidiary of the international Zetax Corporation, well-known in the security and theft prevention industry.

Would you please send us your current sales literature and price list? Of course, we will be glad to provide the usual credit and trade references if we decide to order from your company.

Yours sincerely

Dear

One of our business associates Mr. Mike Nevins of Gorham Brothers in Hong Kong-informed us that your company is a major manufacturer of pure cotton-striped or solid polo shirts and crew neck sweaters in all sizes for young women. We would like you to send us detailed information and your export price list, as well as several samples of the shirts and sweaters.

Thank you very much!

Yours sincerely

Dear

We are interested in ordering 175 new 20" widescreen monitors for our new direct main facility at Erdington, Sidney. Could you please send us an estimate? The enclosed sheet provides the necessary details.

Yours sincerely

Dear

We have heard from the German Consulate in Chicago that you are leading producer self-installation, all-solar panels in Germany. Since there seems to be a growing interest in and demand for such high-quality solar panels in the UK, we would like to know the frame styles that are now available for EU.

We are importers of solar panels in UK.

Please, send us your illustrated collection ; export price list, and terms of business. As a rule our domestic and international suppliers allow us to settle by monthly statements. We can supply of course, with business and bank references. We look forward to your reply.

Yours sincereley

Dear

We would be grateful if you would send us patterns and prices for your floral-print, comforters and geometric-design bedspreads (sizes: Twin, Full, Queen, and King). Please, also inform us whether you could supply these goods from stock, because we need them prior to the holiday season, which begins September 15th.

Yours sincerely

Dear

We are the U.S. buying agents for a direct mail organization in Japan offering quality retailers at bargain prices. Products, which carry an unconditional money-back guarantee, Include tools, do-it-yourself aids, automotive supplies, plus a whole range of hobby and sporting supplies.

Would you please send us your latest price lists and illustrated list for all the products you stock, including detailed information on your discount system for substantial orders?

We look forward to hearing from you soon.

Yours sincerely

Template 30

Replies to LETTER of Inquiry x12

Dear

Thank you for your e-mail of April 29 requesting dealer information about our company's newest Grand Mobile Homes.

With over 4,000 Grand Mobile Homes sold and in service in UK our unique concept has been proven popular. Built with the latest technology and materials and with simplicity of maintenance in mind, our rugged and durable Mobile Homes offer flexibility available in no other mobile home on the market today.

The enclosed brochures as well as the detailed technical and dealership information you why our Grand Mobile Homes have become an outstanding sales success during past three years. After you have reviewed our information package, please feel free to us for further information. We also want to invite you to visit our manufacturing facilities in Wales. We would be pleased to show you how our Grand Mobile Homes meet your requirements of mobile homes in southern Florida, efficiently and economically.

Yours sincerity

Dear

Thank you for your recent communication.

We cannot supply the wooden picnic basket (Model 4A). This item is out of I and we do not' have a firm date for further supplies. However, if we receive a shipment in the near future, we will contact you.

Yours sincerely

Dear

Thank you for your interest in our sales management-training Software. As promised in our telephone conversation of yesterday, I am enclosing detailed information about this Software

If you have any questions, please do not hesitate to contact me.

Yours sincerely

Dear

Thank you for your inquiry. I hope that the enclosed information about our direct-mail marketing course will be of use to you. Just give me a call at (000) 000-0000 I will be happy to answer any questions you may have.

Yours sincerely

Dear

In reply to your web inquiry of September 12, we are pleased to enclose a copy of our recent sales collection which features the complete range of our new corduroy sports for men* These handsome and versatile jackets-in beige, navy, chocolate, or rust-can be worn from the office to informal dinners to weekend activities in great style and The medium-wale corduroy is made from a long-wearing blend of long staple cotton and polyester and is soft and easy to wear. The models that you are interested in are presented pages 9 to 15.

Mrs. Lisa Dillon, our regional sales manager, will telephone your office next week in order to arrange a meeting. He will be able to provide you with complete details of our other new sportswear lines.

Yours sincerely

Dear

Thank you for your request for additional in formation on the Large Carpet Machine, which we have been producing since 2010. This professional vacuum cleaner removes deep-down dirt.

Large Company Inc. has an excellent reputation for high-quality products, reliability, and service. Our products are designed and manufactured in the EU, Romania with distribution channels all over the world.

I have enclosed a special folder on the Large Carpet Machine and a collection that describes our other professional floor care products, including the Silent Power canister and the Full-Power Upright Vacuum Cleaner. Please call me at (000) 000-0000 if you have any questions.

Yours sincerely

Dear

Thank you for your e-mail of February 19.

Enclosed is our current summer sales collection for the complete range of Fair Email communication products you asked for, together with full details of our liberal terms of business. As you can see on page 3 of our price list, we allow you a special discount off all net prices for orders of the value you stated in your e-mail. Delivery will be within four weeks of receipt of your order. However, to take full advantage of these special summer sales offers, we J advise you to place your order promptly. We expect considerable response to our summer sale and supplies are limited.

If you have any further questions, please contact us. We look forward to hearing from you as soon as possible.

Yours sincerely

Dear

Thank you for your e-mail of December 2 in which you asked for detailed about our new range of Sou'wester Rain Hats, styled after the classic foul weather hat by Scottish fishermen for more than a century. We now have designed these rain hats contemporary fabrics and colours and they can be supplied from stock.

Our export prices in the enclosed collection and price list are quoted for delivery in Tokyo payment is to be made by irrevocable letter of credit.

We look forward to hearing from you soon. If you need any further information, please contact us.

Yours sincerely

Dear

Thank you for expressing an interest in Max/Automated Simulations. In response to request for further information on our product line of computer games, we enclose our online collection and price lists.

We are in the process of expanding our distribution channels internationally as the demand for highly sophisticated computer games increases. Our games are unique and positioned your market. Take a few minutes and review the enclosures, and you will see why many top retailers have added the Max computer games to their product mix.

Please contact us if you have any questions regarding the product line or material we look forward to hearing from you in the near future.

Yours sincerely

Dear

We are pleased to enclose the Master Film Classic collection you requested in your e-mail of April 2. Also included is a collection of titles available on the Master Famous Films label. You may order these titles using either the Film Classic or Famous Films order form.

Please note that postage rates listed in both collections apply to UK and USA destinations only. Parcel postage to countries within the European Union is £10 per movie; outside the European £7 per movie.

Kind regards

Dear

Thank you for inquiring about Digital Corporation and our products. The enclosed literature details the capabilities of our digital technology systems. We understand the need for information management and let it guide the research and development of our software, hardware, and web utilities.

If you have additional questions after reading our literature, please call our company's regional office in your area. Our sales or technical representatives would be happy to discuss pricing or arrange a demonstration at your office. A list of regional offices and telephone numbers is enclosed for your convenience.

We appreciate your interest in Digital Corporation.

Yours sincerely

Template 31

Follow-Up Letter X5

Dear

You have probably received the brochures you requested about our sales management training Software. However, since these booklets only provide general information about this Software, I suggest that we get together for a brief personal discussion. In this way, I can answer your questions and tell you how this training Software can benefit you and your company.

I will get in touch with you early next week to determine your interest in this Software.

Yours sincerely

Dear

We wondered whether you received our sales collection and export price lists you e-mail of October 10.

We would be pleased to discuss the possibility of having our products distributed in We will call you to set up a meeting.

We hope that we will be able to meet soon, either in London , London or Chicago.

Yours sincerely

Dear

The collection and price list e-mailed to you last week provided descriptions of our portable hard drives. However, you may have some specific questions on these new models. For that reason, I would welcome the opportunity to answer your questions and, if necessary, advise on how these new models can best suit your company's requirements.

I would be happy to arrange a brief demonstration for you and key members of your staff at a mutually agreeable time. There is, of course, no cost or obligation. Please, contact me so I can reserve a date for you.

Yours sincerely

Dear

Last month's Catering Trade Exhibition in Miami, you visited our stand and showed a considerable interest in our Sabatini carbon steel knives. They are the sharpest knives you can buy and also the easiest knives to use, according to our kitchen tests and conversations with professional cooks and meat cutters. Sabatini carbon cutlery has been manufactured in Italy for more than a century.

We enclose our newest brochure and suggest that the special set of four steel knives please see enclosed which would be of particular interest to you. We are sure that you will find our prices very competitive and our export service outstanding.

We look forward to doing business with you.

Yours sincerely

Dear

It was a pleasure meeting you last Thursday. Thank you for letting me show you and key staff members how our company can handle your company's specific needs. I pleased to send you the rate sheet you requested on our temporary staffing services. I will call you early next week to see whether you have any questions.

Yours sincerely

Tamplate 31

Letter Of Complaint X8

Dear

We are writing to inform you that your delivery of 28 four-drawer chests finish on February 19 has given us cause for serious complaint. They were delivered in standard condition and cannot be fixed. We have been doing business with your for the past four years and have always been satisfied until today. For that reason, us know as soon as possible what your company intends to do to rectify this situation.

Yours sincerely

Dear

On checking the waterproof parkas with taffeta lining (Models 666L and 999XL; our No. 7778) we received this morning, we find that 32 parkas listed on your packing lists well as on your invoices have not been included in this shipment. For that reason, we en a list of the missing articles. Please check with your packers before we make a formal claim.

Yours sincerely

Dear

On 1 June, I ordered an anywhere speaker dock (Article No. 452A) from your Winter Sales Collection . On opening the parcel, I found that it did not contain the ordered item. Instead it contained an entirely different machine. I am therefore returning the item for a replacement.

Yours sincerely

Dear

We write to inform you that the bulk of the acrylic loungewear (button-front robe with V-neck; our order No. SSLW-V2) that was delivered is not up to the samples which we [received on March 15.]

On comparing the loungewear received with the samples, we were unpleasantly surprised to discover that the models are not the same high quality. We can only assume that a was made and that the loungewear we ordered has been wrongly delivered.

We cannot accept this delivery because we pride ourselves on the fact that our stores carry the very best quality in ladies' fashions. For that reason, we must ask for replacement of this entire collection. Please let us know what you wish to do with this order.

Yours sincerely

Dear

I am writing for the third time to complain about the colour photocopying machine installed in our office only three months ago. This machine has not met our staff has high expectations. Contrary to the description in your sales and instruction booklets, the (at least of our colour copier) are not consistent to colour match standards. In addition, y service representative who has examined this machine on various occasions has not able to correct this continuing serious problem.

We shall expect you to deal with this problem without further delay.

Yours sincerely

Dear

The seven-piece wood-and-glass dining set (Order No. 13899) I ordered on April 2. Since I was away on business that day, my neighbour (who has apartment) accepted the packaged set and signed for it without question. However, with unpacked the oak-finished table myself with great care, I discovered that one glass t-he table's three glass inserts was badly scratched. I can only assume that this be due to careless handling at some stage prior to packing. I cannot accept the table in this are due to careless handling at some stage prior to packaging.

I cannot accept the table in state and want to receive a replacement as soon as possible.

Yours sincerely

Dear

On April 13, 1 purchased a brand-new, four-door Excellent Model XXX automobile from   [the Frank Smith Car Dealership in London] Right from the begin have experienced serious stalling problems with this car, even while driving the automobile on the highway. Moreover, the Frank Smith service department seems to be unable solve this very annoying and extremely dangerous problem. My wife does not even want to drive this car, because she is truly scared that this new automobile will accident-tally stop running. Nine trips (!) to the service department have failed to solve or correct this stalling problem.

I am sure that you will agree that this is a ridiculous situation. My direct question to you is: what are you going to do about this very serious as well as dangerous situation? If you, in your capacity as the manufacturer's district manager, cannot solve this situation in a   I satisfactory way within ten days, I will address my complaint directly to both the president of your company and the Automobile Industry Safety Board.

Yours sincerity

Dear

Two weeks ago we ordered a Roomer Folding and Inserting Office Machine Mode, which was delivered this morning. However, when we opened the box, we discovered that t machine (with serial number ADD-595001-X) was damaged. As a matter of fact, it like a used model that has served as a demonstration sample. It is obvious, of course, that we not accept this. We have been doing business with your company during the past six yea without complaint. Since your company prides itself on first-class equipment, we expect you will take the necessary steps to rectify this situation.

Please contact us to pick up machine and provide a replacement.

Yours sincerely

Template 32

Responding To Letter Of Complaint X8

Dear

Thank you for telling us about your problems with the electric oven that you store on January 14. Since this oven is covered by our unconditional refund policy, we provide you with a new oven or else give you a full refund. Please, let us know your decision.

We value your patronage and are very sorry for the inconvenience the problems oven have caused you.

Yours

Dear

We are sorry to hear that you were not satisfied with the shipment of wine glasses you by Associated Parcel Service last week, because we always check our shipments will be sent to your company by air express. Please return the damaged glassware to us. We much regret this inconvenience.

You for your cooperation.

Yours sincerely

Dear

Thank you for your correspondence of July 30. Of course, we are deeply concerned when one of our customers is not satisfied with one of our products. Our company takes great pride in trying co produce only top products. Unfortunately, we sometimes fail.

If you return the defective cappuccino coffee machine to the dealer who sold it to you, he will replace it with a new one. However, if you prefer, we are also willing to refund the purchase price to you.

We are sorry to have inconvenienced you and offer our apologies.

Yours sincerely

Dear

We are sorry your laptop notebook arrived in a damaged condition. As described in your letter, the damage apparently happened during shipment. A replacement will be delivered to your home on Wednesday morning, April 17. Our driver, who delivers the replacement, is authorized to pick up the damaged laptop. We regret your inconvenience and thank you for your understanding and cooperation in this unfortunate matter. We value your business.

Yours sincerely

Dear

I have received your e-mail of April 9 and regret the error on your bimonthly invoice. When this invoice was made up, two items had been duplicated on invoice 778, with the result your company was overcharged £1311.29. I have deducted this amount from your invoice and will mail you a new one for the correct amount of £10000.

Thank you for bringing our billing error to our attention. Again, I apologize for any inconvenience this has caused you.

Yours sincerely

Dear

Thank you for calling the billing error in your last weekly statement to our attention. This error was caused by an oversight in our accounting department. We have statement and a new statement is enclosed. Please accept our sincere apologies for any inconvenience caused. We look forward to our continued good business relations.

Yours sincerely

(Reply and apology for a delay in delivery)

Dear

We have received your Email communication of November 28 and regret the delay in delivery of your order No.MDS-89796AA for floor lamps and pole lamps.

We received your order in late our supplier was out of stock. However, we are pleased to advise you that your order will be filled by December 8. We apologize for any inconvenience caused by this delay. Thank you very much for your patience and cooperation in this matter.

Yours sincerely

(Reply and apology for a damaged desk)

Dear

We are sorry to learn about the damage to the four-drawer desk that you purchased at our store in London on September 26. Our delivery-person informed us that the damage probably occurred during the shipment from the furniture manufacturer to our warehouse from London to Delaware.

Meanwhile, we have ordered an exact replacement from the manufacturer and expect that delivery will take place within one month. As soon as the desk arrives, we will telephone you immediately and will arrange a convenient delivery time.

We regret the inconvenience this has caused you.

Yours sincerely

Template 33

Letter Of Apology X3

Dear

Thank you for your e-mail of June 17 pointing out the error in our invoice No. A-531 dated January 9. We would like to apologize for this billing error and we are sorry for any inconvenience that our error has caused you. We try our best, but occasionally errors do slip by our accounting department. Therefore, we have cancelled the old invoice and now enclose? Please see revised invoice for the correct amount.

We would like to thank you once again for bringing this matter to our attention.

Yours sincerely

Dear

I apologize most sincerely for any discourtesy by our employee, Lisa Foster, last afternoon. None was intended. Because of this unfortunate incident, we would like to you as a token of good faith, a gift certificate for £100 of merchandise valid at any of our department stores in Fay County. Please be assured that we have taken steps to prevent a recurrence of such inexcusable rudeness by our sales staff.

Yours sincerely

Dear

Our local council will be doing some electrical. Work in our office building between March 21, and Wednesday, March 23.

During this time there may be some short interruptions to electrical supply.

Please accept our apologies for any inconvenience that this may cause.

Yours sincerely

Template: 34

Letter Of Congratulation X5

Dear

My congratulations to you on your recent promotion to national sales manager. I know that you have worked hard for Newton Corporation and therefore I am delighted that you have been promoted to this new and challenging position.

Your company is very fortunate to have benefited from your expertise as well as loyalty during the past nine years.

Yours sincerely

(Congratulating A Top Salesperson)

Dear

Congratulations to you on establishing a new sales volume record last year. I know worked hard to achieve this and it is great to see that you were able to attain your goal.

We need people like you, Richard. Keep up the good work!

Yours sincerely

(Congratulating A Top Salesperson Two)

Dear

My congratulations to you on being the Number One Salesperson in the Southwest Sale Group during the past quarter. You outsold all other salespersons during that quarter in both volume and gross margins. An outstanding achievement. If this continues, you will be in line for promotion to Assistant Regional Sales Manager next year.

Keep up the good work for the next quarter!

Yours sincerely

(Congratulating A Top Sales Team)

Dear

Congratulations! Lux Sofas and Chairs is, once again, leading the Northeast zone sales standing report for both the month of July and calendar year to date.

Please pass along my thanks to your sales team for an extraordinary comeback effort during month of July.

Yours sincerely

(Congratulations On Being Elected President Of An Association)

Dear

Congratulations on your election to the presidency of the United Association of Engineers can be proud of this election, because it is a well-deserved recognition of your out-standing work as well as long-time commitment to the activities of the Association. I am also certain that the members appreciated the excellent job you did last year as director of the Association's international activities Software.

My best wishes for success in your new position.

Yours sincerely

Template 35

Letter Of Appreciation X5

Dear

On behalf of the management and staff of St. Marry Relief Services, we want to express our deepest appreciation for your hard work during our recent fund-raising activities untiring energy and labour made this fund-raising drive the most successful one foundation began six years ago. Thank you very much!

Yours sincerely

Dear

Please accept my sincere appreciation for all the assistance you gave me in planning our recent customer seminar at the Cambridge Hotel. Being a novice at planning this type of event, I am certain its success was directly related to your suggestions and directions.

All the people who attended were extremely pleased with their accommodations as well as I the friendliness and attentiveness of your entire staff Please extend my appreciation to the staff and, in particular, to Lisa and Ana.

Yours sincerely

Dear

I would like to take this opportunity to express my appreciation to the staff of your conference centre for the prompt and courteous service that we received during our NBD sales meeting on March 9. We were quite pleased with your facility and with the friendly and helpful service we experienced.

I am sure we will be at your conference centre again in the future.

Yours sincerely

Dear

Often, in our industry, when an innovative plan or project is successfully brought to completion, we tend co remember the problems and the disputes rather than the pleasure of accomplishment. Happily, this is decidedly not the case with the completion and implementation our new marketing and advertising plan thanks to you and your dedicated and creative team.

Leonard Finch joins me in extending our particular appreciation to Fred Frith, , Warren Silverberg, and of course, to Ruth Money and Michael Jonas.

Yours sincerely

Template 36

Thank-You LETTER x2

Dear

Thank you for the excellent job on our recent two-day sales conference. You and your entire staff were so supportive and always available for our last minute changes. It was a real pleasure working with such a helpful and committed group of professionals.

I look forward to future successful meetings at the Summit Conference Centre.

Yours sincerely

Dear

Thank you for taking the time to complete our guest comment card during your stay with us on May 15th to 18th.

Were certainly pleased to have you as our guest here in the hotel and welcome the comments that you provided. You may be assured that the air conditioning unit in Room 815 has been repaired and adjusted to provide a consistent cool airflow. I have also taken the liberty of forwarding your kind mention of William Dodd, our Front Office Clerk, whom you found to be of great assistance during your stay.

We thank you and we do look forward to welcoming you back to the Chest Hotel during your next trip to Atlanta.

Yours sincerely

Template 37

Announcing the acquisition of a new distribution company x8

Gerald M. Winter & Partners
Certified Public Accountants
Is pleased to announce the opening
Practice of international tax consulting

HOME DESIGHN & CO Business Center
Telephone (000)
000 West Appleton Street
Email communication (000)
Boston, MA
Email: ooooo-oooo

Dear

We are happy to announce that on Saturday, March 15, at 6.00 P.M., the Fin & Claw Seafood Restaurant will open its doors in the Cedartown Shopping Centre. To welcome to our new seafood restaurant, we offer special reductions of 25 percent on all items on lunch on and dinner menu during our Grand Opening weekend.

The Fin & Claw Seafood Restaurant features the most extensive selection of seafood dishes in town.

The Management

Reservations for Luncheon and Dinner: tel. (000) 000-00001

(Announcing A New Product. To Customers)

Dear

Benson & Baker Company is proud to announce our newest product: London Dutch Farmer Stainless Cookware Set. It combines copper-clad bottoms for responsiveness to heat, with attractive stainless steel for unsurpassed durability. The transparent tempered glass lids have our full ten-year warranty.

The London Dutch Farmer Stainless Cookware Set is beautifully functional and to last. The nine-piece set includes the covered oven, steamer insert, covered saucepans, open.

The London Dutch Farmer Stainless Cookware Set is beautifully functional and to last. The nine-piece set includes the covered oven, steamer insert, covered saucepans open skillets.

Yours sincerely

(Letter Announcing The Acquisition Of A New Distribution Company)

Dear

Because you are a valued customer, we want to share some interesting news with you. Our company has signed a letter of intent with the XYZ Corporation in Chicago to acquire the XYZ Distribution Company in Miami, Florida. Completion of the sale is subject to various conditions and is expected to occur by year end.

The new organization will retain its own name. The management team of the new company consist of Herald B. Fisher, currently executive vice president of the XYZ Corporation. Mr.Fisher has been directly involved with the XYZ Distribution Company for the past two years.

We will now have the distribution resources necessary for continued growth and viability in providing the services and products demanded by our customers. In addition, we strongly that this acquisition will. Benefit our existing relationship with your company.

We appreciate your continuing support and business and look forward to the opportunities .

We appreciate your continuing support and business and look forward to the opportunities that lie ahead.

Yours sincerely

(Letter announcing a price increase)

Dear

Due to an unexpected price increase from our manufacturer in Italy, we are forced to raise dealer's prices of all our imported fox fur and leather women's shoes (all sizes and all by 4.7 per cent) effective September 1. Orders entered before that date will be invoiced at our old price levels.

We sincerely regret the need for increased prices. However, we know you will understand I that this across-the-board increase, which is caused by imflation as well as higher service and labour costs, is beyond our control.

We do appreciate your business and look forward to a continuing association with you company.

Yours sincerely

(Hotel announcing an environmentally friendly Software)

Dear To help protect our environment; The Manchester Hotel Chain has gone "green" by implementing a new Towel-Saver Software. In doing this we hope to reduce the amount of laundry detergent being released into our waterways. Imagine the tons of towels that are unnecessarily washed each day in all hotels worldwide, and then picture the enormous quantity of laundry detergent that are polluting our water.

Make your choice:
Towels in the bathtub or showers mean:
Please change.
Towels back on the towel rack mean:
I will use them once again.

Help us preserve our environment. Thank you for your support!

Help us preserve our environment. Thank you tor your support!
The Manchester Hotels

(Notice about an electronic security system in use in a store)

Dear

Theft causes losses, and losses push up the costs of operating a store. Increased costs also mean increased price.

In order to discourage and prevent theft, the management of this store has installed an electronic security system. Products are invisibly marked. Should any item be removed from the store without passing through the checkout, an alarm will sound.

This system is designed in the interests of our customers. Thank you for your cooperation and continued support.

The Management

(Letter announcing a price increase)

Dear

On May 1, a 2.3 percent price increase will become effective on all our multi-purpose manual lifts as a result of increased service.

Orders entered before April 1, with shipment dates prior to May 1, will be invoiced at the price levels. However, orders entered after April 1 will be invoiced at the increased price We feel that, despite this modest price increase, your company will still be able to sell products at very competitive prices.

Please contact our sales department if you have any questions.

Yours sincerely

(Letter announcing a price reduction)

Dear

We have just signed a new contract with our manufacturer and are lad to pass the saving, on to you. Therefore, we are pleased to announce a price reduction of 9 % on the dealer "prices of our entire line of Glenmore household floor and carpet cleaners, including our heavy-duty three-speed shampoo/polisher machines.

We feel that these price decreases will enable you to sell even more Glenmore cleaning and polishing units at very competitive prices.

Yours sincerely

Template 38

Informal and formal invitations x13

Dear

The Executive Council would like to invite you to speak about the new developments in European satellite broadcasting industry at our annual General Meeting of the Marketing Directors to be held in London on October 24. About 200 members will be present at this annual meeting.

Several members have recommended you highly. Your recent article in the hotel industry also addresses this very interesting topic. We usually ask our speakers to pre-pare a 30-minute address, followed by a 10-minute question and answer period.

Our society is prepared to pay all your expenses including overnight accommodation and a modest honorarium of £150.

We do hope that you will consider this invitation and join us on October 24. Please, let us know as soon as possible if you will accept this speaking enf3t!errient so that we can finalize our for that evening at the Roosevelt Room of the American Heritage Hotel in London.

Yours sincerely

(Declining An Invitation To Address An Audience)

Dear

Your letter requesting Ms. Allan Andrews to speak before the Young Managers Club on September 18 arrived the day after she had left on an extended business trip to Europe. Ms. Allen will not be back before September 15. Therefore, it will be impossible for her to address the members of your club.

I know, however, that Ms. Allan will appreciate your kind invitation. I am sure she in touch with you when she returns from Europe.

Yours sincerely

(Informal Invitation In The Form Of A Letter; Reply Expected)

Dear

We are pleased to announce that we have moved our offices to a spacious new building at a new location. For that reason, we cordially invite you to see our new facility and to attend an Open House at 175 Fifth Avenue on Thursday, May 10, from 4:00 P.M. until 7:00 P.M.

We certainly hope you can join us on that day. Please let us know if you can, so that we can finalize our Software.

Yours sincerely

(Sales-Oriented Invitation In The Form Of A Letter; No Reply Expected)

Dear

We will introduce our newest Universal Printer Model MM 29 during the upcoming Computer Hardware Exhibition in San Francisco from April 3 to April 6. Since you probably will attend this major trade exhibition, we would like to invite you to stop by our demonstration booth number 189 so that we might introduce you to and demonstrate this brand new model.

We are looking forward to having the opportunity to meet you.

Yours sincerely

(Sales-Oriented Invitation In The Form Of A Letter; No Reply Expected)

Dear

The iPod is the ultimate in portable entertainment. . . . Colin Ronan Electronics Corporation invites you to the Electronics Trade Exhibition to view its full range of this technology company display at:

        Booth 374, Covent Garden Center
        London   January 18-23

Our sales representatives and product specialists will be on hand to answer any questions you may have.

We looking forward to seeing you in London.

Yours sincerely

(Accepting A Formal Invitation)

Dear

Mr. and Mrs. Charles Drake thank the Management Team of the Winchester Corporation for the invitation to attend the dinner dance honouring 'William R_ Chesterfield on Septem-12, at which they will be happy to attend.

Yours sincerely

(Accepting A Formal Invitation)

Dear

Dr. and Mrs. Lisa McDonald are pleased to accept the Winchester Corporation's kind invitation to attend the dinner dance at the Alexandria Hotel on Saturday, September 12.

Yours sincerely

(Declining A Formal Invitation)

Dear

Mr. and Mrs. Alex Smith thank the Management Team of the Winchester for the kind invitation to attend the dinner dance honouring Lisa Moon on June 12, but regret that they are unable to attend due to a prior commitment.

Yours sincerely

(Declining A Formal Invitation)

Dear

Mr. and Mrs. Frank Hitching sincerely regret that owing to a previous engagement they are unable to accept the kind invitation of the Winchester Corporation for the dinner dance to be held on Saturday, September 12.

Yours sincerely

Tamplate 39

Asking for or Making an Appointment x8

Dear

Ms. Diane Bond, national service manager of our sales collection division, will be in London on Thursday, January 28 and would like to tour your web offset printing plant in nearby Cambridge during that afternoon.

Would it be convenient for you or your assistant to meet her on this date? I will get in touch with you by telephone early next week to make an appointment.

Yours sincerely

Dear

I will be in Manchester on Tuesday, June 7, until Thursday, June 9, and would like to meet you at your office to discuss the brochure layout requirements that we briefly talked about at the recent Technical Trade Exposition in London . Please, let me know when you could see me. I can come to your office at any time during the above-mentioned period.

I will telephone your secretary next week to schedule an appointment. I am looking forward to meeting you.

Yours sincerely

Dear

In reference to our telephone conversation yesterday, I have checked the availability French colleague in September. We would indeed be happy to meet with you in London, September 7, at whatever time would be convenient for you.

I am looking forward to our meeting.

Yours sincerely

Acknowledging Receipt Of A Letter During A Person's Absence

Dear

Thank you for your letter of November 6 asking for an appointment with Ms. Louise Rainer. Unfortunately, she is away from the office and is not expected back until the end of this month. Ms. Rainer will contact you upon her return and I am sure she will be pleased to meet with you.

Yours sincerely

Dear

Thank you for your letter of February 5, addressed to Mr. Ronald Santorin, concerning proposed distribution centre. Mr. Santor in is out of town, but I will see that your proposal is called to his immediate attention as soon as he returns to the office next Tuesday.

Yours sincerely

Template 40

Letter Requesting, Acknowledging, Or Refusing Donations X6

Dear

The local chapter of the National Annual Welfare Fund is starting its annual fund-raising this month. We hope that your company will contribute to this very worthy charitable cause.

Thank you very much for your support.

Yours sincerely

Dear

We are pleased to enclose our company check for £1,000 as our annual contribution to fund-raising drive for the local chapter of the National Annual Welfare Fund.

We wish you well in your drive this year.

Yours sincerely

Dear

In response to your letter asking for support for the March of Dollars Benefit Software, we are enclosing a check for £1,500 for a full page ad to be placed in the event journal. Artwork will follow shortly.

Yours sincerely

Dear

Ms. Lisa Frith, national service manager of our sales collection division, will be in Romania on, January 28 and would like to tour your web offset printing plant in nearby Bucharest during that afternoon.

Sincerely

(Accepting An Invitation To Address An Audience)

Dear

Thank you very much for your invitation to address the General Meeting of the Society of Marketing Directors at the American Heritage Hotel in Chicago on October 24 on the subject of new developments in the European satellite broadcasting industry. I am pleased to accept your invitation.

According to your request, I plan to take about 30 minutes for the main part of my speaking engagement followed by a question-and-answer period of about 10 minutes. Mean while, I am looking forward to receiving additional information about the annual meeting.

Yours sincerely

(Declining An Invitation To Address An Audience)

Dear

Thank you very much for your kind invitation to address the members of your Society of Marketing Directors at their annual meeting in Chicago on October 24. Unfortunate I wont be able attend this meeting owing to a prior speaking engagement on that same date. However, I will be happy to address your organization on another occasion.

As an alternate, I suggest that you contact James Novak of

HOME DESIGHN & CO Advertising in London. He recently addressed the members of the Broadcasting Executives Association with a speech about new developments in the satellite industry in the European Union. Thank you again for your invitation. Best of luck with your annual meeting.

Yours sincerely

Template 41

Reservations Of Meeting Room And Other X2

Dear

As discussed on the telephone, we want to reserve the use of a small conference room where dinner can also be served for 23 people for the evening of Thursday, June 7 from 6:00 until 11:00 P.M.

We also want to reserve your three-course steak dinner (£34.95) for every participant, as well as optional bar service.

Please, confirm this reservation by return mail or post.

Yours sincerely

Dear

Ms. Anna Roberts, national service manager of our new fashion collection division, will be in Paris on Thursday, January 28 and would like to tour your web offset printing plant in nearby Paris during that afternoon.

Would it be convenient for you or your assistant to meet her on this date? I will get in touch with you by telephone early next: week to make an appointment.

Yours sincerely

Dear

In reference to our telephone conversation yesterday, I have checked the availability of my French colleague in September. We would indeed be happy to meet with you in San cisco on Thursday, September 7, at whatever time would be convenient for you.

I am looking forward to our meeting.

Yours sincerely

Template 42

Dealing With Club Membership X8

Dear

Your name has been suggested to me by Alfred Drake as a person who is actively interested in community affairs in our town. For that reason, I would like to request your permission to propose your name for membership at the Centreville Civic Club at the next meeting scheduled for Monday, October 4. Please let me know as soon as possible if you are willing to become a member.

Yours sincerely

(Invitation To Consider Membership In A Club)

On behalf of the Carl Wallace Board of Directors in Paradise, I would like to invite you to consider a membership in the Paradise Business Club.

Proceeds from membership directly benefit the Foundation's mission, which is to help higher education pursuits at the vocational/college level and assist with selected funding various local, state, and regional organizations and projects with an agricultural emphasis.

Established in 1990, the Paradise Business Club facilities offer an atmosphere where friends, family, and business associates can enjoy dining and socializing. In addition, the you give through a membership is directly related to the on going commitment to preserve and enhance our communities and the interests they serve.

Join us in our support of this region's leading industry fashion and digital world.

Yours sincerely

(Proposal To Consider A Person For Club Membership)

Dear

I would like to propose Mr. Carl Lewes for membership in the Alma Omega Society.

Mr. Lewes, who has been very active in community and sports affairs in various parts of the recently moved to our town from Dallas, Texas.

I am certain Mr. Lewes would be a real addition and credit to our membership.

Yours sincerely

(Installation Of A New Club Member)

Dear

Thank you very much for recommending me to the Alma Omega Society. I was one of the members and attended the colourful installation ceremony at the Frederick F last week.

Thank you very much for your attention to this request.

Yours sincerely

(Request To Become A Member Of A Professional Organization)

Dear

I believe that, based upon my professional qualifications and business experience, I meet the criteria for membership in the U.S. Association of Certified Travel Agents. For that reason, I would like to receive a membership application form for your organization.

Thank you very much for your attention to this request.

Yours sincerely

(Resignation Of Club Membership)

Dear

It is with considerable regret that I must tender my resignation as vice president of the Mega Style Club. I have not yet fully recovered completely from a recent illness and my business travel schedule for this coming year is such that I would not be able to participate vigorously in the Club's activities. However, I sincerely hope that in a year or two, my health and business affairs will permit me to become active once again in the Club.

Yours sincerely

(Invitation To Members Of A Professional Organization To Attend A Dinner Meeting)

Dear

Our bimonthly dinner meeting scheduled for February 25 should be extremely all members. Our speaker:

William Sokoloff
Service Manager
HOME DESIGHN & CO Photograph Books

He will discuss: A Photo-Journalistic Approach to Book Publishing.

In 2001, HOME DESIGHN & CO Photograph Books became a separate division of HOME DESIGHN & CO Digital Publishing Company Mr. Moon has been in charge of service since 2004. He will cover the wide range of with photojournalists and the problems involved in producing high-quality colour photo books.

See you at the Mandarin Hotel on Wednesday, February 25, at 7:30 P.M.

Yours sincerely

(Announcing A Special Guest Speaker For An Annual Conference)

Dear

During our annual conference of the League for City School Teachers on April 17, we will have a special guest-Dr. Alicia Hobson, Superintendent of Schools, Auburn City-to to us about America's educational system and where it might be in the future.

Meeting the needs of our rapidly expanding educational system, Dr. Hobson has been teacher and administrator for more than 31 years at all levels of public education. Her professional experience in the classroom, her position as head of a large public school system her involvement as a trustee of The Centre for Interracial Urban Education make her greatly qualified to speak about the future needs of our public schools.

We hope to see you in the Auburn City Conference Center on Thursday, April 17 at 9 am.

Yours sincerely

Template 43

Business Offer And Requests X10

(With an unsolicited offer)

Dear

We have seen your name and advertisements in various British trade periodicals and note that you are a major importer of quality garment and shoe racks and accessories, which provide additional hanging space for clothing, shoes, ties, and other personal items. For more than twenty years, our company has been the export agent for the well-known Woodson Racks in London, and we are confident that we can offer your company a great variety of high-quality garment and shoe racks at very competitive prices.

Enclose a copy of our most recent sales collection and price list and hope you will encouraged to place a trial order with us.

Yours s sincerely

(An Uk Manufacturer Offering Merchandise)

Dear

We are a large UK manufacturer specializing in cutlery. As we are particularly keen to pro-mote our high-quality stainless-steel cutlery in Southeast Asia, we are writing to ask if your company would be prepared to allow us to send a representative selection of this cutlery on consignment. In return, we would allow a commission of 11 % calculated on gross profits. No risks are involved, because we will fully reimburse your company for t-he return of any goods that are not: sold within one year. We enclose our collections and price list for your inspection.

We look forward to hearing from you.

Yours sincerely

(Retail chain requesting a sole agency)

Dear

We are a small retail chain with ten sales outlets in the London metropolitan area. Our company specializes in all types of beds (ranging from brass beds, daybeds, French-style and country-style beds, to electric adjustable beds) as well as mattresses (single, twin, queen, and size and so forth).

There is an increasing demand in our sales area for all types of high quality beds and mattresses. For that reason, we are looking for a well-known British manufacturer of these items is willing to offer us a sole agency to retail their beds and mattresses in the San Diego metropolitan area, which includes a large number of suburbs and other communities. Our company is already the sole agent for a major French manufacturer of beds and mattress in the above-mentioned sales territory.

Awaiting your answer to this letter with great interest, we remain.

Yours sincerely

(Request to participate in a survey)

Dear

We are carrying out a survey about the use of business computers in the state of Texas on behalf of the 179 local chapters of the Texas Always Better Business Organization.

The enclosed survey is being conducted among a small, randomly selected sample of medium-sized companies (up to 100 employees). Your participation is very important to our organization. We value your professional opinion. Please feel free, when completing the questionnaire, to include any additional comments you may wish to make.

An independent market research company has been hired to tabulate and analyse you're answers in the enclosed questionnaire. Please be assured that all your answers will be kept strictly confidential and anonymous and will never be associated with your name or used to sell Your answers will only be used to prepare a statistical summary of the survey.

A reply envelope is enclosed and we would very much appreciate your completing and returning the questionnaire to us.

Thank you very much for your kind help and cooperation with this project.

Yours sincerely

(Request to participate in a customer research survey)

Customer Service Questionnaire

Dear

From time to time, we seek the opinion of our customers. We are always trying to the quality of our products and services and the information that you are able to supply will us to serve you better. Your answers will be kept in strict confidence and will only be for statistical analysis.

This questionnaire forms part of our Customer Care Software and we would appreciate to help by completing the enclosed form. Please complete this questionnaire in block and place an "x" in the appropriate boxes. You can return the questionnaire by pre-addressed envelope or by Email communication (000) 000-0000.

Thank you for taking the time to help us.

Yours sincerely

(Letter demanding a retraction in a newspaper)

Dear

We noticed a serious error in the tourism section of the Daily Tribune of September 29. The article "Brave Hearts" about the Native American reservations in Montana, states that our company-John's Trek Tours-only specializes in organizing tours of the Rocky Mountain region. This is incorrect and misleading, because we also offer (since 1991) organized riding and camping tours on Native American tribal lands in Arizona and Utah.

We would appreciate a correction in the next edition of the Daily Tribune. Thank you.

Yours sincerely

(Letter thanking for hospitality)

Dear

You for the kindness and hospitality I enjoyed at your home. Mary is a cook!

I sincerely hope that we may develop some mutually profitable software projects. It would in-deed be advantageous to meet your London representative. Please extend my best wishes to Lisa Green. I will write to him in some detail about the service details we discussed.

Do not forget the standing invitation to visit our home on your next trip to Manchester.

Yours sincerely

(Welcome letter)

Dear

It is certainly a pleasure to welcome you to the Park Hotel.

We are delighted to have you as our guests and I am confident that our services will meet with your satisfaction.

If I may be of any assistance during your stay, please do not hesitate to contact me.

Yours sincerely

Template 44

Placing and acknowledging orders x13

Dear

We acknowledge receipt of your samples and quotation of October 3. Please find our order No. GW/RK 1193-DdeO, for 450 Coats and Dresses.

We would remind you that, as stipulated in our letter of August 29, the blankets must be delivered to our warehouse in Salt Lake City before October 15, because our Sales Week will start on Monday morning, October 27.

Yours sincerity

Dear

We are happy to enclose our trial order No. SidB-8822, for 325 Buda Ladies' Car medium, navy blue colour; at £98.75 per coat, subject to six percent quantity discount sign the duplicate of the enclosed order form and return. It to us as your acknowledgment.

As stated in your quotation of April 8, we may expect immediate shipment from . stock.

As stated in your quotation of April 8, we may expect immediate shipment from stock. We are looking forward to your acknowledgment.

Yours sincerely

Dear

Enclosed you will find our order No. X776 for 550 Brass Finish Table Lamps Model 33D.In 11 accordance with your terms of payment we have instructed International United Commerce Bank to open a credit for £18,710.40 in our favour at their branch office in Newark, New Jersey. This branch office will accept your draft on them for the amount of your invoice.

Yours sincerely

Dear

We thank you for your quotation of July 3 for the supply of vacuum bottles and find your acceptable. We are pleased to enclose our order, No. 993 for 1,.500 unbreakable stain-.less steel vacuum bottles (Cat. No. 330C 1-quart Bottle) at £19.75 per bottle.

We would appreciate delivery within one month and look forward to your acknowledgment.

Yours sincerely

Dear

Thank you for responding so quickly co our telephone inquiry of June 26 about "Rough Country" insulated leather sports boots for men (spring collection : Model X9-22).

We believe that these guaranteed waterproof boots will sell well in Romania and France therefore we enclose that these guaranteed waterproof boots will sell well in UK and US. Therefore we enclose our order form No. 02985B for a substantial trial order. We accept the terms in your quotation of June 28 and also confirm that payment will be made by irrevocable letter of credit.

Please acknowledge this order and also confirm that you will make delivery to Los Angeles, California.

Yours sincerely

Acknowledging an Order

Dear

We acknowledge receipt of your trial order No. MLO-903 for 275 wristwatches (Model X92), which we received today. Your order is now being processed for immediate dispatch and will be ready for airfreight shipment for delivery to Heathrow Airport London early next week. As requested, we will enclose a packing note with the goods.

We are sure you will be pleased with this new line of wristwatches and look forward to working with your company again.

Yours sincerely

Dear

We welcome you as a new customer and appreciate very much your order of May 6, which will be shipped on the 24th by air express. As agreed upon, this order as well as future orders will be shipped to you on our most favourable credit terms.

We are packing our latest window display cards with this order. Within the next few days you will hear from our sales promotion department;, a service that is conducted exclusively for our customers. Please feel free to make use of this service at any time without any charge.

We are looking forward to pleasant business relations with your company.

Yours sincerely

Dear

Thank you for your order (SB-8802) for three general purpose lightweight hand trucks are currently processing this order, which we expect to have ready for shipment by Express Services within two weeks. Our shipping department will notify you in advance.

Thank you for doing business with us.

Yours sincerely

Dear

Thank you for your order No. C 876-DD for 12.5 Do-It-Yourself Design Machines we are unable at this time to fulfil this order due to a fire in our manufacturing plant London three days ago. We intend co resume service next week and expect deliver your order early next month.

We apologize for the delay and hope it will not cause you serious inconvenience.

Yours sincerely

Dear

In our circular letter of September 15 (a copy of which is enclosed with this letter), we ad-our customers of price increases in our entire Speedy Sport Bicycle line which would become effective on October 1. For that reason, we regret that we cannot accept your order No. ACC-18 of October 10 which uses the expired price list.

We look forward to hearing from you soon.

Dear

Thank you for your order No. 396MJ. Much as we would like to accept your order and to do business with your company, we are unable to accept your order at the price you requested of £123.25 per ten units. As indicated in our Email communication of November 14, we stated they £127.50 was our   F lowest price per ten units. Our profit margins, which are already the lowest in the industry, simply do not warrant a further reduction in our quoted price. It stands to reason that we will |simply do not warrant a further reduction in our quoted price. It stands to reason that we will be pleased to fulfil your order 396CF if you will confirm our price of £112.5'0 per ten units.

Yours sincerely

Dear

Thank you for your order No. 00530 of January 19 for 600 Apple Phone Model 18A at £97.95 per unit. We have these clocks in stock and will be able to deliver before the date-March 6-you requested.

However, we are sorry that we cannot supply your order on the credit terms you requested and for that reason request prepayment. Enclosed you will email our preformat invoice. We would be obliged if you would arrange payment for this invoice by either irrevocable letter of credit draft as soon as possible in order that we can ship the goods to PO BOX 235 London.

Yours sincerely

Dear

We have received your most recent order (£98-ZAZ/Bob) and we thank you. Unfortunately, we are temporarily out of stock of Bluetooth headsets in the model you specified. We to receive a new supply shortly and we will send your order as possible.

Thank you so much for your patience during this delay.

Yours sincerely

Template 43: Cancelling an Order

Dear

We are sorry to inform you that we must cancel our order No. MDS:1874 of June 9 due the inexcusable delay in the shipment of the goods, which we still have not yet received.

Yours sincerely

Dear

We are sure you will understand that your very long delay in delivery puts our company in an embarrassing position. For that reason, we can see no alternative but to cancel our order £800 RKTR-741 dated March 28. In addition, we will hold your company liable for all losses caused by this inexcusable delay.

Yours sincerely

Template 44: Collection payment reminders x12

Dear

Just a friendly reminder that we would very much appreciate your payment of £125.50 for copy of our annual Software Digital Tool that you purchased on February 19 you already completed the payment you should disregard this letter. If it is not, please take a moment to complete payment online today.

Thank you very much for your cooperation.

Yours sincerely

Dear

This is just a friendly reminder that your payment of £769.14 will be very much appreciated. This amount is still outstanding in our books. Please check your records.

Dear

In checking our records, we find there is still a balance of £1175.80 due to us for the purchase of website package on October 2. Has the payment been overlooked?

If your check is already in the mail, please disregard this notice. However, if you cannot pay online please inform us when we may expect payment of this balance.

Yours sincerely

Dear

This is just a friendly reminder that your payment of £769.14 will be very much appreciated. This amount is still outstanding in our books. Please check your records. I have attached a link to our online payments methods.

Yours sincerely

Dear

This is just a reminder to inform you that your account is overdue. Please send us the payment due of £1,605.38 vie online payment.

Thank you for your cooperation.

Yours sincerely

Dear

An examination of our records indicate that the following two amounts-for a total £1,605.38-are due from your company:

Invoice A 8763 dated June 18, 20XX for £962.10
Invoice A 8911 dated July 14, 20XX for £643.28

If the above listed amounts are in order, we would appreciate receiving your check £1,605.38 immediately.

Please, inform us in the event there is a valid reason why this balance cannot be paid online immediately. If payment has already been made, you should disregard this reminder.

Yours truly,

Dear

It is some time since we dispatched your order (No. 922) and payment has not yet received. The details are shown on the enclosed statement.

Our terms of business require prompt payment.

Could you please pay the amount due now? If you have already paid, and this email has crossed your payment in the mail, please accept our thanks. If you have any query account, please complete the enclosed form and return it to us.

Yours sincerely

Dear

We are sorry to inform you that your direct debit dated on June 7, and drawn to our in the amount of £374.67 was denied. The Bank of Atlanta returned this notice today with the notation "Insufficient Funds."

It is with reluctance that we now make this formal approach and request you to send us in a certified payment for £374.67. We insist on your prompt attention to this matter.

Yours sincerely

Template 45

Urgent collection payment Reminder x11

Dear

We still have not received payment for the balance of £1,822.58, despite the reminder we sent you on September 2.

Please send us a check for this amount by return mail or inform us immediately about reason this payment is delayed.

Thank you for your cooperation.

Yours sincerely

Dear

In looking over our records, we noticed that your account shows an unpaid balance of.£711.45. Oversights, of course, do happen and therefore we are bringing this immediate attention.

Are sure you will cooperate in keeping your account within the agreed terms payment upon receipt of the monthly statement. A postage-paid envelope has been enclosed for your immediate attention.

We are sure you will cooperate in keeping your account within the agreed terms receipt of the monthly statement. A postage-paid envelope has been enclosed for your convenience.

Your prompt remittance will be appreciated.

Yours sincerely

Dear

Our records indicate that we have had no remittance from your company in response to our letter of May 21. The amount due is £251.87 and we would appreciate your remittance. Thank you for your prompt attention.

Yours sincerely

Dear

A review of your account shows that you have not yet settled your outstanding balance of £331.95, which has been on our books for the past two months. It becomes necessary for us to remind you once again to pay this amount. We really must have a remittance by return mail.

Yours sincerely

Dear

According to our records, your account for our invoice £891 of September 7, amounting to £282.73, is unpaid and past due. We wrote you about this account on July 23, but we received no answer. We wish again to call your attention to the need for immediate of this overdue invoice.

Yours sincerely

Reminder Collection LETTER

Dear

We are disappointed that we have not received any answer from you in response to our recent emails as well as two registered LETTER regarding the payment of the bill for £12,21.76 that you owe our company. This amount is now more than four months overdue. Because you are a valued customer who has always been prompt in paying bills on time, we are wondering why we have not heard from you about this matter. However, we are also sure that you do not want to lose our company's credit standing. You know that our company policy prohibits extending credit to customers who have past-due charges outstanding. Is there a reason for the delay of this payment?

Yours sincerely

Dear

Three months have passed since we mailed you our reminder LETTER about your balance of £1,139.07. However, we have not yet received payment of this amount.

Before this unpaid balance will affect your credit standing, please send us your right away or phone me at (000) 000-0000 to inform me of any reason why you should so.

Yours sincerely

Dear

Our records indicate that your company still owes £6,31.00 from your last order. The account is significantly beyond the 30 days we agreed to when we opened your company credit account last year. Please send payment by return mail since we cannot delay. However, if for any valid reason you cannot pay at this time, call me as soon as you can so that we can discuss an alternative. We cannot believe that you would account to become a forced collection matter.

Yours sincerely

Dear

We are at a loss to understand why we have not heard from you regarding payment of £4,400.92, now more than four months overdue. Therefore, we must hear from you immediately, because on May 15, we will send our quarterly report to the Manufacturers' Credit We are certain that you do not want your company' s name on that list since it would seriously affect the national as well as regional credit rating of your organization.

Since we have not received your payment, we have no alternative but to withdraw your company's credit privileges, effective immediately.

This letter also serves as notice to you that unless you contact us by calling or writing within ten days from today, we will turn your account over for collection proceedings.

Yours sincerely

("Ultimatum") Collection LETTER

Dear

Your bill of £2,459.10 is now overdue 120 days. Please remit this amount at once. If your is not received by March 1, your bill will be placed in the hands of our collection agency.

Yours sincerely

Dear

This is to inform you that after three reminders and several telephone calls, you still have not made any effort to settle your past due account of £6,553.00. Therefore, we are now putting the matter into the hands of the Mayfair Collection Agency on May 14.

Yours sincerely

Dear

Your disregard of our previous reminders and personal telephone calls concerning your count, which is long overdue and delinquent, leaves our company no choice but to serve demand upon you for full payment. If your check for £4,480.55 is not in our hands by July 1 your account will automatically be referred to the Mayfair Collection Agency for lection. We do not like to take these drastic measures, but you leave us with no alternative.

Dear

Our Credit Manager has decided that your delinquent account will be referred to our attorney for legal action in order to collect the outstanding balance of £9,881.'72 due to us for than four months.

Your continuing lack of response to our LETTER, Email communications, and telephone calls and your unwell-Inness to cooperate leaves us no other choice.

Dear

Our credit and collection department has just informed me of their intention to take legal action, because you have failed to answer any of our LETTER, email telegrams, and calls requesting immediate payment of £14,100.19, which is now five months overdue. Unless we hear from you within five-business days-on or before February 12-we will turn delinquent account over to our collection agency.

Yours sincerely

Letter For Banking And Credit Concerns Letter

1. Requesting a credit report
2. Adding or removing someone from a credit account
3. Requesting information on available services
4. Requesting status of a loan application
5. Instructing that an overpayment be applied to a mortgage principal
6. Requesting investigation of a possible bank error
7. Disputing denial of a loan or credit card
8. Disputing fee increase or new fee
9. Disputing a charge
10. Requesting a credit card limit increase
11. Negotiating a payment schedule with a creditor
12. Demanding action
13. Closing an account
14. Recognizing good service
15. Closing a long-standing account

Template 1

Requesting a credit report

Dear

Could you please send me a copy of my current credit report?

On November 1, First America Bank recently denied my application for a Visa card, and I understand that I am entitled to receive, without charge, a copy of my credit report within 30 days of this denial.

If you need further information from me to provide this report, please call my home at 214/555-0398.

Thank you for your prompt attention to my request.

Sincerely

Template 2

Adding Or Removing Someone From A Credit Account

Dear

Please add my son's name to my Charge Card account, effective immediately, and provide him a card in his name.

My 18-year-old son, Thomas Mayhem, will begin school out of state in January, and I'd like him to have access to the family Charge Card account.

Currently, this account has two cardholders, my wife, Judith and me. Thomas would be the third cardholder.

Naturally, as primary cardholder, I retain primary responsibility for any charges incurred on this account.(Thomas should be using the card only for agreed-upon school expenses and for emergencies.)

If I can provide additional information about this request, please call me at (122) 555-9734. Otherwise, we'll be looking to receive an additional card in 'Thomas's name by mail sometime before January 1, 1999.

Sincerely

Template 3

Requesting Information On Available Services

Dear

Please send me information about your bank's savings and checking accounts.

I will be moving to Garden Grove within the month and will be looking for a bank to which I can transfer my account balances.

These are the services I'm most interested in:

- No-fee checking when I maintain a minimum balance.
- Overdraft protection or automatic transfer from savings.
- Extended banking hours on Friday afternoons and Saturday mornings.
- No-fee, reliable 24-hour access to ATMs.
- No-fee telephone banking.
- No-fee telephone banking.
- Christmas Club or youth-oriented savings accounts.

Please be sure to include your complete fee schedule, hours of operation, and rules and regulations for these accounts.

If you have questions about my request, please call me at 208/555-4903.

Thank you for your assistance, and I look forward to receiving this information so that I may choose the bank that best meets my family's needs.

Sincerely

Template 4

Requesting Status Of A Loan Application

Dear

I seem to be having some difficulty determining the status of my pending loan. Can you assist me?

My husband and I met with you and applied for a small business loan more than three weeks ago. But we have yet to receive any further information about it. Where do we stand?

Borrowers' names and SSNs: Alfred & Nadine Ireland 312-87-8695 & 307-98-1242.

Type of loan: Standard Small Business
Loan amount: £17,500
Application date: March 18, 2004

Because our plans to build additional office space hinge on receiving this loan and we are already negotiating with contractors, please call us by the end of next week with any information you can provide. You may reach me on weekdays at 316/555-7878.

I would greatly appreciate any information or anything you can do to help speed up the processing of our loan. I look forward to hearing from you by the end of next week.

Sincerely

Template 5

Instructing That An Overpayment Be Applied To A Mortgage Principal

Dear

Please apply the £201.48 overpayment I'm making this to the principal of my mortgage loan.

Amount of July payment.   £1,000.00
Amount due: 79852
Additional amount to be applied to principal   £5678

Please call me with any concerns about how this overpayment should be applied: 880/555-1810.

Thank you for your usual efficient handling of my payment request.

Cordially

Template 6

Requesting Investigation Of A Possible Bank Error

Dear

I believe I may have discovered an error in my February checking account statement. Could you please check into this and help me reconcile the discrepancy?

My statement shows a deposit February 26 of £280. The next day, February 27, a check for £872 was returned for non-sufficient funds, and I was assessed a £20 overdraft fee.

My records indicate, however, that the February 26 deposit was actually for £2,800, which would more than have covered the February 27 check.

Attached is a copy of my February 26 deposit receipt.

Please call me with your assessment of this situation. You may reach me weekdays at 787-1500.

Thank you for helping me resolve this situation as promptly as possible. ! look forward to hearing from you within the next few days.

Sincerely

Deposit receipt attached

Template 7

Disputing Denial Of A Loan Or Credit Card

Dear

Please reconsider my application for a First America Visa card. I believe my original "pre-approved" application has been denied in error.

On October 1, I was denied a credit card based on "accounts with past due balances." As your letter suggested, I obtained a copy of my credit report, which lists every account I've ever held as "reported with no adverse information.

If this was, in fact, a legitimate offer to which I responded, I would appreciate your taking a second look at my credit history-or providing a legitimate reason for my denial. A copy of my original application is attached.

I look forward from hearing from you in the next few with either good news or a reasonable explanation for my denial.

Thank you for your reconsideration

Attachment: original First America Visa card application

Template 8

Disputing Fee Increase Or New Fee

Dear

I have noticed new ATM fees on my last two bank statements but don't recall receiving a notice explaining the reason for fees. Could you please explain why I'm now being every time I use an automated teller machine? I do not feel I should be charged, especially without notice, for using ATMs.

As you probably know, I've banked with you for nearly 20 years. In the last few years, I've found ATMs a convenient solution to my odd work schedule, which means often handling my banking before or after banking hours.

I've also appreciated the fact that I could use the most convenient ATM, even if it wasn't one at a Second National branch, all of which tend to be located on the outskirts of town. The fact that so many ATMs have been available to me, free of charge, is no doubt a key reason I've stayed with Second National in spite of my moving several times to different homes and different jobs around the city.

I do not feel I should be charged to use ATMs to conduct my banking business, and further feel that the fees, totalling £12.50, on my last two statements, those for July and August, should be refunded to me.

Please call or write me to fully explain your policies regarding ATM fees and how I might receive a refund of these fees charged without my consent. Phone: 075 8776666.

Yours truly

Template 9

Disputing A Charge

Dear

Please remove the May 9 Hospitality Hotel charge of £89 from my account; this charge was placed on my account in error.

I did reserve a room with Hospitality Hoteling Houston for this date and held the reservation with my MasterCard, but two days prior to this date I cancelled the reservation. Because the hotel's policy allows for cancelations up until 6 p.m. the day of arrival, Miss Taylor at the hotel assured me I would not be charged.

I have also called the hotel, whose staff assures me the charge will be removed. However, because I am not completely confident the hotel will handle this competently, I decided to write to you as well.

I will look for an £89 adjustment on my next statement; if you have further questions about this situation or if you difficulty meeting my request, please call me: 110/897-4643.

Thank you for removing this charge with your usual promptness. Unlike my dealings with Hospitality Hotel, my dealings with Cardholder Services have consistently been good ones. I appreciate that!

Yours truly

Template 10

Requesting A Credit Card Limit Increase

Dear

Raise the limit on my Visa card account from its current £1,500 to £3,000.

As your records can confirm, I've kept this account in good standing for more than two years. I've never even been late with a payment and almost always pay above the minimum due each month. If you need more information about my financial situation, I would be happy to discuss this with you or any forms required to complete my request.

If I need do nothing more, please simply inform me of my new limit when it has been raised. Lf I need to provide more information, please write or call me with that information. My phone numbers are 990/555-8393 (daytime) or 990/555-9185 (evenings).

I would appreciate your prompt consideration of my request for this limit increase I feel completely confident I can handle.

Sincerely

Template 11

Negotiating A Payment Schedule With A Creditor

Dear

1 would like to propose establishing a regular payment schedule with you to help me pay my unpaid balance of £1,039.25.

Unfortunately, my financial situation has changed rather significantly in the month since you removed Rebecca's braces. The company with whom I've worked for the past eight years recently laid me off, and I am in the process of finding another job.

Until my employment situation changes, I'd like to make monthly payments of £50. Enclosed is my first monthly payment.

As you can perhaps imagine, I find having to make these arrangements with you a little embarrassing. J fully expect this to be a temporary situation; you can expect full payment as soon as I've secured another job.

I hope you find this payment schedule acceptable, Thank you for your understanding in this matter.

Sincerely

Template 12

Demanding Action

Dear

I'm concerned that I haven't seen a change in my account or heard from you regarding my March 8 letter. Will you help me, or should I be working with the branch manager?

My March 8 letter detailed how a £2,800 deposit was mistakenly entered as £280 and then resulted in a NSF check when the accurate balance should have covered the check. Attached is a of my first letter.

I expect my checking account to be corrected immediately and to I I be notified within the next week to 10 days that it has been corrected. If I do not hear from you in that time, I will discuss my concerns with your branch manager and lodge a formal complaint with the Coiorado Department of Financial Institutions and the local Better Business Bureau.

My daytime phone number, again, is 787-1500.

I look forward to hearing from you with good news.

Sincerely

Attachment: March 22 letter

Template 13

Closing An Account

Dear

Please accept the enclosed check as payment in full on my First America Visa card, and close my account

The 5.9 per cent interest rate for the first year was a great deal; however, both the mediocre service I've received during that year and the current, non-negotiable 14.9 per cent interest rate make keeping the account foolish when so many better options are available.

Thanks, again, for a year of credit with an outstanding interest rate.

Sincerely

Check enclosed

Template 14

Recognizing Good Service

Dear

Your representative, Craig Randall, handled a disputed charge for me with such speed and professionalism that I felt compelled to write to you.

As the attached letter suggests, I was concerned that the merchant involved, Hospitality Hotel, would not act to remove the charge. When they did not do so even two weeks after they had agreed to, Mr. Randall took the initiative to call them directly and made sure the problem was resolved on the spot.

Again, I commend Mr. Randall on his outstanding service; the quality of training your representatives receive is clearly evident in the above-and-beyond acts I've received many times from representatives at Second National Bank.

Thank you from a loyal customer!

Attachment

Template 15

Closing A Long-Standing Account

Dear

Thank you for answering my questions about the ATM I've recently been seeing on my bank statements.

Thank you, to, for refunding your bank's fees from my previous two months' statements since J was not aware of your new fee policy. I also understand that what other banks charge   U Second National customers to use their machines is quite out of your control.

With the established fee structure of all the banks involved, though, I guess I should expect to pay extensive bank machine fees from now on. You see, I must use ATMs (to do my banking at odd hours), and Second National machines are rarely the most convenient for me.

Because I cannot accept such extensive fee increases, I will be moving my accounts to First Mutual, whose ATM fee policy seems much more reasonable.

Thank you for the nearly 20 years of outstanding service you've given my family. Especially when I've had concerns over the last few years about the bank's two buy-outs, you've been extremely helpful.

Yours truly

Medical And Insurance Concerns Letter

1. Authorizing release of medical records
2. Requesting medical information for an employer
3. Requesting information on a pending claim
4. Requesting a change in beneficiary
5. Requesting information about a disease
6. Disputing a straightforward billing error
7. Disputing a less-than-straightforward billing error
8. Disputing denial on insurance coverage or a claim
9. Arranging for monthly payments
10. Complaining about medical services or staff
11. Terminating poor medical care
12. Showing appreciation for good care or service
13. Terminating a long-standing healthcare relationship

Template 1

Authorizing Release Of Medical Records

Dear

With this authorization, please release all medical records my son, Robert T. Smith (birth date: 5/11/2022), related to his knee injury last.

Please send the records to:

Dr. John Murdock

9011 Medical Plaza

Crossroads, IN 45444

If you need further information from me about my request, please call me at 233 5678.

Because we have an appointment for a second surgical we have an appointment for a second surgical your prompt attention to my request.

Sincerely

Template 2

Requesting Medical Information For An Employer

Dear

My employer has requested a letter from you detailing medical condition. Could you please provide such a letter within the next week, if possible?

With my recent back injury, I have requested temporary placement in a position that does not require the bending and lifting I typically do in our warehouse. My employer is generally supportive but would like more information about what I should and should not do at work.

With this letter as authorization, please provide such information to:

Mainline Pipe & Conduit

London

SW45PS

Thank you for you assistance.

Sincerely

Template 3

Requesting Information On A Pending Claim

Dear

I need your assistance with a claim I filed more than six weeks ago but have yet to receive any information about.

Here are the relevant details:

Patient name and DOB: Sharon Moon, 6/28/57

Date of treatment: April 28, 2004

Doctor's name: Theodore Willson

Amount of claim: £678.92

Please call or write me with a response to my claim. You may reach me weekdays at 616/555-2262.

I would appreciate your prompt attention to my claim.

Sincerely

Template 4

Requesting A Change In Beneficiary

Dear

Effective immediately, please change the beneficiary on my term life insurance policy.

With my recent marriage, I'd like the following people named as beneficiaries on my policy:

Primary beneficiary: Simon More SSN 307-96-9878

Secondary beneficiaries: Charles and Mary Martinez 304-78-9646

If you have questions about my request, please call me at 555/622-0393 (days) or 555/547-9630 (evenings).

Thank you for handling this important matter for me.

Sincerely

Template 5

Requesting Information About A Disease

Dear

Could you please send me information about Alzheimer's disease? My mother was recently diagnosed with this and her doctor referred me to your organization for more information.

Here are my key concerns:

- What do we know about how quickly the disease typically progresses?
- What stages can we expect to go through?
- What medications seem most effective in postponing the onset of advanced symptoms?
- What, if anything, can we do to stimulate her mental functioning?

I would appreciate any literature or research results you can provide. I don't have a medical background, but (as you can imagine) I'm extremely interested in learning all I can to help my mother and our family to live with this difficult disease.

If you need more information about my request, please call me at 696/455-9878.

Thank you for your assistance. This information will be invaluable to my family.

Sincerely

Template 6

Disputing A Straightforward Billing Error

Dear

My August 4 statement of charges contains an error, and I will appreciate your making an adjustment as soon as you can.

After I left your offices last Tuesday, I noticed that my statement lists a £68 charge for x-rays. While Dr. Gum and I discussed a possible x-ray, we ultimately decided it was not necessary and that my ankle was merely sprained. I'm Dr. Gum can verify that she did not order an x-ray.

For your convenience, a copy of my statement is attached. If you have any questions, please call me: 467 8888.

Thank you for addressing this promptly with my insurance company, United Heath care, with whom you filed this claim.

Sincerely

Attachment: August 4 statement of charges

Template 7

Disputing A Less-Than-Straightforward Billing Error

Dear

I recently received a second notice for lab charges my insurance company tells

me I am not responsible to pay. Please remove these charges from my account immediately, and stop sending me these insulting LETTER. (Copies of your LETTER and one from my insurance company are attached.)

As a preferred provider, your organization has agreed to provide services for "usual and customary rates." My insurance company, United Healthcare, has explained to that I am not responsible for fees above the "usual and customary rates," to which you have agreed and for which Healthcare has already paid you.

I hope this letter clears up the matter, but if I can provide more information, please call me at 555-8732.

I hope this letter clears up the matter, but if I can provide more information, please call me at 555-8732.

I'm willing to assume that these LETTER have resulted from a misunderstanding and that your company will quickly resolve this situation-without sending me more form LETTER.

Thank you

Attachments

Template 8

Disputing Denial On Insurance Coverage Or A Claim

Dear

Please reconsider your denial to pay for my daughter's Retin-A prescription. This is a medication that certainly should be-and in the past, has been-covered under our policy.

My daughter's dermatologist, Dr. Frith, has prescribed this medication for acne several times in the two years. This is the first time we've had any difficulty receiving reimbursement. Enclosed is a copy of the doctor Verification of Medical Need form, which she submitted to you last month.

Please reconsider this claim (I've also enclosed a copy of the claim), and if you will not reimburse us, please explain why. You may reach me days or evenings at 555/201-8111.

Thank you for your understanding in this matter. I Look forward to hearing from you soon.

Sincerely

Template 8

Arranging For Monthly Payments

Dear

The fees on my January 12 statement seem to be in order. I would like to work with you to establish a regular payment schedule to help our family pay our unpaid balance.

As you might suspect, this automobile accident has hit my family hard financially. Even with medical insurance, the bills family hard financially. Even with medical insurance this bills are much more than we can afford immediately .

I'd like to suggest monthly payments of £200. This amount is the very most we can afford especially in light of other expenses related to the accident. Enclosed is my first monthly payment.

I've never been comfortable owing large amounts of money to a creditor. Believe me, if I had any choice at all, you would already have payment in full.

I hope you find this payment schedule acceptable. Thank you for your understanding in this matter.

Sincerely

Template 9

Complaining About Medical Services Or Staff

Dear

Earlier this summer my husband (then my fiancé) and I received the most incompetent medical care from one of your doctors that either one of us has ever received. I would strongly encourage you to remove him from your medical staff.

Just days before our wedding, we both developed a mysterious rash from head to toe. It seemed enough to warrant a visit to your East Side MedCheck early on a Friday evening, June 5. (The wedding was that Sunday.)

Dr. Craig Simpleton saw us and quickly diagnosed it as scabies, which I was appalled to learn results from a parasite laying eggs under the skin! I was almost more appalled by his prescription: an insecticide with which we were to dowse ourselves from head to toe morning and night for several days. The diagnosis seemed odd, but we dutifully followed his advice, yes, even on our wedding day and night.

Imagine my amazement when a (not a doctor) asked us just as we were leaving the next day for our honeymoon, where we had gotten into so much "poison ivy.' (We had even told Dr. Simpleton we'd both been working in the yard all that Friday).

I will never return to a National Centre. I sincerely hope this doctor is not representative of your entire staff, and I encourage you to get rid of such incompetence before a more serious mistake costs someone much more than a romantic wedding night.

Sincerely

Template 10

Terminating poor medical care

Dear

I will no longer be returning to your office for my gynaecological care. Please forward my medical records to:

Dr. Anna Frith
7287 Medvale Pike, Suite 90
London SW34MR

I'm a relatively new patient, and I've found working with your dehumanizing. Your staff is neither courteous nor conscientious. When I call for Jab results, I'm put on hold for long periods without explanation; I end up explaining the same information to several people, each of whom expresses the same ignorance and indifference about my questions. Then I'm told "The doctor will call you back." Yet I never get a return call.

I have also yet to schedule an appointment for which I didn't have to wait at least 45 minutes. Couldn't appointments be scheduled better to show respect for your patients' time?

If you would like to hear more about one patient's first impressions, I would be happy to discuss my experiences further. You can call me during work hours at 315-6457.

J'm sure your reputation as a physician is well-deserved, but I would never feel comfortable entrusting my care to a doctor whose office management shows so little respect for her patients.

Sincerely

Template 11

Showing Appreciation For Good Care Or Service

Dear

Your care of my father during his recent heart difficulties was nothing less than exceptional, and I'd like to thank you.

I imagine thousands of doctors are, like you, quite competent with the technical aspects of performing an angioplasty. But I've rarely (if ever) seen a doctor handle these less technical aspects with such grace. You met with my several times, always with diagrams in hand; to make sure he understood and was comfortable with what was happening to him. You answered all of our questions with patience and genuine concern, never confounding us with medical Language-as I've so often experienced with doctors.

My profession is that of an adult educator, so I know qui a bit about how adults learn, how fearful they can be when they feel ignorant, and how they like to be treated as they learn. Your skills in this area are among some of the best I've seen among my professional colleagues. Commend you and thank you.

Respectfully

Template 13

Terminating A Long-Standing Healthcare Relationship

Dear

Thank you for your care and attention during the last six years I've been a patient. You've always been competent and attentive with my medical needs and have worked hard to accommodate, even on short notice, any appointment changes my challenging work schedule has required me to make.

As you may already be aware, your move to the far west side of town, creating a 30-minute drive for me each way, has made keeping my appointments even more challenging.

Because I cannot expect this situation to become easier for either of us, I feel I must find a physician more centrally located. I'd like next Thursday to be my last appointment with you.

I regret having to make this decision. I have always trusted your judgment regarding my care, and I would greatly appreciate your recommendation of a physician with offices on the north side of town. Could we discuss this when I see you on Thursday?

Kind regards

Consumer letter samples

1. Making a reservation 231
2. Requesting information from a merchant 233
3. Requesting information from a utility
4. Placing an order for merchandise or service
5. Following up on an order for merchandise or service
6. Following up on an order for merchandise or service
7. An alternative to complaining: Requesting information on a rent increase or maintenance problem
8. Cancelling an order for merchandise or service
9. Returning merchandise
10. Requesting return of a deposit
11. Requesting repair or replacement
12. Requesting repair or replacement
13. Requesting a refund
14. Informing utility of a billing error
15. Breaking a service contract
16. Breaking a lease; requesting security deposit return
17. An alternative to complaining: : Requesting help
18. Informing of hazardous

19. Demanding action

20. Your intention to go to a third party

21. Reporting to a third party

22. Recognizing good service

23. Ending a long-standing business relationship

24. Requesting information on placing a classified ad

25. Voicing an opinion

26. Demanding a correction or retraction

27. Thanking a reporter for fair coverage

28. Template for a cold e-mail

29. Professional Email for Salary Negotiation

Template 1

Making A Reservation

Dear

Will you please reserve a double room for my husband and me for Friday, February 6 through Sunday, February 8?

We plan to arrive before 6 p.m. Friday evening. I understand that you do not need a credit card to hold our reservation so long as we arrive before 6 p.m. If you have questions about my request, please call me: 898 87654.

Please confirm our reservation by January 12. Thank you.

Sincerely

Template 2

Requesting Information From A Merchant

Dear

Please send me information and literature on midrise copiers appropriate for my home office.

These are the features I'm looking for:

- Copy speed at least 10 pages per minute.

- Copy surface large enough for 11 1/2" x 14" documents.

- Multiple paper trays.
- Enlarging capabilities to 200 percent.
- Easy toner replacement (ideally a cartridge versus roller).

I am writing to several companies for information and will make a purchase in the next month based on the information I receive. Please include copier prices, as well as details and fees for any maintenance plans you offer.

Please do not have a sales representative contact me.

However, if you have questions about my request, call me at 67786988.

Thank you for your assistance, and I look forward to receiving this information.

Sincerely

Template 3

Requesting Information On A Rent Increase Or Maintenance Problem

Dear

Your letter explaining the increase in my rent raised some questions for me; could you please answer them?

1. As you know, when I moved in three years ago, I was told As you know, when I moved in three years ago, I was told has?

   Rent November 1995:   £425
   Rent as of October 1996:   £480
   Rent as of November 1997:   £510
   Rent proposed November 2004:   £530

2. Are you also aware that my rent has increased nearly 25%

3. Are you aware that comparable apartments in this area rent more in the range of £400-£480?

4. Finally, when might I expect the next increase, and are you willing to guarantee no increase before that time?

Please drop me a note or call me (555-8293) with answers these questions. I'd appreciate hearing from you before my November rent payment is due.

Sincerely

Template 3

Cancelling An Order For Merchandise Or Service

Dear

Please stop delivery of The Clinton Daily Times to my home effective immediately.

My wife and I have enjoyed receiving your publication for years. Unfortunately, our jobs now have us both traveling most weeks, and we simply cannot keep up with a daily paper.

I believe we have prepaid for April; please send us a refund for the issues we will not receive. If you have questions about this cancellation request, please leave a message at (199) 555-5612, and either my wife or I' will call you back as soon as we can.

Thank you for years of reliable delivery of a top-notch newspaper. If our situation changes, we'll call you to resume delivery. In the meantime, we will expect delivery to stop no later than the end of this week.

Sincerely yours

Template 4

Returning Merchandise

Dear

Enclosed is the Auto Lock De-Icer I received by mail two weeks ago. I'd like a refund for this product because it does not suit my needs.

Your collection seemed to describe a device that was exactly what I've needed for door locks that continually freeze throughout the winter. And the small heated metal rod seemed a more environmentally sound solution than those disposable tubes of alcohol I'd been using.

But this flimsy device falls into pieces when I try to install the batteries. Couldn't such a device be better made so it won't fall apart in my hands (let alone in a coat pocket, where I'd need to keep it)? Lf you offer such a device, I'd love to hear it 345 0000.

As for this device, however, I expect a full refund-including my cost to ship it back to you. Copies of both my sales receipt and a receipt for return postage are enclosed. Please send me my refund within the next two weeks.

Thank you

Template 5

Requesting Return Of A Deposit

Dear

Please return the £20 deposit I left with you for the Eco sound shoes you ordered for me two weeks ago. (Enclosed is my receipt for the deposit.)

When you called last week to tell me your distributor could not get the shoes for six to eight weeks, I checked around here in Flamingo and was able to find a pair immediately.

In case my number isn't handy and you have any questions, it's 3456 000.

Thank you for checking into this for me-and especially for letting me know you were experiencing a delay. You still have the best prices in London for Earth-friendly shoes. You can bet Ill shop with you again.

Sincerely

Template 6

Requesting Repair Or Replacement (Under Warranty)

Dear

Please replace the enclosed pair of defective sunglasses.

I purchased these glasses from your shop four months ago. As you can see, the colour already wearing off the metal frames.

Enclosed with the sunglasses is a copy of my sales receipt. If you have questions or concerns about my request, I can be reached at 078 09876898.

Thank you for your understanding and prompt response.

Sincerely

Template 7

Requesting Repair Or Replacement (No Longer Under Warranty)

Dear

Please repair or replace the enclosed pair of defective sunglasses.

I purchased these glasses from your shop just over one year ago. While they are no longer under warranty, you can see that the is wearing off the metal frames.

These are not inexpensive sunglasses, and I certainly did not expect them to show such wear in just a year's time. They receive no unusually harsh treatment; in fact, when I'm not wearing them, sunglasses show wear better than these are showing?

Enclosed with the sunglasses is a copy of my sales receipt. I do not feel should be charged for a repair or replacement. If you have questions or concerns about my request, I can be reached at 076 00000.

My preference would be to receive a replacement pair unless you can assure me that a repair will really solve the problem. I do not want to be writing you again in a few months.

Thank you for your understanding in this matter. I've purchased sunglasses from your company for years, and I feel certain you'll make this right.

Sincerely

Template 7

Requesting A Refund

Dear

Please refund my purchase price and return postage cost for the enclosed blouse.

I've also enclosed a copy of my sales receipt. Although you'll find I purchased this blouse more than two months ago, I only recently experienced a problem with it when I washed it for the first time. It fell apart!

Your clothes are generally very high quality. I am quite surprised at the how poorly this blouse seems to have been made. In fact, I was somewhat afraid to wash it at all, but I liked the look of the blouse so much, I decided to keep it. When I did wash it, I followed the washing instructions on the label to the letter. If you have any questions about my handling of the blouse, please call me: (211) 555-3902.

Is this an indication of the quality I can expect from Best Dressed Collection Fashions in the future?

Because I paid for it online, I would appreciate returning my purchase price, £39.99, along with the my cost (postage receipt also enclosed) by check as by check as well.

Thank you for your prompt handling of my return.

Yours truly

Template 8

Informing Utility Of A Billing Error

Dear

I need your help in resolving what must be a billing error on my March bill.

My average monthly bill for wintertime gas usage runs £80.40.

With the unusually warm weather we've had in February and March, my family has actually turned our heat off for weeks at a time during these months.

How, then, could our March gas bill be £115.80?!

Please call or write me with either a revised amount due or a detailed explanation for these charges before this bill's due date, April 28. My phone number is 078 09789.

I look forward to hearing from you within the next two weeks.

Sincerely yours

Template 9

Breaking A Service Contract

Dear

Please cancel my service contract and refund the monthly fee I've paid for the past three months.

As we discussed on the telephone yesterday, I have had virtually no opportunity to take advantage of your service given repeated busy signals and the apparently limited ability of our repeated busy signals and the apparently limited ability of that I've been able to use your service perhaps a half dozen times over the past three months.

I understand that you typically do not refund customers' monthly fees beyond the trial period (the first month after sign-up) or in situations in which they've used the service at all during a given month; however, I'm sure you'll agree that my circumstances are unique. I have, in fact, been prevented from using the service I've been paying for.

Please call me at the phone number I've listed above with any questions or concerns about my request. I will expect the automatic billing through my local phone company to end with my next month's bill. Please send my refund check to my home address (above).

Thank you for your cooperation and understanding in this matter.

Regards

Template 10

Breaking A Lease; Request Security Deposit Return

Dear

I will be moving out December 1, 2004, and request that that my security deposit, £425, be returned to me at that time.

As you're already aware, I've had concerns about regular rent increases resulting in a monthly rent now well beyond that for comparable apartments in this area. Since we spoke on October 13, I understand your inability to provide me with a that my rent won't continue to go up. Unfortunately, I simply cannot afford such increases.

I'm sure you'll agree I've been a model tenant for the past three years; I can also assure you that the apartment is in terrific shape-better shape, in fact, than when I moved in, terrific shape-better shape, in fact, than when I moved in, given the landscaping improvements I've made over the years.

I plan to vacate the apartment on December 1 and would appreciate receiving my returned deposit as close to that date as possible. In fact, could I pick it up from you that afternoon?

Thank you for your understanding of my situation. I will call you in the next week to find out when I might receive my security deposit.

Sincerely

Template 11

Another Alternative To Complaining: Requesting Help

Dear

I need your help with a situation I'm finding increasingly frustrating.

Approximately six months ago, I purchased your top-of-the-line plain paper Email communication machine Model 6000. This model's features clearly make it one of the best machines on the market.

But here's my dilemma. I've had endless difficulties getting help in using even the machine's most basic features (for instance, redialling, speed dialling, and broadcast Email communication).

Here's a synopsis of the trouble I've experienced:

Instructions in the owner's manual are very difficult to follow.

Calls for technical support have kept me holding 20 to minutes!

Your voice-mail system has disconnected me numerous times, generally after these long waits.

'The technicians I finally reach offer ample advice without fully understanding my difficulties.

Their quick answers-and unwillingness to remain on the line while I try their advice do not solve the problem.

I'm faced with starting all over with another long wait, another technician, and a machine I still cannot use.

Please call me within the next couple of weeks with your 078 09999.

1 was willing to pay more for quality. Now what can I do to get your organization's help in using my machine? Now what can I do to get your organization's help in using my machine?

Thank you

Template 12

Informing Of Hazardous Product

Dear

Subject:

My family has experienced what I'm sure you'll agree is a serious problem with one of your products. My sincere hope is that you will act to either fix this problem or remove this product from the market.

The product is your Handy Gate safety gate, Model QL780, your only model (to my knowledge) with a spring-loaded handle that allows an adult to "open" the safety gate to pass through while leaving the gate still anchored in the doorway.

On three occasions over two months, my 22-pound toddler has pushed the gate over and gone tumbling over with it. Fortunately, we keep the gate on a level surface, so her injuries negligible. But know people who use these gates to keep toddlers away from stairways and other uneven surfaces; a spill in these cases could be disastrous.

Rest assured, we've made eve' possible adjustment to keep the gate anchored in the doorway. We've spoken to your customer service representatives and even exchanged one gate for another, hoping our first one was simply defective; the second was no different.

Your company has graciously accepted our return of the gate. I would appreciate a response, by mail or telephone, to this letter. I fully expect that you will look into this matter before a child is seriously hurt.

Yours truly

Template 13

If Previous Requests Fail

Dear

We apparently have a problem, and 1 need your assistance.

We apparently have a problem, and 1 need your assistance order I placed nearly two months ago; in addition, no one I speak to by phone seems to have the authority to help me.

You cashed my check for £83.44 more than a month ago for bulbs I have not received. My order, once more, was for:

S7893 24 Mixed Giant Crocus @ £ 8.99   . £ 8.99
S8882 16 Giant Jonquils @ £l0.99   = 10.99
S9770 10 White Narcissus @ £13.99 = 13.99

I expect to receive my order express mailed to me within week. If I do not receive my order, I am prepared to lodge a formal complaint with the Bulb town Chamber of Commerce and the Better Business Bureau. If you need to speak with me, my number is 123/555-1011.

I expect to receive my order express mailed to me within the week. If 1 do not receive my order, I am prepared to lodge formal complaint with the Bulb town Chamber of Commerce and the Better Business Bureau. If you need to speak with me, my number is 123/555-1011.

I look forward to receiving my order within one week.

Sincerely

Attachments: copies of previous LETTER and cancelled check

Template 14

Declaring Your Intention To Go To A Third Party

Dear

Because I have not received a response to any of three previous LETTER I've sent you regarding an order I've paid for but never received (nor a satisfactory response from several phone calls), I will be taking my concerns to the Bulb town Chamber of Commerce and the Better Business Bureau.

Copies of my previous LETTER are attached.

I regret having to take this action-particularly with a company from which I've purchased merchandise for years.

I feel I have no other option.

Sincerely

Template 15

Reporting To A Third Party

Dear,

I have received what I consider unusually poor service from a company in your area and felt that reporting the situation to your chamber was important. I'm sure you will share my concern about the unreasonable treatment I've received from this Bulbtown company.

Copies of my LETTER to this company, The Dutch Touch (P.O.Box 345, Bulbtown, Illinois 074 00000), dating from early August to early October, detailing my difficulties, are attached. My situation involves an £80 order for which I have   I paid and never received merchandise.

If I can provide you with more information or if you can be helpful to me in recouping my £80, please call me 074 00700.

Sincerely

Attachments: copies of previous LETTER and cancelled check cc: President, The Melbourne Sound

Template 16

Recognizing Good Service

Dear

Your technician, Ms. Ana Almstadt, really helped me out of a frustrating situation, and I'd like to commend both her work and your company for the help I've received.

I had purchased your top-of-the-line plain paper Email communication machine Model 6000 but was having endless difficulties getting help in using even the machine's most basic features. A copy of my original letter to you outlining my difficulties is attached.

Ms. Almstadt called me not once, but several times. To make sure I was getting the answers 1 needed to make my Email communication fully operational. On one occasion she spent more than an hour on the telephone with me-even staying beyond her normal work hours-to help me sort out a problem we learned resulted more from a faulty phone line than from any deficiency with your product.

If making talented technicians like Ms. Almstadt truly available to your customers is an indication of the service I can expect in machines to all of my business associates.

Sincerely yours

Attachment

Template 17

Ending A Long-Standing Business Relationship

Dear

Your move to a new salon and change to working fewer hours-so you can pursue other career goals-sound exciting, and I'm happy for you.

Over the 15 years you've been my hairdresser, I have you from salon to salon, waited devotedly for you to return to hairdressing after an eight-month hiatus, and remained devoted as your availability has decreased (no doubt you've been in greater and greater demand) and your prices, over time, have increased.

Unfortunately, your new far-Northside location, your change to working part-time hours, and your recent 20-percent price increase have made it necessary for me to find another hairdresser.

I am sorry I won't be able to keep the appointment we set next month; but I know you'll have no difficulty filling the slot.

Thank you for years of making me look good. You're a talented hairdresser, and I sincerely wish you the very best your career (and personal) goals continue to evolve. Best wishes, to, to you and your fiancé.

Take care

Template 18

Requesting Information On Placing A Classified Ad

Dear

Please help me to place a classified ad in The Gazette for Sunday, August 9.

I've never advertised in The Gazette before, so I'm not sure how to go about it. But I've reviewed other ads in the paper, here's what I'd like my ad to say:

Moving Sale August 15-16, 8 a.m. to 4 p.m
8092 Trestle Way Court, one block east of 80th and
Boulevard. Dining and bedroom furniture, small appliances,
Lawn equipment. Must sell; moving out of country.

Please call or write me to confirm my request and inform me of the cost of the ad and your payment policy. My phone number is 076 0606060.

I look forward to hearing from you and appreciate your assistance.

Sincerely

Template 19

Requesting A Correction Or Retraction

Dear

Today's Times published an incorrect date for the opening of First Central Church's Soup Kitchen; I'd like a correction made as soon as possible this week.

A copy of our original press release is attached for your information.

To help us recruit the volunteers still needed and to get word out to those who need it, please print a correction in the first weekday issue possible and again next Sunday. Many people who could be involved or who could use a good hot meal rely on word-of-mouth to hear about such events, so the sooner you can print a correction, the more our community stands to benefit.

Here is the correct information:

The grand opening of Homeless Shelter will be Sunday, May 3, from 11 a.m. to 2 p.m. The Soup Kitchen is located next to the church at 456 North Central Avenue. All in need are welcome; volunteers are still needed. For more information, call First Central Church at 076 505055.

Please call me if you need further information or are unable to comply with my request. You can reach me at 076 060606.

Thanks for making this correction as quickly as possible.

Thank you,

Chair

Attachment: Original press release

Template 20

Voicing An Opinion

Dear

I've noticed a troubling trend recently in the coverage that that Newsweak Magazine has given to issues related to the threat of terrorism. If your publication still strives to be a top source of no-nonsense, objective reporting, I encourage you to change your policy regarding your coverage of these issues.

For quite some time now, Newsweak has seemed determined to present people who practice Islam in an unflattering, extremist light. As a devoted Muslim, I can tell you that the mainstream of our religion does not advocate the distorted and sick "holy war" notion that figures such as Osama Bin Laden have promoted. Your reporters need to research more carefully the sects of Islam that hold themselves responsible for terrorist acts.

That trend alone would be troubling enough. But now I'm seeing photographs of Muslim women in Middle Eastern countries, their faces shielded in veils and their arms dirty children, which seem to present these people as objects of oddity, a spectacle to be marvelled at by the reader. Such photographs are accompanied by headlines blaring the words such as terrorist nation or hell in a land of extremism. If you're hoping to continue to attract an audience interested in an objective portrayal of real news, not propaganda, I fully expect to see News weak discontinue such irresponsible use of photographs and language.

With the line between news coverage and sensationalism becoming increasingly blurred, publications such as News weak I   usual quality standards usual quality standards.

Sincerely

Template 21

Demanding A Correction Or Retraction

Dear

Because several phone calls over the last few days have failed to secure the promise of a retraction of comments made on your August 3 newscast, I am now writing to you, the station manager, to insist on such a retraction.

In the August 3 evening newscast, your reporter, Carole Ness, stated that United Church Federation members arriving at the scene of a violent murder "may have interfered with police attempts to apprehend the suspect." She further referred to the group of three people as "religious extremists" wh, she suggested, had no business being there.

In fact, that United Church Federation's purpose in going to such gruesome scenes is to offer prayer and healing. We believe that through prayer, the systemic problem of violent crime in our cities can come to an end. The group is an ad hoc gathering of "members" who actually belong to churches, temples, and synagogues around the city. The Federation itself espouses no specific religious teachings other than a firm belief in the power of prayer.

As for Federation members interfering with Dolice business at such scenes, it simply never happens. Federation members generally gather long after the police have left a scene of violence; when occasionally the police and our group are there simultaneously (as was the case in the four-hour ordeal that day), the relationship between the Federation and police is always one of mutual cooperation and respect.

I would encourage your reporter to talk to Police Chief Robert Gray to verify my position. His number is 076 05050404.

Because television wields such power in influencing people's minds (as demonstrated by the flood of angry phone calls I've received in the last few days), I really must insist on a public retraction that includes only factual statements and an objective depiction of the Federation's activities.

I would welcome a conversation with you or your reporter. My phone number, day or night, is 076 05050404.

Thank you for your prompt attention to this matter. I look forward to hearing from you.

Sincerely

Template 22

Announce The Event

Dear

For immediate release. Please announce the following not-for-profit event.

I'd be particularly grateful if you could announce this information during before- and after-work drive times so we may recruit the needed volunteers.

Here are the details:

The grand opening of First Central Church's Soup Kitchen Sunday, May 3, from 1 a.m. to 2 p.m. The Soup Kitchen is located to the church at 345 Central Avenue. All in need are welcome; volunteers are still needed. For more information, please call First Central Church at 076 05050404.

For more information on this event, you can also call me at 076 05050404.

Thank you for your help in spreading the word to those in need and those who can help!

Sincerely

Template 23

Thanking A Reporter For Fair Coverage

Dear

Your report on last night's broadcast was a fine example of quality reporting.

Your depiction of United Church Federation's activities was both balanced and fair. I particularly valued your including the direct quotes from Police Chief Robert Gray.

You may never be fully aware of the benefits our city will reap by your quality work. I sincerely thank you.

Yours truly

Station Manager

Template 24

Cancelling A Long-Held Subscription

Dear

Back in February I expressed my concerns to your photo editor about the direction I saw Newsweak heading with regard to irresponsible use of photography. A copy of my February letter is attached.

Since February, I've unfortunately seen continued use of the photographic techniques I described in that letter. What's more, Newsweak's cover photos and cover designs now look even more like those of tabloid magazines, and its content strays further than ever into the territory of propaganda.

For these reasons, I have decided to end my subscription to a newsmagazine whose quality standards I have held in esteem for more than 20 years. Please consider this letter my official subscription cancellation.

The editorial staff of Newsweak is clearly quite talented. If the magazine's editorial policies ever get back to no-nonsense, objective news reporting, you can bet I'll reinstate my 20-year subscription.

Sincerely

Template 25

Sales Reply

Dear

YOUR ORDER NUMBER

Thank you for your letter of 23 March.

I am very sorry to hear about the mistake made with your order. I have looked into this and found that the mistake happened in the packing section. Unfortunately it was not discovered before the goods were sent to you.

I have arranged for a repeat order to be sent to you today, and I hope this meets your requirements.

Once again, please accept my apologies for the inconvenience caused.

I enclose a copy of our new collection and I hope you find it interesting.

Please give me a call soon on 076 05050404 if you have any questions.

Yours sincerely

Template 25

Sales Enquiry

Dear

My name is Jen Frith and I work for the Procurement Department at a company called Idyllic Earth Health Market. We are a London-based health food store and we would like to expand our range of medicinal herbs – I'm particularly interested in the cancer bush.

Could you please provide me with a price list of all the products that supply?

Many thanks

Regards

Template 26

Response To Sales Enquiry

Dear

Many thanks for your enquiry. Yes we have Cancer Bush (Sutherlandia Frutescens) in stock and can deliver to your area at no extra charge. How many would you like to purchase?

We have many more wonderful medicinal plants in stock, even rare Marshmallow (Althea Officialise) seeds.

I have attached a pricelist of all our products for you.

Please let me know if you require any more assistance.

Kind Regards

Sates Executive

Template 27

Template For A Cold E-Mail

Dear

I represent a medicinal plant and raw materials supplier called Sage Health. Our specialty is organic ingredients, especially hard –to-find ones.

We have rare Marshmallow gel (Althea Officinal) is available first time in London . I thought you might be interested in this product as it is a highly popular organic anti-aging substance used in in beauty creams, and I noticed that your store sells their own range of natural beauty products. I am confident that this product will greatly enhance your offering and increase your long-term revenue.

I am available in your area on Thursday April 18 if you would like to meet and receive some free Templates for your store. I could then answers any questions you may have about the product.

Thank you for your time and look forward to hearing from you.

Kind Regards

Template 28

Professional Email For Salary Negotiation

Dear

I have greatly enjoyed working at Transom Enterprises as a Melon Clerk. In the years since I joined the company in 2001, I have become a loyal and integral member of the team, and have developed innovative ways to contribute to the department.

For example, in the past year alone, I have achieved the following goals:

- Brought in two new major clients to the company, increasing total sales revenue by 5%
- Voluntarily trained 5 new members of staff, totalling 35 hours voluntary service

I believe I have gone above and beyond the benchmarks we set for my position in our last yearly appraisal.

I would therefore appreciate the chance to set up a meeting with you to discuss raising my salary by five per cent, which I believe reflects my performance and current competencies, as well as the industry averages.

Once again, I feel very lucky to be a member of this s departments and I look forward to taking on my next projects in the near future.

Thank you for your time. I look forward to speaking with you soon.

Sincerely

Template 29

Salary Negotiation

Dear

I have worked loyally and efficiently for Trincom Enterprises as a Debtors Clerk since 2001. I hardly take sick leave, my performance reviews are always positive and my work is always done meticulously and on time.

I would therefore appreciate the opportunity to come and speak to you about a small raise in my salary. I am not asking for a lot, merely 10% on top of what I currently earn.

Please be assured that I understand if my request is denied due to factors beyond the company's control and I will continue working as I always have as I enjoy my work and my team.

Warm Regards

Template 30

Letter Of Reference/Reference

To whom it may concern,

Ana and I worked together at P&L in Marketing for 10 years.

It is my pleasure to recommend her for the position of Online your XL Consulting.

Firstly, Jane is a self-confident and outgoing person, who finds it easy to relate to people from all kinds of backgrounds.

During her time at P&J Marketing, Jane proved to be passionate, communicative, hard-working and excellent at managing her time. In addition,. Jane is the kind of person who works well with others, as she displays great sensitivity and empathy. She was always willing to the team and help her colleagues. Moreover, (Furthermore). P&J Marketing she was popular and fully committed to the organization's objectives.

Ana mentioned to me that this role at your company would involve dealing with corporate clients, and I believe that she is remarkably well item for this task. By way of example, way of example, (For instance) at. P&J Marketing, Jane demonstrated excellent communication skills dealing with corporate clients on a daily basis. . She also has a keen interest in new media, which J am sure will stand her in good stead when she is helping g clients.

I recommend Jane without reservation she would be an excellent asset to your company.

Please do not hesitate to contact me if you have any question

Sincerely

Sales Orders And Their Fulfilment

1. Placing orders
2. Confirmation of telephone order
3. Tabulated order
4. Order based on quotation
5. Covering letter with order form
6. Formal acknowledgement of routine order (by Email communication)
7. Acknowledgement of a first order
8. Acknowledgement of order pointing out delayed delivery
9. Acknowledgement of a first order
10. Acknowledgement of order pointing out delayed delivery
11. Supplier refuses price reduction
12. Supplier rejects buyer's delivery terms
13. Refuses to extend credit
14. Supplier sends a substitute article
15. Supplier makes a counter-offer
16. Request for forwarding instructions
17. Advice of goods ready for despatch
18. Notification of goods despatched
19. Report of damage in transit
20. Report of non-delivery of goods
21. Complaint to carrier concerning non-delivery
22. Covering letter with invoice

23. Supplier sends debit note
24. Buyer requests credit
25. Supplier refuses request for credit note
26. Supplier reports underpaid
27. Buyer reports errors in statement
28. Customer requests time to pay (granted)
29. Customer requests time to pay (not granted)
30. Supplier questions partial payment
31. Supplier asks customer to select terms of payment
32. Late Payments explains inability to pay
33. Customer explains late payment
34. Personalised collection LETTER
35. Specimen final collection LETTER
36. Customer requests open-account terms
37. Customer requests credit extension due to bankruptcy
38. Supplier requests references
39. Supplier asks for completion of credit application form
40. Customer supplies a banker's reference

Template 1

Placing Orders

Dear

Thank you for your quotation of 4 June.

Please supply:100 reams of A2 quality Printing Paper, white, at 2.16 per kg, including delivery. Delivery is required not later than the end of this month.

Yours sincerely

Template 2

Confirmation Of Telephone Order

Dear

Thank you for your quotation of 5 July.

Our order number 237 for four of the items is enclosed. All these items are urgently required by our customer so we hope you will send them immediately.

Yours sincerely

Template 3

Tabulated Order

Dear

1   Please accept our order for the following books on our usual discount terms of 25% off published prices:

NUMBER   TITLE   AUTHOR   PUBUSHED

OF COPIES

50 for   Rose Taylor   8.99

40 for   Essential Communication   Rose Taylor   7.99

We look forward to prompt delivery.

Yours faithfully

Template 4

Order Based On Quotation

Dear

Thank you for your quotation of 4 June. Please supply:

100 reams of A2 quality Printing Paper, white, at 2.16 per kg, including delivery.

Delivery is required not later than the end of this month.

Yours sincerely

Template 5

Covering Letter With Order Form

Dear

Thank you for your quotation of 5 July. Our order number 237 for four of the

Items is enclosed.

All these items are urgently required by our customer so we hope you will send them immediately.

Sincerely

Template 6

Formal Acknowledgement Of Routine Order (By Email Communication)

Thank you for your order number 237 for bed coverings.

As all items were in stock, they will be delivered to you tomorrow by our own transport.

We hope you will find these goods satisfactory and that we may have the pleasure of receiving further orders from you.

Many thanks

Template 7

Acknowledgement Of A First Order

Dear

We were very pleased to receive your order of 18 June for cotton prints, and welcome you as one of our customers.

We confirm supply of the prints at the prices stated in your letter. Delivery be made by our own vehicles early next week. We feel confident that you will be completely satisfied with these goods and that you will find them of exceptional value for money.

As you may not be aware of the wide range of goods we have available, we enclosing a copy of our collection.

We hope that our handling of your first order with us will lead to further business between us and mark the beginning of a happy working relationship.

Yours sincerely

Template 8

Acknowledgement Of Order Pointing Out Delayed Delivery

Dear

Thank you for your order of 15 March for electric shavers. We regret that we cannot supply them immediately owing to a fire in our factory.

Every effort is being made to resume

service and we fully expect to be able to deliver the shavers by the end of this month.

We apologise for the delay and trust it will not cause you serious inconvenience.

Yours sincerely

Template 9

Acknowledgement Of A First Order

We were very pleased to receive your order of 18 June for cotton prints, welcome you as one of our customer.

We confirm supply of the prints at the prices stated expected. Delivery will be made by post early next week. We feel confident that you completely satisfied with these goods and that you will find them of exceptional value for money.

As you may not be aware of the wide range of goods we have available, we are enclosing a link to our range.

We hope that our handling of your first order with us will lead to further business between us and mark the beginning of a happy relationship.

Yours sincerely

Template 10

Acknowledgement Of Order Pointing Out Delayed Delivery

Dear

Thank you for your order of 15 March for electric shavers. We regret that we cannot supply them immediately owing to a fire in our factory.

Every effort is being made to resume service and we fully expect to be able to deliver the shavers by the end of this month.

We apologise for the delay and trust it will not cause you serious inconvenience.

Yours sincerely

Template 11

Supplier Refuses Price Reduction

Dear

We have carefully considered your counter-proposal of 15 August to our offer of

Woollen underwear, but regret that we cannot accept it.

The prices quoted in our letter of 13 August leave us with only the smallest of They are in fact lower than those of our competitors for goods of similar quality.

The wool used in the manufacture of our THERMALINE range undergoes a patented process, which prevents shrinkage and increases durability.

We hope you will give further thought to this matter, but if you then still feel you cannot accept our offer we hope it will not prevent you from contacting us on some future occasion.

We will always be happy to consider carefully any proposals likely to lead to between us.

Yours sincerely

Template 12

Supplier Rejects Buyer's Delivery Terms

Dear

YOUR ORDER NUMBER

We were pleased to receive your order of 2 November for 24 ATLANTIS SONY sets. However since you state the firm condition of delivery before Christmas, we regret that we cannot supply you on this occasion.

The manufacturers of these goods are finding it impossible to meet current for this popular television set. We placed an order for 100 sets one month ago but were informed that all orders were being met in very Strict Rotation. Our own order will not be met before the end of January.

I understand from our telephone conversation this morning that your customers are unwilling to consider other models. In the circumstances I hope you will be able to meet your requirements from some other source. May I suggest that you Television Services Ltd of Leicester. They usually carry large stocks and may be able to help you.

Yours sincerely

Template 13

Refuses To Extend Credit

Dear

Were pleased to receive your order of 15 April for a further supply of USB..

However, owing to current difficult conditions we have had to try to ensure that many customers keep their accounts within reasonable limits. Only in this way we meet our own commitments.

At present the balance of your account stands at over 1800. We hope that we may be able to reduce it before we grant credit for further supplies.

In the circumstances we should be grateful if you would send us your payment for, say, half the amount owed. We could then arrange to supply the goods now requested and charge them to your account.

Yours sincerely

Template 14

Supplier Sends A Substitute Article

Dear

We were pleased to receive your letter of 10 April together with your order for a number of items included in our quotation reference RS980.

All the items ordered are in stock except for the 25 cushion covers in strawberry pink. Stocks of these have been sold out since our quotation, and the manufacturers inform us that it will be another 4 weeks before they can send replacements.

As you state that delivery of all items is a matter of urgency, we have substituted cushion covers in a red and pink, identical in design and quality to those ordered. We hope you will find them satisfactory. If not, please return them at our expense. We shall be glad either to exchange them or to arrange credit.

All items will be on our delivery schedule tomorrow. We hope you will be pleased with them.

Yours sincerely

Template 15

Supplier Makes A Counter-Offer

Dear

Thank you for your letter of 11 May ordering 800 metres of 100 cm wide watered silk.

We regret to say that we can no longer supply this silk. Fashions change and in recent years the demand for watered silks has fallen to such an extent that we no longer produce them.

In their place we can offer our new GOSSAMER brand of 100. This is a woven, hardwearing, non-creatable material with a most attractive product. The range number of repeat orders we regulate receive from leading distributors and manufacturers is clear evidence of the widespread popularity of this brand. At the low price of only £3.20 per metre, this rayon is much cheaper than silk and appearance is just as attractive.

We also manufacture other cloths in which you may be interested and are sending a complete range of patterns by separate post. Alt these clothes are selling very well in many countries and can be supplied from stock. If you decide to place an order we can meet it within one week.

Please contact me if you have any queries.

Yours sincerely

Template 16

Request For Forwarding Instructions

Dear

We are pleased to confirm that the 12 Olivetti KX R193 word processors which you ordered on 15 October are now ready for despatch.

When placing your order you stressed the importance of prompt delivery, and I am glad to say that by making a special effort we have been able to improve by a few days on the delivery date agreed.

We await your shipping instructions, and immediately we hear from you we wiu send you our advice of despatch.

Yours sincerely

Template 17

Advice Of Goods Ready For Despatch

Dear

We are pleased to confirm that all the books which you ordered on 3 April are packed and ready for despatch.

The consignment awaits collection at our warehouse and consists of two cases, each weighing about 100 kg.

For shipment, for Singapore, have already been made with W Watson & Co Ltd, our forwarding actents.9 As soon as we receive their statement of charges, we will arrange for shipping documents to be sent to you through Barclays Bank against our draft for acceptance, as agreed.

We look forward to further business with you.

Yours sincerely

Template 18

Notification Of Goods Despatched

Dear

The mohair rugs you ordered on 5 January have been packed in four special waterproof-lined cases. They will be collected tomorrow for consignment by passenger train and should reach you by Friday.

We feel sure you will find the consignment supports our claim to sell the best rugs of their kind and hope we may look forward to further orders from you.

Yours sincerely

Template 19

Report Of Damage In Transit

Dear

We regret to inform you that of the four cases of mohair rugs which were sent on 28 January, one was delivered damaged. The waterproof lining was badly torn and it will be necessary to send seven of the rugs for cleaning before we can offer them for sale.

Will you therefore please arrange to send replacements immediately and charge them to our account.

We realise that the responsibility for damage is ours and have already taken up I the matter of compensation with the railway authorities.

Yours sincerely

Template 20

Report Of Non-Delivery Of Goods

Dear

You wrote to us on 1 January informing us that the mohair rugs supplied to the above order were being despatched.

We expected these goods a week ago and on the faith of your notification of

Promised immediate delivery to a number of our customers. As the goods have not yet reached us, we naturally feel our customers have been let down.

Delivery of the rugs is now a matter of urgency. Please find out what has happened to the consignment and let us know when we may expect.

Delivery of the rugs is now a matter of urgency. Please find out what has happened to the consignment and let us know when we may expect delivery.

We are of course making our own enquiries at this end.

Yours sincerely

Template 21

Complaint To Carrier Concerning Non-Delivery

Dear

We regret to report that a consignment of mohair rugs addressed to W Hart &25-27 Gordon Avenue, Warrington, has not yet reached them.

These cases were collected by your carrier on 28 January for consignment by passenger train and should have been delivered by 1 February. We hold your carrier's receipt number 3542.

As our customer is urgently in need of these goods, we must ask you to make enquiries and let us know the cause of the delay and when delivery will be made.

Please treat this matter as one of extreme

Yours sincerely

Template 22

Covering Letter With Invoice

Dear

Our invoice number 23456 is enclosed covering the polyester shirts ordered 24 August.

These shirts have been packed ready for despatch and are being sent to your address. They should reach you within a few days.

Yours faithfully

Template 23

Supplier Sends Direct Debit Note

Dear

I regret to inform you that an error was made on our invoice number 3435 of 1 August.

The correct charge for polyester shirts, medium, is 24.70 and not 28.00 as stated. We are therefore enclosing a debit note for the amount undercharged, namely 17.70.

This mistake was due to an input error and we are sorry it was not noticed invoice was sent.

Yours faithfully

Template 24

Buyer Requests Credit

Returned packing case

Dear

We have today returned to you by rail one empty packing case, charged on your invoice number 678 of 1 August at 23.25.

A debit note for this amount is enclosed and we should be glad to receive your credit note in return.

Yours faithfully

Incorrect trade discount

Dear

Your invoice number 56688 dated 22 September allows a trade discount of only 33% instead of the 40% to which you agreed in your letter of 5 August because of the unusually large order.

Calculated on the invoice gross total of 1,500 the difference in discount is exactly 100. If you will please adjust your charge we shall be glad to pass the invoice for immediate payment.

Yours faithfully

Template 25

Supplier Refuses Request For Credit Note

Retailer's request

Dear

On 1 September we returned to you by parcel post one cassette tape recorder, On 1 September we returned to you by parcel post one cassette tape recorder, and charged on your invoice number 5624 dated 2 August.

The customer who bought this recorder complained about its performance. It was for this reason that we returned it to you after satisfying ourselves that the complaint was justified.

We have received no acknowledgement of the returned recorder or of the letter we sent to you on 1 September. It may be that you are trying to obtain a replacement for us. If this is the case and a replacement is not immediately available, please send us a credit note for the invoiced cost of the returned recorder, namely 175.

We hope to hear from you soon.

Yours faithfully

Wholesaler's reply

Dear

We are sorry to learn from your letter of 16 September of the need to return one of the recorders supplied to you and charged on our invoice number 5624.

We received your letter of 1 September but regret that we have no trace of the returned recorder. It would help if you could describe the kind of container in which it was packed and state exactly how it was addressed and the method of delivery used. As soon as we receive this information we will make a thorough investigation.

Meanwhile I am sure you will understand that we cannot either provide a free replacement or grant the credit you request. If you could wait for about 10 days, could replace the tape recorder but would have to charge it to your account if our further enquiries should prove unsuccessful.

Yours sincerely

Template 26

Supplier Reports Underpaid

Supplier's letter

Dear

We are enclosing our September statement totalling £820.57.

The opening balance brought forward is the amount left uncovered by the payment received from you against our August statement which totalled £560.27. The payment received from you, however, was drawn for £500.27 only, leaving the unpaid balance of £60 brought forward.

We should appreciate early settlement of the total amount now due.

Yours faithfully

Buyer's reply

Dear

We have received your letter of 19 October enclosing September's statement.

We apologise for the underpayment of £90 on your August statement. This was

Due to a misreading of the amount due. The final figure was not very clearly printed and we mistakenly read it as £500.27 instead of £560.27.

Our payment for £820.57, the total amount on the September statement, is enclosed.

Yours faithfully

Template 27

Buyer Reports Errors In Statement

Dear

On checking your statement for July we notice the following errors:

1. The sum of £14.10 for the return of empty packing cases, covered by your credit note number £621 dated 5 July, has not been entered.

2. Invoice Number W825 for £127.32 has been debited twice – once on 11 July and again on 21 July.

Therefore we are deducting the sum of £141.42 from the balance shown on your statement, and enclose our payment for £354.50 in full settlement.

Yours faithfully

Template 28

Customer Requests Time To Pay (Granted)

Customer's request

Dear

We have received your letter of 6 August reminding us that payment of the amount owing on your June statement is overdue.

We were under the impression that payment was not due until the end of August when we would have had no difficulty in settling your account. However it seems that we misunderstood your terms of payment.

In the circumstances we should be grateful if you could allow us to defer

Women's for a further 3 weeks. Our present difficulty is purely temporary. Before the end of the month payments are due to us from a number of our regular customers who are notably prompt payers.

We very much regret having to make this request and hope you will be able to grant it.

Yours faithfully

Supplier's reply

Dear

Having carefully considered your letter of 8 August, we have decided to allow you to defer payment of your account to the end of August.

This request is granted as an exceptional measure only because of the promptness with which you have settled your accounts in the past. We hope that in future dealings you will be able to keep to our terms of payment. We take this opportunity to remind you that they are as follows:

21Wo discount for payment within 10 days
Net cash for payment within one month
We look forward to continuing to work with you.

Yours sincerely

Template 29

Customer Requests Time To Pay (Not Granted)

Customer's request

Dear

Thank you for your letter of 23 July asking for immediate payment of the 687 due on your invoice number SDFG 098.

When we wrote promising to pay you in full by 16 July, we fully expected to be able to do so. . However we were unfortunately called upon to meet an unforeseen and unusually heavy demand earlier this month.

We are therefore enclosing a payment for 200 on account,6 and ask you to be good enough to allow us a further few weeks in which to settle the balance. We fully expect to be able to settle your account in full by the end of August. If you would grant this deferment, we should be most grateful.

I hope to hear from you soon.

Yours sincerely

Supplier's reply

Thank you for your letter of 25 July sending us a payment for 200 on account and asking for an extension of time in which to pay the balance.

As your account is now more than 2 months overdue we find your present payment quite insufficient. It is hardly reasonable to expect us to wait a further month for the balance, particularly as we invoiced the goods at an especially low price, which was mentioned to you at the time.

We sympathise with your difficulties but need hardly remind you that it is in customers' long-term interests to pay their accounts promptly so as to qualify for discounts and at the same time build a reputation for financial reliability.

In the circumstances we hope that in your own interests you will make arrangements to clear your account without further delay. We look forward to receiving your payment for the balance on your account within the next few days.

Yours sincerely

Template 30

Supplier Questions Partial Payment

Dear

We thank you for your letter of 10 October enclosing your payment for £58.67. Our official receipt is enclosed as requested.

As you do not say that the payment is on account, we are wondering whether the amount of £58.67 was intended to be 88.67 – the balance on your account as shown in our September statement.

In any case we look forward to receiving the un-cleared balance of 45 within the next few days.

Yours sincerely

Template 31

Supplier Asks Customer To Select Terms Of Payment

Dear

Thank you for your letter of 8 April, but you do not say whether you wish this transaction to be for cash or on credit.

When we wrote to you on 56 March we explained our willingness to offer easy credit terms to customers who do not wish to pay cash, and also that we allow generous discounts to cash customers.

We may not have made it clear that when placing orders customers should state whether cash or credit terms are required.

Please let me know which you prefer so that we can arrange your account accordingly.

Yours sincerely

Template 32

Late Payments Explains Inability To Pay

Dear

Your invoice number 527 dated 20 July for 1516 is due for payment at the of this month.

Unfortunately a fire broke out in our Despatch Department last week and destroyed a large part of a valuable consignment due for delivery to a cash customer. Our claim is now with the insurance company but it is unlikely to be met for another 3 or 4 weeks. Until then we are faced with a difficult financial problem.

I am therefore writing for permission to defer overdraft of your invoice until the of September.

As you are aware, my accounts with you have always been settled promptly and are with regret that I am now forced to make this request. I hope that you will find possible to grant it.

Yours faithfully

Template 33

Customer Explains Late Payment

Dear

Further to your letter of 4 July, I enclose a payment for £1182.57 in full settlement of your invoice number WW563. Many apologies for the late payment.

This is due to my absence from the office through illness and my failure to leave

Instructions for your account to be paid. I did not discover the oversights until returned to the office yesterday.

I would not like you to think that failure to settle your account on time was in any intentional My apologies once again for this delay.

Yours sincerely

Template 34

Personalised Collection Letter

To a regular payee

Dear

As you are usually very prompt in settling your accounts, we wonder whether there is any special reason why we have not received payment of this account, which is already a month overdue.

In case you may not have received the statement of account sent on 31 May showing a balance owing of £105.67, a copy is enclosed. We hope this will receive your early attention.

Yours sincerely

To a new customer

Dear

We regret having to remind you that we have not received payment of the balance {I of 105.67 due on our statement for December. This was sent to you on 4 January and a copy is enclosed.

We must remind you that unusually low prices were quoted to you on the understanding of an early settlement.

It may well be that non-payment is due to an oversight, and so we ask you to be good enough to send us your payment within the next few days.

Yours faithfully

To a customer who has sent a part payment

Dear

Thank you for your letter of 8 March enclosing a payment for 500 in part payment of the balance due on our February statement.

Your payment leaves an unpaid balance of £825.62. As our policy is to work on small profit margins, we regret that we cannot grant long-term credit facilities.

We are sure that you will not think it is unreasonable for us to ask for immediate payment of this balance.

Yours sincerely

Template 35

Specimen Final Collection Letter

Dear

As we have not received a reply to our letter of 5 July requesting settlement of the above account, we are writing again to remind you that the amount still is £105.67.

No doubt there is some special reason for the delay in payment, and we should welcome an explanation together with your remittance.

Yours sincerely

Template 36

Customer Requests Open-Account Terms

Dear

Have been very satisfied with your handling of our past orders, and as our business is growing expect to place even larger orders with you in the future.

As our dealings have extended over a period of nearly 2 years, we hope you will agree to allow us open-account facilities with, say, quarterly settlements. This arrangement would save us the inconvenience of making separate payments on invoices?

Bankers and trade references can be provided if required.

We hope to receive your favourable reply soon.

Yours sincerely

Reply

Dear

Thank you for your letter of 18 November requesting the transfer of your business payment on invoice to open-account terms.

As our business relations with you over the past 2 years have been entirely satisfactory, are quite willing to make the transfer, based on a 90-day settlement period. In your case it will not be necessary to supply references.

We are pleased that you have been satisfied with our past service and that expansion of your business is likely to lead to increased orders. We can assure you of our continued efforts to give you the same high standard of service as in the past.

Yours sincerely

Template 37

Customer Requests Credit Extension Due To Bankruptcy

Dear

We have received and checked your statement for the quarter ended 30 September and agree with the balance of £785.72 shown to be due.

Until now we have had no difficulty in meeting our commitments and have always settled our accounts with you promptly. We could have done so at this time but for bankruptcy of an important customer whose affairs are not likely to be for some time.

We should be most grateful if you would allow us to defer payment of your present account to the end of next month. This would enable us to meet a temporarily difficult situation forced upon us by events that could not be foreseen.

During the next few weeks we will be receiving payments under a number of large contracts. 1f you grant our request we shall have no difficulty in settling with you in full in due course.

If you wish to discuss this please give me a calf on 076 404040.

Yours sincerely

Template 38

Supplier Requests References

Dear

We were pleased to receive your first order with us dated 2 May.

When opening new accounts it is our practice to ask customers for trade references. Please be good enough to send us the names and addresses of two other suppliers with whom you have dealings.

We hope to receive this information by return, and meanwhile your order has been put in hand for despatch immediately we hear further from you.

Yours sincerely

Template 39

Supplier Asks For Completion Of Credit Application Form

Dear

Thank you for your order number 526 of 15 June for polyester bedspreads pillow cases.

As your name does not appear on our books and as we should like you to take advantage of our usual credit terms, we enclose our credit application form for your completion and return as soon as possible.

We should be able to deliver your present order in about 2 weeks, and look forward to receiving your further orders.

We hope that this first transaction will mark the beginning of a pleasant business connection.

Yours sincerely

Template 40

Customer Supplies A Banker's Reference

Dear

Our payment for 2513 is enclosed in full settlement of your invoice number 826 for the stereo tape recorders supplied earlier this month.

My directors have good reason to believe that these particular products will be a popular selling line in this part of the country. As we expect to place further orders with you from time to time, we should be glad if you would arrange to provide open-account facilities on a quarterly basis.

For information concerning our credit standard we refer you to Barclays Bank

Ltd, 4567-988 The Arcade, Southampton.

Yours faithfully

Reports And Proposals

1. 'Brevity' memo to the War Cabinet from Sir Winston Churchill
2. Memorandum
3. Report
4. A longer proposal
5. Sale Letter appeal to economy
6. Sales appeal to efficiency
7. Sales appeal to security
8. Sales appeal to comfort
9. Sales appeal to leisure
10. Appeal to sympathy
11. Appeal to comfort
12. Sales appeal to heat
13. Offer to a newly established trader
14. To a regular customer
15. Offer to new home owners
16. Offer of a demonstration
17. Press release announcing new hotel wing
18. Article in staff newsletter
19. Announcing dinner and dance

Template 1

"Brevity" Memo To The War Cabinet From Sir Winston Churchill

Looking back to memos, in 1940 Sir Winston Churchill could see the benefits of cutting out padding and overuse of passive writing.

"To do our work, we all have to read a mass of papers. Nearly all of them are far too long. This wastes time, while energy has to be spent in looking for the essential points.

I ask my colleagues and their staff to see to it that their reports are shorter.

The aim should be reports which set out the main points in a series of short, crisp paragraphs.

If a report relies on detailed analysts of some complicated factors, or on statistics, these should be set out in an appendix .

Often the occasion is best met by submitting not a full-dress report, but an aide-memoire consisting of headings only, which can be expanded orally if needed.

Let us have an end of such phrases as these:

'It is also of importance to bear in mind the following considerations', or 'Consideration should be given to the possibility of carrying into effect'. Most of these woolly phrases are mere padding, which can be left out altogether, or replaced by a single word. Let us not shrink from using the short expressive phrase, even if it is conversational.

Reports drawn up on the lines I propose may first seem rough as compared with the flat surface of officialise jargon* but the saving in time will be great, while the discipline of setting out the real points concisely will provide an aid to clearer thinking."

Sir Winston Churchill, 9 August 1940

Template 2

Memorandum

To

From

Ref

Date

VISIT OF MR JO CHWEE LEONG, SMITH IMPORTING IN LONDON

Mr Jo Chwee Leong is to visit us on (date). As we can expect a large order his company, Smith Importing Company of Hong Kong, it is important that he receives a good impression of our company. The following are the arrangements for the visit.

ARRANGEMENTS MADE

1. Accommodation has been arranged for Mr Ho at Hotel Modeme and I have arranged for a taxi to collect him from the hotel at 9.30 am to bring him to Shazini Shoes.

2. When Mr Ho arrives at Shazini Shoes at 10.00 am he well be met by Mr Lee and senior staff who will take him on a visit of the factory.

3. A buffet lunch has been arranged in the guest room at 12.30 am. Vegetarian food has been provided.

4   The board room has been booked for a conference for the whole afternoon for Mr Ho, Mr Lee and senior staff. Refreshments have been laid on during the afternoon.

5   A taxi has been booked to take Mr Lee to the airport at 5.30 pm, so he can check in for his flight before 6.00 pm.

ARRANGEMENTS STILL TO BE MADE

1   Up to date price lists, collections and samples of shoes will be provided in the boardroom.

2   Staff will be informed that Mr Lee and senior staff will not be available next Friday.

Template 3

Report

Maruman Stores, Notting Hill Branch Report On Possibility Of Opening A Creche

INTRODUCTION

I was asked to investigate the opening of a crèche at the Notting Hill branch by Mrs Lillian Cheng. In order to do this the following steps were taken.

1. I obtained a breakdown of figures showing the number of customers with young children.
2. I discussed this issue with several customers who brought children to the store.
3. The accommodation, staffing and insurance issues were considered.
4. I investigated the experience of other shops that already have a crèche.

DISCUSSION

1. 7.3% of Coats customers have at least one child under the age of 3.

2. The majority of customers interviewed said they would use a crèche if the cost was reasonable. Some of these customers also commented that other friends who are not presently customers might also consider using the shop if there was a crèche.

3. There are strict laws and regulations concerning accommodation and staffing of crèche. The site would have to be approved to run a crèche before we could start one.

4. Staff appointed to run the crèche would have to be fully qualified.

5. A suitable space would have to be found. This would require running water as well as toilets, The crèche would have to be close to the store entrance but due to noise levels it should be kept separate from the main store.

6. The company would be required to ensure adequate insurance.

7. Many rival stores in the neighbourhood are offering crèche facilities.

CONCLUSIONS

A crèche would be popular and well-used if we decided to go ahead with this.

RECOMMENDATIONS

I suggest that the company should give further consideration to offering a crèche and investigate the financial aspects that would be involved.

Anna Moon
Customer Services Executive
LC/ST
20 April 2024

Template 4

A Longer Proposal

FLEXIBLE WORKING HOURS
An initial study for HOME DESIGHN & CO Ltd
By

An initial study

Objective

To identify the factors involved in introducing flexible working hours, to examine their benefits and disadvantages and to recommend the best approach to take.

Summary

At present, almost all employees of HOME DESIGHN & CO Ltd work from 9.00 to 5.00. A handful from 9.30 to 5.30.

Many, though not all, staff are unhappy with this and would prefer a more flexible Some are working mothers and would like to be able to take children to and from school. Some, particularly the older employees, have sick or elderly relatives who make demands on their time which do not fit comfortably with their working hours.

For the company itself, this dissatisfaction among staff leads to low morale and reduced productivity. It also makes it harder to attract and retain good staff.

There are three basic options for the future:

1   Leave things as they are. This is obviously less demanding on resources implementing a new system. At least we know it works even if it isn't perfect.

2   Highly flexible system. Employees would clock on and clock off anytime with a 12'h hour working day until they have 'clocked up' 35 hours a week. This be the hardest system to implement.

3   Limited flexibility. Staff could start work any time between 8.00 to 10.00 am   I and work through for eight hours. This would not solve all employees' problems but it would solve most of them.

Proposal

Introduce a system of limited flexibility for now, retaining the option of increasing flexibility later of this seems appropriate.

Position

The current working hours at HOME DESIGHN & CO Ltd are 9.00 to 5.00 for most employees, with a few working from 9.30 to 5.30.

Problem

Although this works up to a point, it does have certain disadvantages, both for the organisation and for some of the employees.

The organisation: The chief disadvantage of the current system is that many of   the staff are dissatisfied with it. This has become such a serious problem that it is becoming harder to attract and retain good staff. Those staff who do join the company and stay with it feel less motivated: this, as research has shown, means they are less productive than they could be.

The employees: Some employees are satisfied with their current working hours, but many of them find the present system restrictive. There are several reasons for the employees most strongly in favour of greater flexibility are, in particular:

The parents, especially mothers, who would prefer to be able to take their children to and from school, and to work around this commitment employees, many of them in the older age range, who have elderly or sick relatives who they would like to be more available for.

An initial study questioned nearly 140 employees in a cross-section of ages. A large majority were in favour of a more flexible approach, in particular the women and the younger members of the company. It is worth noting that a minority of staff were against the introduction of flexible working hours, Appendix I gives the full results of this study.

Possibilities

Since this report is looking at the principle and not the detail of a more flexible approach, the options available fall broadly into three categories: retaining the present system, introducing limited flexibility of working hours, and implementing a highly flexible system.

Although the system is not perfect, at least we know it works. The staff all signed their contracts on the understanding that the company worked to standard hours of business, and while it may not be ideal for them it is at least manageable. Better the devil you know.

Implementing any new system is bound to incur problems and consequently retaining the present working hours is the least expensive option in terms of direct cost.

Highly flexible system. A highly flexible system would mean keeping the site open !from, say, 7.30 am to 8.00 pm. All staff are contracted to work a certain number of hours a week and time clocks are installed. Employees simply clock on and off whenever they enter or leave the building, until they have reached their full number of hours each week.

System has the obvious benefit that it can accommodate a huge degree of flexibility which should suit the various demands of all employees. They could even elect to work 35 hours a week spread over only three days. A further benefit to the company would be that doctors' appointments and so on would no longer happen 'on company time' as they do at present. This system does have several disadvantages, however:

Many staff regard occasional time oft for such things as doctors' appointments or serious family crises as a natural "perk" ' of the job.. With this system they would have to make up the hours elsewhere. Not only would they lose the time off, but many would also feel that the company did not trust them. This would obviously be bad for company morale.

It would be difficult to implement this system fairly. The sales office, for example, must be staffed at least from 9.00 to 5.30 every day. What if all the sales staff want to take Friday off? How do you decide who can and who can't? What if the computer goes down at 4 o'clock in the afternoon and there are no computer staff in until 7.30 the following morning?

Limited flexibility: This would make asking employees to continue to work an eight hour day, but give them a range of, say, ten hours to fit it into. They could start any time between 8.00 and 10.00 in the morning, so they would finish eight hours later – between 4.00 and 6.00.

On the plus side, this would give the employees the co-operation and recognition of their problems that many of them look for, and would therefore increase staff motivation. For some it would provide a way around their other commitments.

Proposal

The number of staff in favour of more flexible working hours, and the importance of staff motivation, it seems sensible to adopt some kind of flexible approach. But it is probably advisable to find a system that allows the significant minority who prefer to stay as they are to do so.

So which is the best system to choose? It is harder to go backwards than forwards in developing new systems: if the highly flexible approach failed it would be difficult to pull back to a less flexible system (in terms of keeping the staff happy). On the other hand, a limited degree of flexibility could easily be extended later if this seemed appropriate.

So at this stage it seems that the most workable system, which contains most of the benefits required by the employees, is the limited flexibility of working hours.

Template 5

Sale Letter Appeal To Economy

Are you nervous when asked to propose a vote of thanks, to take the Chair at a meeting, or to make a speech? If so this letter has been written specially for you!

Would you like to cut your domestic fuel costs by 20 per cent? If your answer is 'yes', read on.

'The common cold,' says Dr James Carter, 'probably causes more lost time at ,work in a year than all other illnesses put together.'

More than 50 per cent of people have eye trouble and in the past year no fewer than 16,000 people in Britain have lost their sight. Are your eyes in danger?

This hi-fi system is carefully designed and incorporates the latest technological developments to give high-quality sound including full stereo recording and playback on the twin-cassette deck. Its clearly arranged controls make for very !   simple operation. It is supplied with two detachable loudspeakers separately mounted in solid, polished teak cabinets, as finely finished as a Rolfs-Royce.

Remember, we have manufactured cotton shirts for 50 years and are quite confident that you will be more than satisfied with their quality.

This offer is made on the clear understanding that if the goods are not completely to your satisfaction you can return them to us without any obligation whatever and at our own expense. The full amount you paid will be refunded immediately.

If you will return the enclosed request card we will show you how you can have all the advantages of cold storage and at the same time at the same time.

The special discount now offered can be allowed only on orders placed by 30 June. So hurry and take advantage of this limited offer while there is still time.

Template 6

Sale Appeal To Economy

Dear

Have you ever thought how much time your typist wastes in taking down your dictation? It can be as much as a third of the time spent on correspondence. Why not record your dictation on our Software and she can be doing other jobs while you dictate?

You will be surprised at how little it costs. For 52 weeks in the year your Software works hard for you, and you can never give it too much to do all for less than an average month's salary for a secretary! It will take dictation anywhere at any time – during lunch-hour, in the evening, at home – you can even dictate while you are travelling or away on business. Simply post the recorded messages back to your secretary for typing.

The Software is efficient, reliable, time-saving and economical. Backed by our international reputation for reliability, it is in regular use in thousands of offices all over the country. It gives superb eService quality with every syllable as clear as a bell. Ft is unbelievably simple to use just slip in a preloaded cassette, press a button, and it is ready to record your dictation, interviews, telephone conversations, reports, instructions or whatever. Nothing could be simpler! And I   with our unique after-sales service contract you are assured lasting operation at the peak of efficiency.

Some of your business friends are sure to be using our it asks them about it before you place an order and we are sure they will back up our dreams. If you prefer, return the enclosed prepaid card and we will arrange for our representative to call and arrange a demonstration for you. Just state the day and time that will be most convenient for you,

Yours sincerely

Template 6

Sales Appeal To Efficiency

Dear

Reports from all over the world confirm what we have always known that the RELIANCE solid tyre is the fulfilment of every car owner's dream.

You will naturally be well aware of the weaknesses of the ordinary air-filled tyre punctures, outer covers which split under sudden stress, and a tendency to skid on wet road surfaces, to mention only a few of motorists' main complaints. Our RELIANCE tyre enables you to offer your customers a tyre which is beyond criticism in those qualities of road-holding and reliability.

We could tell you a lot more about RELIANCE tyres but would prefer you to read the enclosed copies of reports from racing car drivers, test drivers, motor dealers j and manufacturers. These reports really speak for themselves.

To encourage you to hold a stock of the new solid RELIANCE, we are pleased to offer you a special discount of 3% on any order received by 1 July.

Yours sincerely

Template 7

Sales Appeal To Security

Dear

A client of mine is happier today than he has been for a long time – and with good reason. For the first time since he married 10 years ago he says he feels really comfortable about the future. Should he die within the next 20 years, his wife and family will now be provided for. For less than 2 a week paid now, his would receive 50 per month for a full 20 years, and then a lump sum of £5000.

Such protection would have been beyond his reach a short time ago, but a and novel scheme has enabled him to ensure this security for his family. The scheme does not have to be for 20 years. It can be for 15 or 10 or any other number of years. And it need not be for 10,000. It could be for much more or much less so that you arrange the protection you want.

For just a few pounds each month you can buy peace of mind for your wife, your children and for yourself. You cannot – you dare not – leave them unprotected.

I would appreciate an opportunity to call on you to tell you more about this scheme which so many families are finding so attractive. I shall not press you to join; I just give you all the details and leave the rest to you. Please return the enclosed prepaid reply card and I will can at any time convenient to you.

Yours sincerely

Template 8

Sales Appeal To Comfort

Dear

What would you say to a gift that gave you a warmer and more comfortable home, free from draughts, and a saving of over 20% in fuel costs?

You can enjoy these advantages, not just this year but every year, simply by installing our SEALTITE panel system of double glazina. Can you think of a better gift for your entire family? The enclosed brochure will outline some of benefits which make SEALTITE the most completely satisfactory double-glazing system on the market thanks to a number of features not provided in any other system.

Remember that the panels are precision it is made to fit. By experienced craftsmen to fit your own particular windows. Remember too that you will be dealing with a well-company which owes its success to the satisfaction given to scores of thousands of customers.

There is no need for you to make up your mind right now. First why not let give you a free demonstration in your own home without any obligation If you are looking for an investment with an annual average return of over 20%, then here is your opportunity. If you post the enclosed card to reach us by the end of August, we can complete the installation for you in good time before winter sets in.

Secure your home with SEALTITE!

Yours sincerely

Template 9

Sales Appeal To Leisure

Dear

'Modern scientific invention is a curse to the human race and will one day it,' said one of my customers recently. Rather a rash statement.4 and quite untrue for there are modern inventions which, far from being a curse, are real blessings.

Our new AQUAMASTER washer is just one of them. It takes all the hard work of the weekly wash and makes washing a pleasure. All you have to do is put your soiled clothes in, press a button and sit back while the machine does the work. It does everything – washing, rinsing and drying – and we feel it does it quicker better than any washing machine on the market today.

Come along and see the AQUAMASTER at work in our showroom. A demonstration will take up only a few minutes of your time, but it may rid you of your dread of washing day and make life much more pleasant.

I hope you will accept this invitation and come along soon to see what this latest of domestic time-savers can do for you.

Yours sincerely

Template 10

Appeal To Sympathy

You can walk about the house, at work, in the streets, in the country. You take this ability for granted, yet it is denied to thousands of others those who are born crippled, or crippled in childhood by accident or illness.

It is estimated that every 5 minutes in Britain a deformed child is born or a child is crippled by accident or illness. This means that every day there could be 288 more crippled children.

Does this not strike you as unfair? Most of what is unfair in life is something we can do little about but here is one very important inequality, which everyone can help with. The enclosed leaflet explains how you can help. Please read it carefully while remembering again just how lucky you are.

Yours faithfully

Template 11

Appeal To Comfort

Dear

At half the actual cost you can now have SOLAR HEATING installed in your home.

As part of our research and development scheme introduced two years ago we are about to make our selection of a number of properties throughout the country as 'Research Homes' yours could be one of them.

The information received from selected 'Research Homes' in the past 2 years has proved that SOLAR HEATING is successful even in the most northern parts of the United Kingdom. This information has also enabled us to grow and improve our designs, which we will continue to do.

If you are interested in helping our research Softwareme in return for a half-price solar heating system, please complete the enclosed form and return it by the end of May. Within three weeks we will inform you if your home has been selected for the scheme.

Yours sincerely

Template 12

Sales Appeal To Heat

Dear

Thousands of people who normally suffer from the miseries of cold, damp, changeable weather wear THERMO. Why? The answer is simple tests conducted at the leading Textile Industries Department at Leeds University have shown that of all the traditional underwear fabrics THERMO has the highest insulating.

THERMO has been relieving aches and pains for many years, particularly those caused by rheumatism. It not only brings extra warmth but also soothes those aches caused by icy winds cutting into your bones and chilling you to the marrow. THERM absorbs much less moisture than conventional underwear fabrics, so perspiration passes straight through the material. It leaves your skin dry but very, very warm.

Don't just take our word for it – take a good look at some of the testimonials shown in the enclosed collection. The demand for THERM garments grown so much in recent years that we often have to deal with over 20,000 garments in a single day.

The enclosed collection is packed with lots of ways in which THERM keep you warm and healthy this winter. Just browse through it, choose the garment you would like, and send us your completed order form our FREEPOST address means there is even no need for a postage stamp!

Warmth and health will soon be on their way to you. If you are not satisfied with your purchase, return it to us within 14 days and we will refund your money without question and with the least possible delay.

Let THERM keep you warm this winter!

Yours faithfully

Template 13

Offer To A Newly Established Trader

Dear

We would like to send our best wishes for the success of your new shop specialising in the sale of toys. Naturally you will wish to offer your customers the latest toys toys that are attractive, hard wearing and reasonably priced. Your stock will not be complete without the mechanical toys for which we have a national reputation.

We are sole importers of VALIFACT toys and as you will see from the enclosed price list our terms are very generous. In addition to the trade discount stated, we would allow you a special first-order discount of 5%.

We hope that these terms will encourage you to place an order with us and feel sure you would be well satisfied with your first transaction.

We will be happy to arrange for one of our representatives to call on you to ensure that you are fully briefed on the wide assortment of toys we can offer.

Yours faithfully

Template 14

To A Regular Customer

Dear

We have just bought a large quantity of high quality rugs and carpets from the bankrupt stock of one of our competitors.

As you are one of our most regular and long-standing customers, we would like you to share in the excellent opportunities, which our purchase provides. We can offer you mohair rugs in a variety of colours at prices ranging from 55 to 1500;also premier quality Wilton and Lister carpeting in a wide range of patterns at 20% below current wholesale prices.

This is an exceptional opportunity for you to buy a stock of high-quality products prices we cannot repeat. We hope you will take full advantage of it.

If you are interested please call at our warehouse to see the stock for yourself not later than next Friday 14 October. Or alternatively call our Sales Department on 074 00000 to place an immediate order.

Yours sincerely

Template 15

Offer To New Homeowners

Dear

Welcome to your new home! We have no wish to disturb you as you settle in but we would like to tell you why people in this town and the surrounding areas are very familiar with the name BAX.

Our store is situated at the corner of Grafton Street and Dorset Road and we invite you to visit us to see for yourself the exciting range of goods which have made us a household name.

Our well-known shopping guide is enclosed for you to browse through at your leisure. You will see practically everything you need to add to the comfort and beauty of your home.

The enclosed card is valid for one calendar month and it will entitle you to select goods of your own choice as your free gift.

We sincerely hope that you enjoy living in your new home.

Yours faithfully

Template 16

Offer Of A Demonstration

Dear

The Ideal Home Lex opens at Earls Court on Monday 21 June and you are

certain to find attractive new designs in furniture as well as many new ideas.

The exhibition has much to offer which you will find useful, but we would like extend our special invitation to our own display on Stand 26 where we shall be revealing our new WINDSOR range of unit furniture

WINDSOR represents an entirely new concept in luxury unit furniture at very modest prices and we hope you will not miss the opportunity to see it for yourself. The inbuilt charm of this range comes from the use of solid elm beech, combined with expert craftsmanship to give a perfect finish to each piece of furniture.

I enclose two admission tickets to the Ideal Home Lux. .I am sure you will not want to miss this opportunity to see the variety of ways in which WINDSOR unit furniture can be arranged to suit any requirements.

Look forward to seeing you there.

Yours sincerely

Template 17

Press Release Announcing New Hotel Wing

DATE

NEW SERVICE CONCEPTS

Service, the magic word in today's hotel industry, gains a new perspective when the new Regency Suites wing of the Pagoda Hotel Singapore opens in early the 2028.

The hotel's new upmarket product is targeted at the corporate traveller. In Line with this, a range of personalised services in major areas can now be by the discerning traveller.

The Business Centre, a vital facility for businessmen on the move, will operate 24 hours 7 days a week. With this extension of operating hours, busy executives will enjoy the convenience of conducing business at any time of the day. Whether it is an urgent Email communication required at 1 am or an e-mail, Email communication or letter by send in the middle of the night, time is no longer an issue. The Business Centre is well equipped with a complete range of secretarial service including a comprehensive reference library, personal computer, access to the Internet private offices and conference room with lounge.

Housekeeping and laundry services will also be available 24 hours daily. Guests arriving late at night will no longer worry about getting a suit pressed for the next morning. Requests for extra pillows, shampoo or stationery, or any other item will be met regardless of the hour.

A professional concierge team will answer queries and provide the wealth of information often required, from dinner reservations to theatre shows, or even finding the best shoe-maker in town.

The hotel's airport representatives will not only greet guests upon arrival at airport but also meet them during departure too. In addition to its 2 limousines, a fleet of 14 other cars are available at all times for a city tour or business trips.

With 155 Oda Hotels and resorts around the world, the Oda Tokyo positioning itself as a top deluxe hotel, making it the perfect choice for any traveller.

-end-

Contact:

Template18

Article In Staff Newsletter

SUPERSTARS TEAM GAIN SECOND PLACE

Stamina and strength of 3 Global employees were put to the test when they competed in the European finals of the Tech-stars competition held in Paris, France.

Global Inc was invited to the European finals after winning the regional at Leeds and being runners-up in the British final.

All entrants must work with information technology in some way, and Global entered a team every year since 1985 when they won the European final. This year's competition consisted of 8 strenuous, athletic-based events in one day, in which 3 of the 5 team members had to compete.

Unfortunately due to holiday commitments, this year's Global team entered without 2 of their top athletes, leaving Merry Holmes, Martin Wilson and Andrew to compete in this event. After a long day's work the team then had to face the final event, which was a 2000 metre steeplechase, and all team members performed extremely well in this.

The final result was that Global put in a very incredible performance and achieved second place. Well done to the team!

Template 19

Announcing Dinner And Dance

ARE YOU READY FOR THE GLOBAL DINNER AND DANCE?

The year has flown and it's time once again to get ready for the Global Annual Dinner and Dance. Put these details in your diary now:

Where?	Diamond Suite, Shangri La Hotel
When?	Saturday 23 December 2050
What time?	7.30 pm until late

As usual there will be a 10-course Chinese dinner (we can of course cater for any special requirements). Lisa Fashions will be entertaining us with a fashion show as we eat. With lucky draws, spot prizes and after-dinner entertainers and dancing, it's sure to be a great evening that you will not want to miss.

This company-sponsored dinner dance will cost you only £50 each. Partners pay the same price too. If it's anything like previous years' functions, you can be assured of a fabulous time. Get your registration forms from Reception or the Human Resource Department and book early.

If you have any queries please contact:

Yours

Extension 223

E-mail name@domain.com

Template 20

Manufacturer's Confirmation Of Agency Terms

Dear

We were pleased to learn from your Email communication of 14 November that you are willing to accept an agency for marketing our goods in Saudi Arabia. Set out below are the terms discussed and agreed with your Mr Williams when he called here earlier this month, but before drafting the formal agreement we should like you to confirm them.

1. The agency will operate as from I January 200- for a period of 3 years, subject to renewal.

2. Agency will be a sole agency for marketing our goods in Saudi Arabia.

3. No sales of competing products will be made in Saudi Arabia either on own account or on account of any other firm or company.

4. All customers' orders will be transmitted to us immediately for supply direct.

5. Credit terms will not be given or promised to any customer without our express consent.

6. All goods supplied will be invoiced by us direct to customers with copies to you.

7   A commission of 5% based on fob value of all goods shipped to Saudi Arabia, whether on orders placed through you or not, will be payable at end of each quarter.

8   Customers will be required to settle their accounts with us direct. A statement will be sent to you at the end of each month of all payments received by us.

9   A special credited commission of 2h% will be added.

10 All questions of difference arising under our agreement will be referred to arbitration.

Please confirm your agreement to these terms. A formal agreement will then be drafted and copies sent for your signature.

Yours faithfully

Announcing Changes In Business

1   Change of company name

2   Opening of a new store

3   Expansion of existing business

4   Opening of a new business

5   Establishment of a new branch

6   Removal to new premises

7   Reorganisation of a store's departments

8   Death of a colleague

9   Retirement of a partner

10 Appointment of a new partner

11 Conversion of partnership to private company

12 Dismissal of firm's representative

13 Appointment of new representative

14 Announcement about new working

15 Letter regarding outstanding holiday entitlement

Template 1

Change Of Company Name

Dear

Change of Company Name/Transfer of Business

In November 2020 Amman Communications was acquired by Stigma Pte Ltd. As a result of this acquisition and renaming the company, we are amending the registered name for direct debit processing.

This change will not affect the service you receive in any way, except that direct debits will be collected by Stigma Pte Ltd instead of Amman Communications with immediate effect. The only change you will notice is the different name on your bank/building society statement for this direct debit.

You need not take any action. Details of the change have been sent to your bank/building society. Your rights under the direct debit guarantee are not affected, as detailed on the attached guarantee.

Yours sincerely

Template 2

Opening Of A New Store

Dear

BEST SUPERSTORE OPENS AT BEDFORD -12 JULY 2024

Have you seen the great news in the national newspapers recently? Best International are opening a chain of furniture superstores throughout the UK. The first one will be open at Bedford on Monday 12 July 2024

Special discounts will be given to the first 50 customers who come through our doors from 0900 on our opening day.

Open times are   0900-2000 Monday to Saturday

A variety of kitchens, bathrooms, dining rooms and lounges will be on display. A full planning service is available so you can leave it to the experts to design just what planning service is available so you can leave it to the experts to design just what staff.

The store will be of particular interest to the DIY enthusiast. You will find everything you may need – paints, wall coverings, tiles, carpets, and so much everything you may need paints, wall coverings, tiles, carpets, and so much more. We will deliver free of change any orders over £100 for smaller orders there will be a minimal charge. Credit facilities are available at low interest rates.

Our car park has spaces for 400 cars but if you prefer to take the bus, number 214 stops right outside the Best Superstore. Do don't miss our grand opening on Monday 12 July remember there's a special discount waiting for you if you are among the first 50 customers.

See you at the superstore!

Template 3

Expansion Of Existing Business

Dear

To meet the growing demand for a hardware and general store in this area we decided to extend our business by opening a new department.

Our new department will carry an extensive range of hardware and other domestic goods at prices which compare very favourably with those charged other suppliers.

We would like the opportunity to demonstrate our new merchandise to you so we are arranging a special window display during the week beginning 24 June. The official opening of our new department wilt take place on the following Monday 1 July.

We hope you will visit our new department during opening week and give us the opportunity to show you that the reputation enjoyed by our other departments for giving sound value for money will apply equally to this new department.

Yours sincerely

Template 4

Opening Of A New Business

Dear

We are pleased to announce the opening of our new retail grocery store on Monday 1 September.

Mrs Victoria Chadwick has been appointed Manager. She has 15 years' experience of the trade and we are sure that the goods supplied will be of quality and reasonably priced.

Our new store will open at 0800 hours on Monday 1 September. As a special celebration offer a discount of 10% will be allowed on all purchases made first 50 customers. We hope we can look forward to your being one of them.

Yours sincerely

Template 5

Establishment Of A New Branch

Dear

Owing to the large increase in the volume of our trade with the Kingdom of Jordan, we have decided to open a branch in Amman. Mr Faisal Shaman has been appointed as Manager.

Although we hope we have provided you with an efficient service in the past, this new branch in your country will result in your orders and enquiries being dealt with more promptly.

This new branch will open on 1 May and from that date all orders and enquiries should be sent to

Manager

Co Ltd

18 London Avenue

Tel: 087 987600

Template 6

Removal To New Premises

Dear

The steady growth of our business has made necessary an ready move to new and larger premises. We have been fortunate in acquiring a particularly good site

On the new industrial estate at Chorley, and from 1 July our new address will be as follows:

Unit 20
Grange Road
London
SW235PS
Telephone 078 777777

This new site is served by excellent transport facilities, both road and rail, enabling deliveries to be made promptly. It also provides for better methods of service, which will increase output and also improve the quality of our goods even further.

Have very much appreciated your custom in the past and confidently expect to be able to offer you improvements in service when the new factory moves into full service.

Yours sincerely

Template 7

Reorganisation Of A Store's Departments

Dear

In order to provide you with even better service, we have recently extended and relocation on a number of departments in our store.

1. On the ground floor we have a wide selection of greetings cards, both boxed and single Christmas cards.

2. In the Children's and Babywear Department on the first floor there is a 'Ladybird' section.

3. Basement displays a good collection of wallpapers, most of which we able to supply within 24 hours.

We thank you for your past custom and hope we may continue to be of service you.

Yours sincerely

Template 8

Death Of A Colleague

Dear

It is with much sadness that I have to tell you of the sudden death of our Marketing Director, Michael Spencer. Michael had been with this company for 10 years and he made an enormous contribution to the development of the business. He will be greatly missed by all his colleagues.

I am anxious to ensure continuing service to you. Please contact me directly with any matters which Michael would normally deal with.

Yours sincerely

Template 9

Retirement Of A Partner

Dear

We regret to inform you that our senior partner, Mr Harold West, has decided to retire on 31 May due to recent extended ill-health.

The withdrawal of Mr West's capital will be made good by contributions from the remaining partners, and the value of the firm's capital will therefore remain unchanged. We will continue to trade under the name of West, Webb & CO, and there will be no change in policy.

We hope that the confidence you have shown in our company in the past will continue and that we may rely on your custom in the future.

Yours sincerely

Template 10

Appointment Of A New Partner

Dear

A large increase in the volume of our business has made necessary an in the membership of this company. It is with pleasure that we announce the appointment of Mrs Lisa Mith as partner.

Mrs Mith has been our Head Buyer for the past 10 years and is well acquainted with every aspect of our policy. Her expertise and experience will continue to of great value to the company.

There will be no change to our firm's name of Taylor, Hyde & Co.

We look forward to continuing our mutually beneficial business relationship with you.

Yours sincerely

Template 11

Conversion Of Partnership To Private Company

Dear

The need for additional capital to finance the considerable growth in the volume of our trade has made it necessary to reorganise our business as a private company. The new company has been registered with limited liability in the Hoole Umited.

We wish to stress that this change is in name only and that the nature of business will remain exactly as before. There will be no change in business policy.

The personal relationship which has been built up with all customers in the past will be maintained; we shall continue to do our utmost to ensure that you are completely satisfied with the way in which we handle your future orders.

Yours sincerely

Template 12

Dismissal Of Firm's Representative

Dear

We wish to inform you that Miss Rona Smart who has been our representative I North-West England for the past 7 years has left our service. Therefore she no longer has authority to take orders or to collect accounts on our behalf.

In her place we have appointed Mrs Tracie Coole. Mrs Coole has for many years had control of our sales section and is thoroughly familiar with the needs of customers in your area She intends to call on you some time this month to introduce herself and to bring samples of our new spring fabrics.

We look forward to continuing our business relationship with you.

Yours sincerely

Tempalte13

Appointment Of New Representative

Dear

Mr Samuel Frith who has been calling on you regularly for the past 6 years, has now joined our firm as junior partner. His many friends will doubtless be sorry that they will see him much less frequently and we can assure you that he shares regret.

Mr Frith hopes to keep in touch with you and other customers by occasional to his former territory.

Mr Lionel Tufnell has been appointed to represent us in the South West and Mr Frith will introduce him to you when he makes his last regular call on you next Mr Tufnell has worked closely with Mr Frith in the past and he will to do so in the future. Mr Frith will continue to offer help and advice in matters affecting you and other customers in the South West, and his intimate of your requirements will be of great benefit to Mr Tufnellin his new 'responsibilities.

Our business relations with you have always been very good, and we believe we have succeeded in serving you well. It is therefore with confidence that we ask you to extend to our new representative the courtesy and friendliness you have always shown to Mr Frith.

Yours sincerely

Template 14

Announcement About New Working

NEW WORKING HOURS

With effect from 1 September 2050- working hours will be amended to 0930 to 1730 Monday to Friday instead of the present working hours of 0900 to 1700.

I hope you will find these new hours convenient. If you anticipate experiencing any difficulties please let me know before 14 March.

Template 15

Letter Regarding Outstanding Holiday Entitlement

In the past it has been a policy of the company that all staff must take their holiday entitlement within one calendar year. Any holiday entitlement not taken before 31 December each year has been forfeited.

It has now been decided to amend this rule to provide staff with more flexibility regarding holidays.

With immediate effect anyone who has up to 5 days' holiday entitlement outstanding at 31 December may carry this over to 31 March the following year.

Any days that have not been used by 31 March will be forfeited. Unused holiday entitlement may not be converted to pay in lieu.

The approval of staff leave is still subject to agreement with your manager/supervisor. This will take into account the business and operational needs of the department and especially clashes with other staff.

If you have any questions about this new policy, please telephone the Human Resource Department on extension 459.

Chapter 2

Legal Letter

General

Whilst the drafting in general focuses primarily on contracts, you need to be
aware there are many types of legal documents you could encounter in practice, which serve a variety of different purposes and take very different
forms. For example, in Civil Litigation there are certain formalities that need to
be followed when drafting court documents to comply with the Civil Procedure
Rules.

Most commercial agreements will broadly contain the following elements:

- ✓ Front cover
- ✓ Contents page
- ✓ Commencement, date and parties
- ✓ Recitals (not essential but desirable)
- ✓ Definitions and interpretation

Operative provisions:

- Terms defining the scope of the agreement (such as the duration

- of the agreement)
- Conditions precedent (setting out any conditions to be satisfied
- before the agreement comes into force)
- Obligations of the parties
- Options or rights in favour of one of the parties
- Warranties and indemnities (if numerous, in a Schedule)
- Boilerplate clauses (standard clauses inserted into all agreements, but
- which may be very important and may be subject to negotiation)
- Schedules
- Testimonium and Execution clauses

Although much is it is relevant to all documents.

Types of contracts

There are generally two types of contract:

1. a contract/agreement under hand (i.e. an agreement which is not intended to take effect as a deed); and

2. a deed (i.e. an agreement requiring an additional execution formality beyond a simple signature).

DRAFTING

Generally, a contract will take the form of an agreement under hand unless it should take the form of a deed for one (or more) of the following reasons:

1. it is a document which is required to be executed as a deed (e.g. certain transactions relating to land, certain mortgages of property, or the grant of a power of attorney);

2. it is desirable to have a limitation period for an action arising from the contract of twelve years (a deed) rather than six years (an agreement under hand); or

3. it is questionable whether valuable consideration is being provided by a party to the document. If a document takes the form of a deed, valuable consideration need not be given for the document to be binding.

To ensure that you have included all the relevant information, it may help to use the "6 Ws". When drafting the parties' obligations, consider the following questions.

1. Who is to perform the obligation?
2. What is the obligation to be performed?
3. When is the obligation to be performed?
4. Where is the obligation to be performed?
5. To Whom is the obligation to be performed?
6. What if - What are the consequences of a failure to perform an obligation?

Avoid using 'redundant pairs' e.g.
'alter or change'
'any and each'
'custom and usage'
'full and complete'
'have and hold'
'known and described as'
'made and entered into'
'save and except'
'separate and distinct'
'undertake and agree'

Use:
'on or before' rather than 'by';
'after' or 'from and excluding' rather than 'from';
'to and including' or 'to but excluding' rather than 'until' or 'to';
'between'—state whether the period is inclusive or exclusive of the first and last days.

Rules of construction

a) Recitals

The recitals (a brief background to the document – see paragraph 4.5 below) may be relied upon to resolve any ambiguities in the operative parts.

b) 'Ejusdem generis' ('Of the same kind')

General words following specific words are treated as limited in meaning to the class or concept expressed in the specific words.

For example, a provision in a bill of lading (a document used in shipping transactions) referring to a port becoming 'unsafe in consequence of war, disturbance or other cause', would not cover the port becoming unsafe because of icy conditions, since that is not a cause ejusdem generis with war or disturbance.

c) 'Noscitur a sociis' ('It is known from its associates')

This rule has both a wide and narrow meaning. In its wider sense,

the rule requires that a document be construed as a whole and that the construction of a particular part of the document that is consistent with the whole is preferred. In its narrower sense, the rule requires that general words be limited by reference to the subject matter with which they are concerned.

Both senses express the basic principle that the interpretation of words is governed by the context in which they appear.

Example: What is the term "Property" in conveyancing unlikely to include? Intellectual property? Personal property?

'Expressio unius exclusio alterius' ('The express mention of one thing implies the exclusion of another')

Where a provision is expressed in detail, or a detailed list of particulars is enumerated, any unexpressed detail or particular is presumed to be excluded. The application of this rule can be avoided either by avoiding the specification of detail (unless it is possible to be certain of complete accuracy and exhaustive coverage) or by the inclusion of general words (but bearing in mind the other rules of construction set out above).

d) 'Contra proferentem' ('Against the one putting it forward')

Ambiguous words will be construed against the interests of the party attempting to rely on the clause in question.

Termination

15.1 The Company is entitled to terminate this Agreement immediately on giving written notice to the Contractor if:

(a) the Contractor is in material breach of this Agreement;

(b) a liquidator, administrator or administrative receiver is appointed in respect of the Contractor; or

(c) any of the representations made in clause [ ] proves to have been incorrect or misleading as at the date of this Agreement.

15.2 Any notice given under clause 15.1 must be delivered to the Contractor at [address], or by facsimile to [Email communication number] or by email to [email address] or to such other address, facsimile number or email address as the Contractor may notify to the Company from time to time.

As a starting point the drafter needs to understand the business points to go into the legal document, translate them comprehensively into the most appropriate contractual terms and achieve clarity and certainty. (BPP Law)

LEGAL TEMPLATES LETTER

1. Legal Research
2. Share Purchase Agreement Sample Advise
3. Dispute Advice
4. Consumer sale of goods Certificate of guarantee
5. Unsolicited goods
6. Goods sent on approval
7. Confirming contract ended
8. Claim payment for work done under contract and for extra work requested
9. Claiming for work done over and above the contract
10. Claiming to have completed the contract
11. Ending a contra which has been frustrated
12. Accepting a breach of contract as repudiation
13. Giving notice to end a contract
14. Contract entered into under a mistake of fact and requesting return of moneys paid
15. Request for repayment
16. Recording a rectification of a mistake
17. Comfort letter

18. Request for time

19. Referring to lapse of an offer

20. An offer not accepted in time

21. Deferred acceptance

22. Accepting subject to conditions

23. Accepting subject to conditions

24. Correcting a quotation

25. Accepting an offer

26. Following an acknowledgement of order

27. An offer

28. An option to purchase

29. Contractual letter of offer to buy property

30. Negotiating to sell property

31. Negotiating a contract

32. Giving a trade reference

33. Declining to give a reference

34. Reference for an employee

35. Claiming payment for a secret profit

36. Holding agent liable as principal

37. To undisclosed principal

38. Claiming commission

39. Recording agency

40. Agent claiming indemnity

41. Warning agent that he is exceeding his authority

42. Notifying a customer that an agent has exceeded his authority

43. Agent confirming sale

44. Appointing a sales agent

45. Answering a claim for an alleged debt

46. Making an offer of payment

47. Statutory demand for debt from an individual

48. To a company making statutory demand for a debt

49. Before action is brought

50. Stopping further work

51. Retaining goods for non-payment

52. Second application for debt

53. Reminder of outstanding account

54. Claiming damages for failure to take delivery

55. Claiming liquidated damages

56. Claim for damages

57. Claim for damages

58. Agreeing to arbitrate

59. Rejecting a claim

60. Settling a claim 'without prejudice'

61. Answering a claim in a conciliatory manner

62. A claim in a conciliatory manner

63. Complaining of breach and keeping open all rights

64. To insurers notifying a claim

65. Reserving title on a

66. Making interest payable

67. Suspending services

68. Notifying delivery of service

69. Accepting goods and notifying claim for damages

70. Where carrier left t goods

71. Rejecting goods because of late delivery

72. Rejection of goods Reply to claim by liquidator

73. To receiver claiming goods

74. Complaining of a slander of goods

75. Complaining of a passing off

76. To ex-employee who is using trade information

77. To ex-employee in breach of contract against competition

78. An employee leaving for pregnancy

79. To the court notifying ending of employment

80. To employees following take over

81. Appointing an independent contractor

82. Giving discharge from a guarantee

83. Claiming discharge by operation of law

84. Release of a guarantee

85. Request payment made under a guarantee

86. Agreeing to give a guarantee

87. Protective form of guarantee

88. Letter of guarantee

89. Declining to give a trade reference

90. Making a claim under an insurance policy

91. Auditors appointment

92. To solicitors asking for a quotation

93. To solicitors making a complaint

94. Authorizing a bank to disclose information

95. To a bank following agreement for a facility

96. Creating a service tenancy

97. Requesting permission to change use

98. Requesting permission to carry out improvements

99. Consent to alterations not improvements

100. Real-estate opening negotiations for a new lease

Template 1

Legal Research Letter

Dear

Here are my conclusions in respect of Lara concerns about Mona Choi's directorship and employment in Marry Furniture Ltd (the "Company"). My understanding of the factual situation is set out in the attached report.

Review of Research

To achieve Monica's proposal that Mona is removed from the board, there are two options: either Mona can resign, or James, Monica and Delyth can vote together as shareholders to remove Mona from the board.

To achieve Monica's desire to keep Mona as an employee pending trial, she may not need to take any action, although Mona's employment contract may provide for termination of her employment on her dismissal as a director. However, James may have implied authority, as managing director, to dismiss Mona from her job without Monica's approval. James' authority can be removed by a board decision and Monica can pass such a resolution using her casting vote. In the event that James does not attend any board meeting where his powers of dismissal are to be restricted, Monica may need to be ready to ask Mona to support the appointment of Delyth as a director so that the meeting is quorate and the resolution can be passed. Therefore, if

Monica is concerned that James may act alone to dismiss Mona from her job straight away, Monica would be able to prevent this.

To ensure Mona has no involvement in financial matters and does not contact clients in her continued employment, Monica could follow the same process of obtaining a board resolution to take away Mona's responsibilities which involve finance or contact with the public, subject to any advice of the employment team on varying the service contract.

Monica needs to know about the consequences of a custodial sentence on Mona's employment. If Mona is subject to a custodial sentence (as opposed to remanded in custody pending trial), it is likely that her employment will terminate and that any dismissal will be fair and lawful.

Advice

Whilst a resignation could preserve Mona's personal dignity and would be quicker than holding a shareholders' meeting, Mona may resist resigning. In order to reduce the likelihood of this happening, we could prepare a formal notice to the Company proposing Mona's removal (signed by James, Delyth and Monica) in order to make it clear that if Mona refuses to resign she will be forcibly removed if the matter has to go to a vote. Faced with the prospect of being removed against her will, Mona may then relent and tender her resignation. This would avoid the need for further formal meetings, and would mean Monica can assure her personal clients (or their parents) that the Company acted robustly in response to the allegations, and was poised to secure Mona's forcible removal had she not agreed to resign.

Monica should hold a board meeting to remove Mona's responsibility for contact with customers and financial matters. That is a crucial role for the Company, which cannot be left vacant, so Monica will need to do this herself. The board will then need to either approve a service contract for Monica or else decide how to allocate Mona's responsibilities.

Monica wants to prevent Mona losing her job unless she is sentenced to a custodial sentence. As James may have implied authority to dismiss Mona, Monica should be prepared to call a board meeting to withdraw any implied authority. This should be on a date when Delyth can attend so that Monica and Mona can appoint her if James does not turn up. Monica should send us Mona's employment contract for us to check whether it contains a clause automatically terminating her employment in the event of her removal from the board.

Taking these steps to prevent James from dismissing Mona will be complicated, and could result in creating unnecessary divisions between family members. It is also possible that Delyth will not necessarily want to be a director (even though she can resign at the end of the meeting). I therefore recommend that Monica asks James to agree to have his managing director's powers limited so that it is absolutely clear that he cannot dismiss Mona from her job. Monica could explain to him that this would avoid the need to find a replacement for the whole of Mona's work. Monica could also point out that imposition of a custodial sentence will likely result in termination of Mona's employment in any event, and any such termination resulting from a custodial sentence is likely to be fair and lawful, so is a lower risk strategy than instant dismissal.

To maintain the good relationship with Mona, Monica should explain to Mona in advance why they propose dealing with things in this way. Monica should confirm it in writing, for clarity. I recommend that we draft this letter to go from Monica to ensure that it is accurate. A formal letter from us directly to Mona appears inappropriate in the family circumstances.

In terms of practical steps, I suggest that we do the following:

- Prepare a Form TM01 for Monica to date and file immediately after the meeting; and

- Show Monica the kind of formal wording used in a resignation letter to ensure that it sets out the specific date for termination required by Model Article 18(f).

I suggest we do not actually draft a full resignation letter, as that may appear unnecessarily aggressive. If you or Monica need any further assistance do give me a call, especially if you need me to plan how to set up and run the shareholders' meeting in the event that Mona has to be forced off the board.

Kind regards

Template 2

Share Purchase Agreement Sample Advise

Dear

Share Purchase Agreement dated 12 May 2025

Thank you for your instructions to review your sale of Mona LMB Limited ("LMB") to Paradise Hotels Limited (Paradise ") under the above Share Purchase Agreement. I have had the opportunity to read all of the documentation which you sent to me, including all of the accounting information which you provided to Paradise Hotels Limited and the letter before claim which you recently received from Mike Moris LLP.

Allegation to be investigated

The allegation made against Mona Estate PLC is that it failed to disclose a downturn in the profits of De Halve Moris, LMB' sole hotel in Holland, and that this constituted a material adverse change in the turnover, financial position or prospects of LMB. Such downturn is alleged to have taken place between 30 April 2015 and the completion date of the sale, 24 June 2015.

Profit Forecast for LMB as at 30 April 2015

One of the documents provided to Paradise Hotels Limited on the date the parties signed the Share Purchase Agreement was a Profit Forecast dated 30 April 2015 ("the April Profit Forecast")

The forecast for De Halve Moris for the quarter ending 24 June 2015 was:

- Turnover 190,500.00
- Profit 53,250.00

The management accounts of LMB for the quarter ending 24 June 2015 show that the actual performance of De Halve Moris was as follows:

- Turnover 95,250.00
- Loss 34,750.00

The difference in profits was therefore 88,000.00. I am not sure how Paradise Hotels Limited calculated their alleged loss of 400,000.

Upon further investigation, I have discovered that there was a general decline in hotel trade in Holland during May and June 2015, resulting from unprecedented rainfall which caused major flooding in the region. This clearly had an adverse effect upon the trade at De Halve Moris.

The Disclosure Letter dated 24 June 2050

The disclosure letter says nothing about De Halve Moris or its decline in profits during May and June 2015. On the face of it, therefore, there was a failure to disclose facts relating to the financial position of the Dutch operation of LMB.

Material adverse change?

The overall turnover of LMB for its financial year ending 31 December 2015 was 73.23 million. The turnover of De Halve Moris during that period was 742,857.

The-loss in profits at De Halve Moris for the quarter ending 24 June 2015 of 88,000 is insignificant in that context and would not, in my opinion, have affected the value of LMB as at the date of the sale. It does not represent a "material adverse change".

I trust that my conclusion provides some comfort to you. Incidentally, I did see that .there is something in the Share Purchase Agreement about notice of a claim, and I wondered whether that is something that you had looked at. This is outside of my remit and so I leave that to you and your lawyers.

Please let me know if I can be of any further assistance.

Yours sincerely

Solicitor

Template 3

Dispute Advice Sample

Dispute with Construction Limited

I spoke with our expert, Marisa Smith on 20 August 2018. Mr Smith has now considered your architect's designs for the glass roof. Unfortunately, his conclusion may now have an adverse impact on your case against Smithmon Construction Limited ("Smithmon"). Mr Smith has indicated that he is amenable to omitting this from his final report, but for the reasons detailed below I do not consider this to be appropriate.

Impact on your claim against Smithmon

Mr Smith has concluded that the design of the roof was flawed; he says that its metal structure was far too heavy and was not sufficiently supported. He thinks that the cracks in the walls could have been caused by the structure pulling inwards and downwards and that there is a small possibility that the roof collapsed completely of its own accord, rather than through the fault of Smithmon. If this information comes to the attention of the court, you may not succeed in demonstrating that the excavating and pile-driving caused the damage to the roof and this would mean that your nuisance claim would fail.

The consequences of Mr O'Leary omitting his conclusion

If we allow Mr Smith to omit his conclusion about the glass roof from his report, then he will be in breach of his obligations to the court:

The court rules state that Mr Smith has a duty' to be independent and uninfluenced by the pressures of litigation and to be unbiased. These duties are owed to the court and not to you as the party instructing him. He also has a duty to consider all material facts including those which might detract from his opinion; this therefore includes the glass roof designs.

Mr Smith has to make a statement at the end of his report that he has complied with his duties to the court and that he believes that the contents of his report are true. Clearly if he omits the information about the glass roof, he has not complied with his duties and he will potentially be liable for contempt of court due to his breach of his statement. This could result in a fine or even imprisonment.

If I allow Mr Smith to omit his conclusion from his report, then I myself will be in breach of my professional duties as a solicitor. I am not permitted to knowingly allow someone else to mislead the court.

Possible steps which Smithmon could take before the trial

Copies of the plans and specifications for the glass roof were provided to Smithmon during the disclosure process. Smithmon ' expert is likely to see these and he may come to the same view as Mr Smith. This could lead to Smithmon taking one or all of the following steps:

Smithmon' solicitor may ask Mr Smith questions about the roof design in order to clarify his report. Mr Smith is obliged to answer these questions; if he tries to avoid the issue then Smithmon may become suspicious about the nature of our instructions to him.

Any suspicion about our instructions may lead Smithmon' solicitor to make an application to the court for disclosure of our instructions to Mr Smith. Whilst the court will not routinely order the disclosure of the instructions given to an expert, it may order that the instructions be disclosed if it has reasonable grounds to believe that the substance of the instructions set out in the report are inaccurate or incomplete. It could become apparent that we requested Mr Smith to omit the information from his report. This might result in your claim being struck out or an adverse costs order against you.

Mr Smith will have to meet with Smithmon' expert in. order to identify areas of agreement and disagreement between them. Again, if Mr Smith tries to avoid the issue then Smithmon may become suspicious about the nature of our instructions to him. In his report, Mr Smith is obliged to set out the substance of all facts and instructions which are material to the opinions expressed in his report or on which those opinions are based.

Smithmon could also apply to disbar Mr Smith's evidence completely on the basis that he does not understand his duty to the court. Without any expert evidence, there is little chance of your claim succeeding.

Possible ways which Smithmon could take at the trial

Even if Smithmon does not take any immediate action, they may wait until the trial to raise the issue. They could cross-examine Mr Smith upon the glass roof in the witness box at trial; Mr Smith is obliged to tell the truth and it could become clear that he had omitted information from his report. This could seriously impact on the credibility of his evidence.

Smithmon may also at that point apply for disclosure of our instructions to Mr Smith and/or for permission to cross-examine him on our instructions. This could, again, lead to your claim being struck out or to an adverse costs order against you or to an order disbarring Mr Smith's evidence.

Advice

For all of the above reasons, we must insist that Mr Smith includes his about the glass roof in his final report.

However, we could obtain an alternative Sava on the glass roof from another expert; if this expert's opinion is more favourable than Mr Smith, then we could serve this report instead of Mr Smith's report. This would involve further costs and we would not be able to recover the costs of instructing Mr Smith from Smithmon even if your claim was to succeed.

Alternatively, we could start negotiations to try to settle the claim out of court.

Once you have had a chance to consider the contents of this letter, please me with your instructions.

Yours sincerely

Template 4

Consumer Sale Of Goods Certificate Of Guarantee

Dear

We are very pleased to have received your letter, and are sending by separate despatch the goods requested. All our goods are sold on our standard trading terms (a copy of which is enclosed), which include our guarantee of reliability. A certificate confirming your guarantee is enclosed. You also enclose our invoice for payment as soon as you safely receive the goods and are satisfied with them.

Yours faithfully

Template 5

Unsolicited goods

Dear

As an introduction to our range of real touch flowers we are sending to you a sample of some of our latest designs, together with a leaflet giving details of the prices and normal business terms which we offer.

All the glasses are made of the finest material. They are fragile, can easily be damaged, and because of the quality should not be allowed to be exposed to extremes of temperature.

We will telephone you within the next few days, after you have an opportunity to inspect the goods, to discuss with you any points you may wish to raise. You are, of course, under no obligation to purchase any of the goods, which since they will belong to us until you purchase them, will be entirely at our risk whilst they are on your premises.

We look forward to speaking to you and hope that we will have the pleasure of doing business with you.

Yours faithfully

Template 6

Goods sent on approval

Dear Sirs

In response to your recent request for an opportunity to inspect our range of teapots, we have sent by separate delivery a sample of each model for your approval. You may retain them for a period of ten days after which they should be returned, for which purpose a redelivery labels enclosed. Any goods not returned within this period will be deemed to have been accepted by you and the full purchase price, as set out on our enclosed price list, will be payable.

Our terms of business, including payment terms, are set out on the reverse of this letter. We particularly draw your attention to condition 3 of our terms, which provides that this delivery is dispatched on the basis that the ownership of the goods will not pass to you until payment has been made in full.

We also draw your attention to the fact that so long as you retain the goods you will be responsible for any loss or damage to them.

We hope that you will be pleased with our range and that we shall have the pleasure of developing a business relationship with you.

Yours faithfully

Template 7

Confirming contract ended

Dear

It is sad to realise that the three years during which we agreed to co-operate in the sale of solar panels will end on 1 April. I hope that we can continue to work together in the future as in the past.

Do you want to agree a new contract or would you prefer that from now on we treat each opportunity as a separate matter to be looked at on its own facts? I am quite open-minded and am happy to see you at any time to work out the way we will proceed in the future.

Any time to work out the way we will proceed in the future.

Yours sincerely

Template 8

Claim payment for work done under contract and for extra work requested

Dear

Under our agreement, as recorded in my letter of 4 April and your reply of 3 April, I agreed that we would write a Software for your stock control. The specification of the Software, as it was to perform, was included with my letter.

During the course of writing the Software you asked on various occasions for alterations and modifications to be made to enable you to use the Software in different ways. I agreed to do this for you but as it was not part of the specification set out in our original agreement, additional charges have been incurred.

The additional work involved has been twelve hours of Softwareing additional work involved has been twelve hours of Software-and accepted rate for this type of work), this involves a fee of £600.

The Software has now been written with the modifications you requested. It has been tested and runs according to specification. I have, therefore, fully performed my contract with you and enclose my account for the fee as stated in the contract, plus an additional charge of £396 for the additional work.

I shall be pleased to receive your online payment by return.

Yours sincerely

Template 9

Claiming for work done over and above the contract

Dear

Now that we have commenced to write the Software specified in our letter of 4 April, it is becoming apparent that you are also in need of an extra Software to cover a full database of capital markets research and customer requirements.

We can incorporate this within the existing software we are at present writing, but it will mean additional charges.

You have the choice of leaving us to carry on with the p existing software, and when that is finished having a new Software written for the additional requirement, or letting us incorporate your additional requirements with the present work. Obviously, it is more economic to do the work now, which will save time and money for the future. Please, though, let us know what you want us to do. We would carry out the additional work for an extra £1500.

Yours sincerely

Template 10

Claiming to have completed the contract

Dear

Under our agreement, as recorded in my letter of 1 April and your reply of 4 April, I agreed that we would write a Software for your stock control. The specification of the Software, as it was to perform, was included with my letter.

During the course of writing the Software you asked on various occasions for alterations and modifications to be made to enable you to use the Software in different ways. As a matter of good client relations, I made the necessary modifications and have not raised any additional charges.

The Software has now been written; it has been tested and runs according to specification. I have, therefore, fully performed my contract with you and enclose my account for the fee as stated in the contract. I shall be pleased to receive your online payment.

Yours sincerely

Template 11

Ending a contra which has been frustrated

Dear Sirs

Re: Software for Mauriton Speed

As a consequence of the Order in Council made yesterday dealing with the supply of advanced technological matter to Mauriton Speed we have been served with an Order made by the Best of Technology forbidding the supply of any software under our contract with you.

In these circumstances, we can only regret that our whole contract is impossible of performance through no fault of either of us. We return herewith the deposit made by you and release you from any further liability under the agreement.

We are disappointed that our business should be frustrated in this way and only hope that when the present emergency has passed we be able to resume discussions to mutual advantage.

Yours faithfully

Template 12

Accepting a breach of contract as repudiation

Dear Sirs

Notwithstanding the clear terms of your agreement with us and despite my repeated telephone calls to you, you have still not called off the third instalment of the goods.

I realise that you are having your own difficulties in achieving sales of the deliveries you have taken to date, but that is not a matter that affects our agreement with you to take £900 loads per month. This failure goes to the root of our agreement and can only be regarded as an intention by you to reject your contractual obligations.

I have considered the matter carefully and have decided that your conduct is such that my company can no longer continue with the association with you. I am advised that your breach of contract amounts to a repudiation by you of the contract and I am therefore seeking legal advice as to my company's remedies for breach of contract.

Yours faithfully

Template 13

Giving notice to end a contract

Dear

In accordance with paragraph (a) of my letter of 6 April 2045 (the letter appointing you our northern area representative), I give you notice to determine your appointment on 5 April 2045, or three months after receipt by you of this letter, whichever shall be the later date.

Will you please write to me with an acknowledgement of receipt of this letter.

Yours sincerely

Template 14

Contract entered into under a mistake of fact and requesting return of moneys paid

Dear Sirs

We were very sorry to hear from you that at the time of our agreement with you the Maersk Carrier had been lost at sea together with its cargo, which included the Tesla new model we had agreed to purchase from you.

We fully accept that at the time that we agreed upon the terms of the deal, neither of us knew the true facts. Now that the facts are known, we regret that we have to say that in the circumstances we are treating the whole transaction as ended.

Will you please return to us the deposit we had made on account of the purchase price.

Yours faithfully

Template 14

Request for repayment

Dear Sirs

We refer to our recent telephone conversation when we informed you of the claim that we had received.

We purchased from you for the sum of £10.000.000 clothing wear believing that they were your property, or that you were entitled to sell them to us. We have now discovered that, in fact, they were the property of Clothing Wear Ltd who has demanded that we either return the goods to that company or pay them the value.

We were very surprised to learn of this situation and, in the circumstances, we must ask that you return to us immediately the amount that we have paid to you, otherwise we will have no alternative but to instruct our lawyers to take the appropriate proceedings for recovery.

Yours faithfully

Template 16

Recording a rectification of a mistake

Dear

Northern area agency

Following our recent conversation confirm that there was an error in the correspondence appointing you our northern area agent. In paragraph (a) the initial period should have read 'three years from today's date' not 'three months'. I do apologise for this error and am pleased to correct it.

Could you please acknowledge this letter and confirm your agreement to this correction.

Yours sincerely

Template 17

Comfort letter

Dear Sirs

We confirm that we are aware of the proposed contract between your company and our subsidiary Reda Fashion Ltd, under which your company will be making available a credit facility of 10,000,000 to Reda Fashion Ltd. We have read and approve of the terms of that contract as set out in your letter of 1 April. We confirm that it is our intention to retain our present financial interest in Brass Reda Fashion Ltd, and that it will be our intention that the company should at all times be in a position to meet its obligations to you.

This letter is given to you at your request. In giving this letter we do so on the basis that there is no intention on our behalf to create any legal relations between us.

Yours faithfully

Template 18

Request for time

Dear

I am sorry that we have not been able to write to you on your offer cf 30 April. We still have some problems to resolve before a decision can be made. Could you please agree that your offer can be extended by three weeks, within which time we hope to be able to respond to you.

Confirmation of your agreement will be very gratefully received.

Yours sincerely

Template 19

Referring to lapse of an offer

Dear

I am sorry to see that you have not yet accepted the offer made in my letter of 1 April. As you will have seen from the terms of that letter the offer has now lapsed.

If you are still interested in discussing the matter, I would be pleased to hear from you to see whether it is possible for us to make a renewed offer.

Yours sincerely

Template 20

An offer not accepted in time

Dear

As you have not accepted the proposition contained in my letter of 12 June, I am sorry, but it is now withdrawn. I am still willing to do business with you, and would be ready to re-open negotiations with you on it if you are still interested.

Yours sincerely

Template 21

Deferred acceptance

Dear

Thank you for your letter setting out your proposals. In general terms I think we are agreed, but before I finally accept I would like to consider some of the implications that affect us here. I will come back to you with a firm reply in two or three days.

Yours sincerely

Template 22

Accepting subject to conditions

Dear

Thank you for your letter setting out your proposals. In general terms I could agree with your proposition but I would like you to consider whether instead of delivery being made on 1 April you could bring this forward to 15 March.

As to your payment terms, it is usual for us to agree to not less than sixty days from delivery rather than the terms you have suggested. Please let me know whether this can be agreed.

When I hear from you on these points I can let you know whether we are finally agreed and the order can be placed.

Yours sincerely

Template 23

Accepting subject to conditions

Dear

Thank you for your letter setting out your proposals. In general terms I might agree with your proposition but I would like you to consider whether instead of delivery being made on 1 December you could bring whether instead of delivery

As to your payment terms, it is usual for us to agree to not less than sixty days from delivery rather than the terms you have suggested. Please let me know whether this can be agreed.

When I hear from you on these points I can let you know whether we are finally agreed and the order can be placed.

Yours sincerely

Template 24

Correcting a quotation

Dear

In our telephone conversation this afternoon, I forgot to mention that delivery couldn't be made until after the works' annual break. This means that the earliest delivery we can offer is 15 September.

I did try to telephone you and tell you of this, but unfortunately you were not available. Please can you let me know whether you will wish to proceed on this basis.

I am sorry that this is the best delivery date I can offer and do hope that it will not inconvenience you.

Yours sincerely

Template 25

Accepting an offer

Dear

Thank you for your letter. I confirm my telephone conversation with you when I told you that I accepted your terms and it was agreed that we would now proceed with all speed.

Yours sincerely

Template 26

Following an acknowledgement of order

Dear Sirs

Order No 10

Your form of acknowledgement of our above numbered order has been received. We have noticed that the printed conditions on the back of the form are at variance with our printed form of conditions of order. We do not accept your conditions and repeat our order in its original form; you may accept this order by proceeding with it without further written acknowledgement.

Yours faithfully

Template 27

An offer

Dear Sirs

As requested, the following is our quotation for the supply of 10.000 fashion items.

1. Price. The price will be £5 per unit plus VAT at the appropriate plus carriage.'
2. Delivery. Delivery will be within two months of the receipt by us of your order.
3. Payment. Payment is due thirty days from the date of despatch from our
4. Offer remains open for one month from the date of this letter
5. This offer remains open for one month from the date of this letter and any acceptance, which must be in writing, will only have effect when it is acknowledged by us.

Yours faithfully

Template 28

An option to purchase

Dear

Re:

I confirm the agreement we reached today when you granted me an option, for which I paid you the sum of £5,000, to purchase the freehold of the above property.

The terms of the option were as follows.

1. For the sum of £5,000 (which I paid to you and you accepted) you granted me the option, exercisable within a period of six months from today's date, to purchase the freehold interest in the shop and living accommodation at 28 The High Street, London.

2. The payment of £5,000 will not be returnable to me but, in the event that I exercise the option, credit will be given to me for that amount against the purchase price payable.

3. The purchase price payable on the exercise of the option will be the sum of 100,000.

4. I may exercise the option by giving you a notice in writing at any time before the expiry of six months from today's date or two weeks after the grant to me of a planning permission

which will permit the use of the whole of the premises for offices, whichever is the first to happen.

5   I will immediately apply for planning permission and I will, at my own expense, use my best endeavors to obtain it. I will not, though, be obliged to make any appeal from a refusal. You will support my application by giving formal consent and support.

6   On my exercising the option, the Law Society's Conditions of Sale shall apply to the sale, you will sell to me as beneficial owner, you will deduce to me a good and marketable title free from branches and, on completion of the sale, you will give vacant possession of the whole of the premises.

7   Completion shall take place at your solicitor's office on or before expiry of four weeks from the date on which I exercise the option.

Will you please sign and return to me one copy of this letter in acknowledgement that you agree these terms.

I am so pleased that we have been able to reach such a mutually advantageous agreement and hope that planning consent will be granted without difficulty.

Yours sincerely

Template 29

Contractual letter of offer to buy property

SUBJECT TO CONTRACT

Dear

Re: Premises at London Bridge

I confirm our discussions of today regarding our warehouse at London Bridge.

Subject to contract, it was agreed that you would offer the sum £400,000 for the residue of the lease, which we hold on these premises. As I told you, the lease is for a term of twenty-one years from 25 December 2000 at a yearly rent of £400,000, which is payable quarterly on the usual quarter days. The rent is subject to review every five the tenant is responsible for all outgoings and for all repairs. I am now instructing my solicitors to send to your solicitors a draft contract, and I hope that the sale will go smoothly. I assume that I will be hearing from the surveyor who will be inspecting the property for you. We talked about many things and you asked various questions about the property. If there are any points that occur to you and that I can help on, please let me know. I must make it clear, though, that I am giving you this information in an endeavour to be helpful.

Please tell me about anything that you are particularly relying on, so that we can see whether or not it should be included in the contract that our lawyers will be preparing. Anything not in the contract will not have any legal effect.

Yours

Template 30

Negotiating to sell property

SUBJECT TO CONTRACT

Dear

Re: Premises at London Bridge

I confirm our discussions of today regarding our warehouse at London Bridge.

Subject to contract, it was agreed that you would offer the sum £400,000 for the residue of the lease, which we hold on these premises. As I told you, the lease is for a term of twenty-one years from 25 December 2000 at a yearly rent of £400,000, which is payable quarterly on the usual quarter days. The rent is subject to review every five the tenant is responsible for all outgoings and for all repairs. I am now instructing my solicitors to send to your solicitors a draft contract, and I hope that the sale will go smoothly. I assume that I will be hearing from the surveyor who will be inspecting the property for you. We talked about many things and you asked various questions about the property. If there are any points that occur to you and that I can help on, please let me know. I must make it clear, though, that I am giving you this information in an endeavour to be helpful.

Please tell me about anything that you are particularly relying on, so that we can see whether or not it should be included in the contract that our lawyers will be preparing. Anything not in the contract will not have any legal effect.

Yours

Template 31

Negotiating a contract

Dear

Proposed investment in Frith Ltd

Following the meeting that we had last Monday, I confirm the changes I made to contact you on the basis that they were 'subject to contract'.

1. Frith Ltd at the moment has an issued share capital of £10.000.000, of which I hold ninety-nine shares and my wife holds one. The proposal is that I will increase the share capital to 10.000.000 shares and I will subscribe for an additional 10.0000 (making the joint holding of my wife and myself 5.000) and you will subscribe for 5.000 so that we are exactly equal shareholders,

2. I will pass the necessary resolutions to appoint you an additional director of the company and I will arrange that my wife resign her directorship.

3. We will then both appoint Christina Smith as a director. I will be chairman of the company without a casting vote,

4. We will ask our solicitors to amend the Articles of Association so as to provide that if either of us wishes to sell his shares he must first offer them to the other at a price to be settled by the auditors.

5 . The existing solicitors and auditors will be retained and Anna Sava will continue to be the company secretary.

If you agree to this suggestion, I will instruct my solicitors to draw up a contract for your solicitors to approve.

I am very pleased to know that you may be joining me and I hope that our association will be a long and happy one.

Yours sincerely

Template 32

Giving a trade reference

Dear Sirs

Fashion & Home Deco Co. Ltd

In answer to your request for a reference for the above-named company, we would say that over the past three years during which they have operated account facilities with us they have discharged their obligations faithfully and in due time. We know of nothing to their discredit.

We are giving this reference as a courtesy to a fellow trader and in an effort to be helpful. In accordance with our invariable custom, we must make it clear that we do so only on the basis that we accept no legal liabilities arising from the reference and must leave you to judge, on whatever other evidence you may acquire, whether or not to do business with the company.

Yours faithfully

Template 34

Declining to give a reference

Dear Sirs

We have received your request for a reference for Mr Mike Time. We do not know whether Mr Smith invited you to refer to us in this way, but in all fairness to him we think it would be better that some other party were approached as his referee.

Mr Smith will no doubt be able to explain to you the difficulty we have.

We regret that we are unable to be of more help to you.

Yours faithfully

Template 35

Reference for an employee

Dear

Re:

Mr Smith was employed by us for a period of five years, originally as a in our buying department and, through promotion, rising to the position of assistant to the chief buyer. He left at his own wish on 20 June last.

Throughout his employment he was a good and conscientious worker. Although we did have occasion to complain about his time keeping, we would have no hesitation in recommending him for employment in a position comparable to that he enjoyed with us.

In accordance with the usual custom of this company we give this reference in an attempt to be helpful but on the strict basis that we accept no legal liability.

Yours faithfully

Template 36

Claiming payment for a secret profit

Dear

We are very surprised to learn that whilst you were acting as our agent on the recent purchase you negotiated for us, you were also paid a commission by the vendor. This is quite clearly a breach of your towards us and calls for an explanation as to the reason why you should act in this manner.

The fact that the vendor was to pay a commission to you should been disclosed to us. In the circumstances we consider that we entitled to demand the payment to us of the commission paid to you. Unless we have a remittance within the next seven days our will be instructed to take the appropriate proceedings.

Yours sincerely

Template 37

Holding agent liable as principal

Dear Sirs

Contract dated

We told you that when the goods ordered under the above contract were delivered we discovered that, contrary to your assurances when we placed the order, they were made of an alloy which was not brass. As we told you when we were discussing the order, any other alloy would cause us considerable expense to adapt for the display we have m mmd.

We intend to pursue our remedies for the losses we will suffer claim that you are merely an agent for the company that manufactures and have denied any personal liability. At no time during our dealings with you have you said that you were an agent, the order we placed was placed with you in your own name, and you made no comment. It was not until we claimed upon you for the misstatement relating to the goods that you claimed to be anything other than a principal.

We are advised that your relationship with Fashion House Ltd is no concern of ours and we irritated to pursue our rights against you personally.

Yours faithfully

Template 38

To undisclosed principal

Dear Sirs

Contract dated

On 30 April we contracted to purchase 100 brass candlesticks. At the time, we were under the impression that Mr. Mike Time, with whom we were negotiating, was acting on his own account. He informed us that the candlesticks were manufactured from brass and our order was placed in reliance upon this claim.

The goods have been delivered and we now find that the literature sent with them expressly states that the goods are manufactured from some other alloy.

On our claiming against Mr. Smith for the losses we have suffered through his misrepresentation, he informs us that he is only an agent Will you please let us know by return whether Mr. Smith is your)Will you please let us know by return whether Mr. Smith is your agent and whether you were aware of the claims that he has been making for your product. We must make it clear that we are reserving all our rights in this matter.

Yours faithfully

Template 39

Claiming commission

Dear

Sales commission

I have been checking the accounts that you have sent me against my own records. I know that the customers whose names are set out on the attached sheet have ordered from you and that you have made deliveries to them. I cannot find that any payment has been made of the commission due to me.

Can you please ask your accounts department to refer to their records and either let me have the payment or an explanation for the non-payment. I am not aware of any reason why payment should be delayed.

Yours sincerely

Template 40

Recording agency

Dear

Sales agency

I confirm the arrangement which we have made which is that on all sales effected by me of your brass candlesticks I will be paid a commission of 2.5 per cent of the invoice value (excluding VAT).

At the end of each calendar month you will send me a showing the amount of the invoices rendered in the month, and you will pay me my commission at the end of the next month.

Although this recognizes that your terms of business say that payment is due to you at the end of the month following the month of delivery, I will be paid commission on orders obtained irrespective of the date of payment to you.

I am very pleased to have this opportunity to work for you and hope I am very pleased to have this opportunity to work for you and hope association.

Yours sincerely

Template 41

Agent claiming indemnity

Dear

I have been told by Frith Corporation PLC that the goods sold to them last are defective and that as a result they are going to claim month damages.

They have told me that they claim that the material used was an alloy and not the pure metal that they said I had promised them. I did not make any promises to them about the product and I certainly did not tell them that pure metal would be used. It seems to me that they may be trying to claim on us both.

If any claim is made on me out of this order, I will expect you to indemnify me against all liability. It seems to me that we shall have to have different solicitors because there may be a conflict of interests. I will be looking to you to give more a complete indemnity against my solicitor's fees, and I would be grateful for your confirmation that this be done.

This is an unhappy business; between us we must see that the claim is properly met and, if possible, defeated.

Yours sincerely

Template 42

Warning agent that he is exceeding his authority

Dear

It has come to my notice that you are telling customers that our goods can be adapted for use with mains electricity, that they are made from pure brass and that they are normally based upon a wooden plinth. None of these is true.

I must warn you that you have no authority to make any representations about the product and that you must keep strictly to the sales instructions that we have given you. Any future repetition of this type of conduct will result in our terminating your agency.

I want you to understand the seriousness of the matter. Quite apart from the damage that you could cause to us, if without authority you make promises or give warranties you will have a personal liability to the customer for any damage caused to him. For our part, if your actions were to result in claim being made upon us, we should seek indemnity from you. In any legal proceedings, we would join you and claim against you for our indemnity and the costs incurred. So you will see that it is vital, for your own protection that you keep well within the bounds of your authority. If at any time you want to be sure of your position, contact us at once and we will give you guidance.

I am sorry that I have had to write such a formal letter but it is best that you know clearly what our attitude is and avoid problems for the future.

Yours sincerely

Template 43

Notifying a customer that an agent has exceeded his authority

Dear

It has come to our notice that our agent Mr Merry Smith has represented to you that our candlesticks are all mounted on wooden plinths, are manufactured from pure brass and are suitable for conversion for connection to the domestic electricity lighting circuits. None of these representations is true. The sticks that are mounted on wooden plinths are a special design which would be charged for at a special rate. The materials from which we manufacture the candlesticks is not pure brass (pure brass would be too soft for the purpose) and we could not in any circumstances agree to an adaptation to permit connection to the mains power supply. Safety considerations would make this a most unwise procedure.

Mr Smith has no authority to make representations of this nature on our behalf. He is a sales representative of this company and any special terms and conditions on any order placed with us must have been agreed by us in writing first.

We apologies most sincerely to you for these unauthorized claims. We would very much like to help you and to supply a product that suits your requirements. Our commercial director, Mr Frith, will be suits your requirements. Our commercial director, Mr will be

Contacting you in the hope that we may be of assistance.

Yours faithfully

Template 43

Agent confirming sale

Dear

I confirm on behalf of Brass Candlesticks Ltd, whom I represent, your order for 100,000 candlesticks. I enclose for you a copy of the company's standard form of conditions of sale, which will apply. You will hear from them direct as to the date of delivery.

I am very pleased indeed to have had this opportunity to meet you and hope that this will be the commencement of a long and mutually profitable association.

Yours sincerely

Template 44

Appointing a sales agent

Dear

I confirm on behalf of Fashion Ltd, whom I represent, your order for 100,000 candlesticks. I enclose for you a copy of the company's standard form of conditions of sale, which will apply will hear from them direct as to the date of delivery.

I am very pleased indeed to have had this opportunity to meet you and hope that this will be the commencement of a long and mutually profitable association.

Yours sincerely

Template 45

Answering a claim for an alleged debt

Dear

Your invoice no.

We have received your above-numbered invoice.

May we make it clear to you at once that we do not owe the sum claimed or any other amount. Your invoice alleges that we owe you 5,000 for goods which you claim to have delivered to us. We can only conclude that this relates to the goods we ordered from you but which, when your carrier attempted to affect a delivery to us, we found did not correspond with the sample previously supplied and we refused to accept them.

Any attempts by you to pursue this claim will be strenuously resisted. Moreover, we consider that your failure to deliver goods in accordance with the sample was a clear breach by you and we are treating any contract that might have existed between us as at an end. We reserve our rights to claim for the losses we have suffered by We reserve our rights

Yours faithfully

Template 46

Making an offer of payment

WITHOUT PREJUDICE

Dear Sirs

Your invoice no.

We apologies to you for the delay in discharging your account.

Because of matters with which you are not concerned we are in the embarrassing position of having to ask for your help and consideration.

We would be grateful if you would allow us to discharge the liability to you by equal monthly payments of £10,000, the first payable forthwith and the remainder each month.

As a token of our good faith, we enclose herewith our payment for the first installment and post-dated payments for the remainder.

We do hope that you will be able to see your way to accept this offer. We are grateful to you for your past indulgence and repeat our apologies for our failure.

Yours faithfully

Template 47

Statutory demand for debt from an individual

Dear

Our invoice no.

We enclose herewith a statutory demand for debt pursuant to the Insolvency Act 1986 and the rules made thereunder.

Please acknowledge receipt.

Yours faithfully

Template 48

To a company making statutory demand for a debt

Dear

Re: Our invoice no.

The debt due to us for £50,000 under the above-mentioned invoice remains unpaid.

Pursuant to section 518 of the Companies Act 1985 we enclose a demand in the prescribed form. Please acknowledge receipt.

Yours faithfully

Template 49

Before action is brought

Dear

Our invoice no. 123

Our invoice for £50,000 for the goods sold to you on 1 August last and delivered to you on the same date remains outstanding.

Unless payment is received within seven days, proceedings for recovery of the amount due will be commenced without further notice to you.

Yours faithfully

Template 50

Stopping further work

Dear

Our invoice no.

Our above-numbered invoice remains unpaid despite repeated demands. All further work on the balance of your order has been stopped and will not be recommenced until payment has been received.

Yours faithfully

Template 51

Retaining goods for non-payment

Dear

Our invoice no.

We regret to see that despite repeated reminders our above-mentioned account remains unpaid.

The goods in question will not be released to you until our account has been discharged in full.

We must ask you to let us have a remittance by return, failing which we shall refer the account to our lawyers for collection.

Yours faithfully

Template 52

Second application for debt

Dear

Our invoice no.

We regret to see that we have received no reply to our letter of 1 August; neither have we received any settlement of the account.

From the lack of communication from you we can only assume that there is no question that you wish to raise over the account or the goods. We cannot, therefore, understand your failure to discharge the debt.

We are sure that you will fully understand that we cannot extend credit to this extent with present-day overheads. Our terms of trade are strictly thirty days.

Please let us have the payment in settlement of our account without further delay.

Yours faithfully

Template 52

Reminder of outstanding account

Dear

We notice that our above-numbered invoice is outstanding. Is there any query that you have in respect of the account or the goods? If there is, please let us know. In the interests of good customer relations we try to assist in any way possible where problems have arisen. If, as we hope, there are no difficulties we look forward to receiving your remittance in settlement by return.

Yours faithfully

Template 53

Claiming damages for failure to take delivery

Dear

Your order no.

Yesterday we notified you that goods against your above-numbered order were ready for delivery. You informed us that because of a change in your requirements you no longer wished to receive them.

Change in your requirements you no longer wished to receive them. Fallen by 10 per cent.

In an endeavor to mitigate the loss that we have suffered by your default, we have sold the goods at the best price that could be obtained on the open market, which was £50.000.

We accordingly enclose our invoice for the amount of 6,000 made up as follows:

Agreed price	£55,000.00
Cost of resale	£10000
	£56,000.00

Less proceeds of resale £50.000

$$6,000.00$$

We trust that the unpleasantness of litigation can be avoided but, unless we receive a remittance from you for this amount, we shall be compelled to instruct our lawyers to commence proceedings for it recovery.

Yours faithfully

Template 54

Claiming liquidated damages

Dear

Our order no.

We refer to condition 5 of our Conditions of Sale. In breach of condition, you have not given us a date for delivery of the third installment of the goods ordered. These goods are now manufactured and have been ready for delivery for the past two weeks.

Damages at the rate of 100 per week are being incurred. This sum will be added to the amount of our next invoice.

Yours faithfully

Template 55

Claim for damages

Dear

Our order no.

Due to the failure of your company to deliver the goods ordered by us in the time stated in the order, we were unable to complete the shipment on SS Export Helper. As you will recall, when we placed the order with you we specifically made known to you that the order had to be delivered in time for us to make a shipment on this particular sailing, and that any late delivery would result in our having to incur the extra expense of flying

the goods out to Sardinia.

The air freight charges which your late delivery has caused us are 10,000. We look to your company to reimburse this sum, failing which we shall place the matter into the hands of our lawyers with a to legal proceedings being instituted for recovery of the amount .

Yours faithfully

Template 56

Claim for damages

Dear

Re: Dispute

We agree to the dispute between us being referred to an arbitrator for decision. The following terms will apply to the arbitration.

1. Mr Jack Jones of 1 New Street, Derby, shall be the arbitrator.

2. The Rules of the London Court of Arbitration, as they apply to a domestic arbitration, shall apply.

3. The costs of the arbitration, including the liability to pay the arbitrator's fees shall be at the discretion of the arbitrator.

4. Only one expert witness per party shall be allowed.

5. The arbitration shall take place at the offices of Mr Jones.

Please sign and return the carbon of this letter to signify your agreement.

Yours faithfully

Template 57

Agreeing to arbitrate

Dear

Re: Dispute

We agree to the dispute between us being referred to an arbitrator for decision. The following terms will apply to the arbitration.

1. Mr Jack Jones of 1 New Street, Derby, shall be the arbitrator.
2. The Rules of the London Court of Arbitration, as they apply to a domestic arbitration, shall apply.
3. The costs of the arbitration, including the liability to pay the arbitrator's fees shall be at the discretion of the arbitrator.
4. Only one expert witness per party shall be allowed.
5. The arbitration shall take place at the offices of Mr Jones.

Please sign and return the carbon of this letter to signify your agreement.

Yours faithfully

Template 58

Rejecting a claim

Dear

Re: Your letter of 1 August

We have received your letter of 1 August and note the claims you are raising.

We do not accept that the goods supplied were defective and do not admit that we have any liability to you.

We are passing all correspondence to our lawyers, London Partners, Deltoid & Dirac, to whom all further correspondence should be addressed.

Yours faithfully

Template 59

Settling a claim 'without prejudice"

Dear

Re: Claim for defective goods

Following our discussions on your above-mentioned claim we confirm that we have made the following offer.

1. We will replace the goods forthwith at no cost to you.

2. We will pay the fees of the expert you engaged to advise you on the condition of the goods and their fitness for the purpose for which you had purchased them.

3. We will pay the sum of £11,000 as an ex gratia payment and by way of recognition of the inconvenience you have suffered.

4. You will accept this offer in full and final settlement of any claim you may have against us arising out of or incidental to this consignment.

If this offer is accepted, please sign and return the copy of this letter and we will let you have our payment to cover items 2 and 3 by return.

Template 61

Answering a claim in a conciliatory manner

WITHOUT PREJUDICE

Dear

We have received your letter of 7 August and are very sorry to hear that you consider that the goods we have supplied are defective. We would ask that you allow us to inspect them either at your premises or here.

We take every care in the manufacture of this product, and the most stringent quality control inspections are made. If it should be that a mistake has occurred we will, of course, replace the goods without any charge to you.

We have noted your claim that in addition to a replacement of the goods, we should compensate you for the additional losses you have suffered. We draw your attention to our conditions of sale and particularly to condition 12, which limits our liability to replacement. However, we would not want any customer to feel that he is being treated unfairly or to have any sense of grievance. We suggest that when we have been able to inspect the goods we meet and see whether some compromise can be reached.

Yours faithfully

Template 62

A claim in a conciliatory manner

Dear

We have received your letter of 7 August and are very sorry to hear that you consider that the goods we have supplied are defective. We would ask that you allow us to inspect them either at your premises or here.

We take every care in the manufacture of this product, and the most stringent quality control inspections are made. If it should be that a mistake has occurred we will, of course, replace the goods without any charge to you.

We have noted your claim that in addition to a replacement of the goods, we should compensate you for the additional losses you have suffered. We draw your attention to our conditions of sale and particularly to condition 12, which limits our liability to replacement. However, we would not want any customer to feel that he is being treated unfairly or to have any sense of grievance. We suggest that when we have been able to inspect the goods we meet and see whether some compromise can be reached.

Yours faithfully

Template 60

Complaining of breach and keeping open all rights

Dear

Your continued failure to call off the third installment of the goods your continued failure to call off the third installment of the goods that agreement.

We intend to pursue our rights, through the courts if With this in mind, we are consulting our lawyers from whom you will be hearing in due course.

Yours faithfully

Template 65

To insurers notifying a claim

Dear

Re: Policy number

We are notifying you of a possible claim under the above-numbered policy and enclose for you copies of the relevant order, consignment note, our conditions of trade and the letter raising the claim.

The facts, which give rise to the claim, are ... [here set out briefly the facts of the matter].

For obvious commercial reasons we wish to dispose of this claim without recourse to litigation, and would like to send to the customer a letter, of which the enclosed is a draft. Could we please have your comments.

Yours faithfully

Template 66

Reserving title on a sale

Dear

Our invoice no.

The goods referred to in the above invoice have been dispatched today. The container is marked with the invoice number and the words 'Fashion Houses Ltd'. These goods have been dispatched on the condition that the legal ownership of them remains yours until such time as you have paid for them in full. Until they have been paid for, they must not be used for your business of manufacturing fashion items, nor may you resell them.

If they are not paid for within sixty days, we shall have the right to enter upon your premises to take them back, and so long as they are unpaid for you must take proper care of them, and see that they are kept separate in your stores from your own goods.

Yours faithfully

Template 67

Making interest payable

Dear

Outstanding accounts

We very much regret to see that our invoices dating back to last August are still unpaid. You will know that our business terms are payment within thirty days. In common with most businesses, we cannot afford to give free credit.

The only basis upon which we are prepared to delay the commencement of legal proceedings to recover the outstanding amount is that you let us have your payment for the August account forthwith, you agree that the balance of the accounts outstanding will carry interest at the rate of 15 per cent per annum from thirty days after their date until payment, and that you discharge the remaining accounts within two months.

Yours faithfully

Template 68

Suspending services

Dear

Your order no.

We have received your above-numbered order.

We regret to find that despite repeated reminders you have still not paid our invoices dated 23 January 2005 and 15 March 2010. In view of our long-standing business relationship, we would like to assist you by accepting this new order, but we are sure that you will understand that we cannot extend further credit. We will accept your order only on terms that no delivery will be made until we have received payment in full of the outstanding invoices, and that in this and in all future orders the goods will be dispatched to you strictly on a cash on delivery basis.

Please confirm in writing that this is accepted by you.

Yours faithfully

Template 69

Notifying delivery of service

Dear

Your order no.

We regret to see that you are now one month in arrears with the interim payment due under your above-numbered contract. These payments were fundamental to the whole transaction.

In the circumstances, unless payment is received within the next twenty-four hours all further service of the goods will be stopped. We shall endeavor to sell those goods already made and will look to you for the damages we have suffered by reason of your breach.

Yours faithfully

Template 70

Accepting goods and notifying claim for damages

Dear

Your order no.

We are now in a position to deliver goods in satisfaction of your above-mentioned order.

Our carriers, Fashion House Ltd, have been instructed that they must obtain your signature to the consignment note as your agreement that the goods conform with your order. This will be a upon which delivery will be made. The carriers inform us that they will make the delivery on Wednesday next.

Unless we hear from you to the contrary, delivery will be made during normal business hours at your premises, Chelsea, London.

Yours faithfully

Template 71

Where carrier left t goods

Dear

Our order no.

[Paragraph 1 as in previous letter.]

The carrier was instructed to return the goods to you. Or, if it is the case, 'The carrier left before we could give him instructions to return the goods to you.'

We have given no permission, expressly or by implication, permit-ting the goods to be left on our premises. We require you to remove immediately and accept no liability for them or for any damage that they may suffer whilst they are on our premises.

Yours faithfully

Template 72

Rejecting goods because of late delivery

Dear

Our order no.

Your carrier today attempted to deliver goods pursuant to our above-quoted order.

"It was a fundamental term of our order that the goods would be delivered by the lost of this month. In view of your failure to comply with this term, we refuse to accept the goods and have instructed your carrier to return them to you.

Your failure has caused us loss and a further letter will be sent to you on this subject.

Yours faithfully

Template 73

Rejection of goods Reply to claim by liquidator

Dear

Our order no.

Your carrier today attempted to deliver goods said to be in fulfillment of our above-numbered order.

On examination we found that the goods offered did not correspond with the sample we had received [with the description given/were damaged] and we refused to accept them. The carrier was instructed to return them to you.

Yours faithfully

Template 74

To receiver claiming goods

Dear

Rose Wholesalers Ltd

We have seen that you have been appointed receiver of the above-named company. On the company's premises is a consignment of goods marked 'Goods from Fashion HOuse Ltd'. These goods belong to us. They were the subject of an order placed by the company of which you are the receiver, and were delivered by us under reservation of title.

No payment for the goods has been received by us and the property in them remains with us. Under the terms upon which they were delivered we have a right of entry to the company's premises repossess our property. We propose to exercise this right on Monday on which day our carrier will call to collect them.

Yours faithfully

Template 75

Complaining of a slander of goods

Dear

We were very surprised to be told by Large Wholesalers Plc that you had told them that our candlesticks were not made of brass, and that the insulation was so defective that we had received repeated claims from customers, one of whom had suffered serious injury by reason of the defective product.

You have been familiar with our product for many years and will be well aware that these statements are completely and utterly untrue. As a result of the information you gave them, Rose Wholesalers Plc have withdrawn the order they were placing with us and have placed their order elsewhere.

We must ask that you give us an immediate undertaking that you will not repeat these falsehoods, that you will write at once (sending us a copy to Rose Wholesalers Plc telling them that the statements were false and totally without foundation.

Unless this undertaking and offer to pay damages is received by return, we shall instruct our solicitors to commence proceedings further notice to you.

Yours faithfully

Template 76

Complaining of a passing off

Dear

We have obtained one of the candlesticks that you are selling under name 'The New Stick'. We find that it is made from the same materials, to the same design as ours and, more seriously, includes our patent insulating process.

We are the holders of patent number 12334 issued to us on 1 April 2020 from the patent office in London. Unless you withdraw from sale all products using our patented method, undertake with us not to continue to infringe our rights, and pay to us damages for the infringement, we shall instruct our solicitors to commence the appropriate proceedings.

Yours faithfully

Template 77

Complaining of an induced breach of contract

Dear

In breach of his contract with us, Merry Smith has left his employment and has joined the organization that you have established. From information that has reached us we have satisfied ourselves that at your instigation and with your encouragement and support that he took this action.

We have suffered damage from this breach and we are immediately instructing our solicitors to take the appropriate proceedings.

Yours faithfully

Template 78

To ex-employee in breach of contract against competition

Dear

It has come to our notice that, in breach of your agreement with us, you are calling on customers in Huntingdon. We remind you of your agreement with us which included a term that for a period of three years from the end of your employment with us you would not compete with us within a radius of five miles of these premises. You are breaking this agreement.

Unless we have your written undertaking that you will abide by the terms of your agreement (and we remind you that this term of the agreement is still effective even though you have left our employment] and will stop all attempts to sell to customers in this area, we shall instruct our solicitors to commence proceedings against you.

Yours sincerely

Template 79

An employee leaving for pregnancy

Dear

Please accept my best hopes for your future confinement. I do that all goes well for you.

As you know, you have a right to return to work after your confinement, and we all hope that you will be back with us. It is going to be necessary for us to cover the work in your absence and I am sure that you will understand that we need to know what, at the moment, you hope to do. If you intend to come back after the confinement, will you please write and let me know. I will need something in writing as a record of your intention, so even though you may telephone I will still need a letter. I am sorry to have to be so formal but this is one of those times when formality is essential.

I will await hearing from you and in the meantime send the best wishes of us all.

Yours sincerely

Template 80

To the court notifying ending of employment

The Chief Clerk

London County Court

Court Offices

SW3504

Dear

Mike Smith, attachment of earnings order no. 12334

We have to inform you that the above-named debtor against whom the above-quoted attachment of earnings order was made ceased to be employed by us on Friday of last week, 13 June.

We have reason to believe that he has taken employment with the firm of Fashion Ltd, of 5 St John's Street, London.

Yours faithfully

Template 81

To employees following take over

Dear

The ownership of the business of Fashion House Ltd has now been transferred to this company. I want to assure you that there will be no changes (except for the better) for any employee. There will be no redundancies, and no changes in your working conditions. I hope that as part of a larger organization we will be able to offer you opportunities and working conditions that will greatly benefit you.

Our business is, for legal reasons, divided into several different companies but we try to see that all employees, no matter which company they actually work for, are treated in the same manner and have similar rights and privileges. For this reason we like to have all who are doing similar work employed under the same contract of employment. This will mean that your existing contract of employment has to be changed. I enclose the new form.

If you have any questions or difficulties over the changes, Mr Tomes (the company secretary) can see you and help you. If you have no questions or objections, you need take no action. If you do have any problems, I am sure that we can resolve them but you should let Mr Tomes know at once.

May I welcome you into our group and hope that we shall have the privilege of your help for many years to come.

Yours sincerely

Template 82

Appointing an independent contractor

Dear

This letter confirms my offer to you of a contract for supplying a complete buying office service for this company commencing on 1 April next. I have already explained to you the range of products we need and the service we require from a buying office. You or an organization headed by you will provide these services upon the following terms.

1. We will make available to you office accommodation at these premises, the extent of the accommodation being limited to two rooms large enough to accommodate you, an assistant and two typists. We will make no charge for this accommodation. Your right to occupy these rooms will be on license and will automatically terminate when this contract ends.

2. You will, at your own expense, provide such office furniture and equipment as may be necessary to enable you to carry out with efficiency the service required. We will, if you require it, make available to you finance to enable you to provide this equipment, the finance to bear interest at a rate equal to charged to us by our bankers and to be deducted monthly from amount due to you for your fees.

3   You will be solely responsible for engaging the staff necessary to provide the service and will indemnify us against all liability to the Inland Revenue and Customs and Excise for taxation and VAT payments. Since your fee is to be paid on a cost plus basis, we will have the right to place limits upon the amount, which you may charge for salaries and other expenses.

4   The manner in which the services are performed will be for you to decide, but will be carried out in a good and efficient manner and so that our business is in no way impeded through lack of supplies.

5   For providing these services we will pay to you a fee, which will be calculated on a cost plus 15 per cent basis, plus VAT. You will render us an account of the costs you have incurred on 1 January and 1 June in each year. Our accountants shall have full access to all your records to enable them to audit the account so rendered all your records to enable them to audit the account so rendered. We will make to you monthly payments on account of the fee at the rate of 2,000 per month commencing on 27 April next. Any overpayment that may be occasioned will be carried forward and any deficiency will be paid within seven days of the agreement of your account.

6   This agreement shall be for an initial period of three years. At the end of the third year the agreement will continue unless either party has given three months' prior written notice to the contrary. If no such notice is given either party may determine the agreement by three months' notice in writing.

7   This agreement shall be for an initial period of three years. At end of the third year the agreement will continue unless either party has given three months' prior written notice to the contrary. If no such notice is given either party may determine the agreement by three months' notice in writing.

8   There is one matter upon which we are most insistent. This concerns the confidentiality of the work. You will in providing the services gain knowledge of our business, our business contacts, our procedures and many of our business secrets. It will be fundamental that on the determination of this agreement no matter how it comes about, you will not disclose to any one and you will not make use for your own benefit or for the benefit of anyone else any of this confidential information that you acquire.

9   Company's premises any records or papers which may relate to our business. Any records or papers which I may permit to be taken will be returned next day, and whilst they are in your possession will be kept in a safe and secure place.

10 Rules of the London Court of Arbitration shall apply to the arbitration.

If you agree to these terms please sign and return one copy of this letter.

Yours faithfully

Template 83

Giving discharge from a guarantee

Dear

Fashion House Co. Ltd

We acknowledge the receipt from you of the sum of 100,000. We confirm that this is the total amount due from you under your guarantee of the above-mentioned company's debts, and that accordingly you are discharged from your guarantee and from all liability to us.

Yours faithfully

Template 84

Claiming discharge by operation of law

Dear

It has come to my notice that, without reference to me, you extended the time for payment of the debt due from the above company. This is contrary to my rights under the guarantee I gave of the debt.

I learn that, without reference to me, you have made substantial variations in the contract terms that existed when the guarantee was entered into. Apart from any other considerations the alteration of contract terms is a breach of the terms upon which I gave my guarantee.

In all these circumstances, I consider myself discharged from all liability under the guarantee.

Yours faithfully

Template 85

Release of a guarantee

Dear Sirs

1 wish to be discharged from my liability to you under the guarantee given for the debts of the above-named company. Please confirm the amount, if any, due under the guarantee amount, if any, due under the guarantee.

Yours faithfully

Template 86

Request payment made under a guarantee

Dear

I have been compelled to meet the liability entered into a guarantee oh the debt of the company to its suppliers. The amount I have had to pay including all interest and costs was £20,000.

Unless the company reimburses me for this amount within the next seven days I shall instruct my solicitors to take all appropriate proceedings for recovery.

[I have the right under my guarantee agreement with the company to require the execution by the company of a charge on the company's assets and to require the allotment to me of shares in the company. My solicitors are instructed to pursue this right on my behalf.]

Yours faithfully

Template 87

Agreeing to give a guarantee

Dear

I am prepared to give a guarantee for the company to cover the liability it will have to its suppliers. The guarantee would be given on the following terms.

1. It will be limited to the sum of £10.000.000.

2. In the event that I am called upon to meet any liability under the guarantee you will understand that I will have the right to recover from the company. In so far as the company is unable to meet its liability to me, the directors will make good any deficiency.

3. So long as the guarantee exists, you will keep me fully informed as to the financial position of the company and will not enter into any contracts or accept any obligations without referring to me first.

4. So long as the guarantee exists, you will keep me fully informed as to the financial position of the company and will not enter into any contracts or accept any obligations without referring to me first.

5. You will ensure that all liability to the Commissioners of Inland Revenue and Customs and Excise is promptly and fully discharged.

6   I will have the right to require the company to pay its debt and procure my discharge from the guarantee and this right I can exercise at any time after the liability of the company to the suppliers exceeds 10,000 or after the period of three months from today. The right will be exercised by my giving one month's notice in writing.

7   I will have the right at any time after I have entered into the guarantee to call for a floating charge on all the assets of the company to secure the liability I will have incurred on the behalf. In addition, I shall have the right, if l have to a call on my guarantee, to call for the allotment to me of a in the company equal to one share for each one pound I am called upon to meet and (if the number of shares so will mean that I would be in a minority) such further shares as will make my total shareholding in the company 51 per cent of the total issued share capital.

If you agree to these terms will you please sign and return to me the carbon copy of this letter.

Yours faithfully

Template 88

Protective form of guarantee

Dear

In consideration of your agreeing to make continued supply of goods to the above-mentioned company I hereby guarantee to you payment by the company for goods to a value of £1,000 inclusive of VAT. This guarantee is given on the following basis.

1. There will be no variation in your normal terms of business as applied on sales to the company without my written consent.

2. Before any liability arises under this guarantee you will give me seven days' notice in writing of the default by the company. Seven days' notice in writing of the default by the company.

3. I will have the right to determine this guarantee at any time upon my giving to you seven days' notice in writing and making payment to you of the then outstanding amount of the company's indebtedness to you, up to a maximum of £10.000,000.

Yours faithfully

Template 89

Letter of guarantee

Dear Sirs

In consideration of your supplying goods to the above company on account terms, I hereby guarantee to you payment for all goods supplied in accordance with your normal payment terms. Any giving of time by you to the company will not release me from the have accepted under this guarantee.

Yours faithfully

Template 90

Declining to give a trade reference

Dear

We have received your request for a trade reference for the above named company. We regret that it is our invariable practice not to give trade references. We apologies for this unhelpful attitude and must make it clear that in taking this line we are in no way intending to suggest that the above-named company is (or is not) unworthy of confidence. On that subject, we regret that we must ask you to form an opinion on whatever other information you may obtain.

Yours faithfully

Template 91

Making a claim under an insurance policy

Dear

We regret to have to inform you that last night during the period when these premises were unoccupied, we suffered a break-in and thieves stole the equipment listed on the enclosed schedule. We are having further checks made to see whether any other property is missing.

In addition, they caused considerable damage to the property breaking down interior doors, which were locked, and forcing open the drawers of locked desks. Estimates are being obtained for the cost of carrying out the necessary repairs and these estimates, when obtained, will be sent to you for your acceptance.

The police have been informed and are making their enquiries. Mean time, would you please note that a claim will be made for the loss of the stolen goods, the damage to the property and the con-sequential loss caused to our business. Full details of these losses are being calculated and will be notified to you in due course.

Yours faithfully

Template 92

Auditors appointment

Dear

This company has been newly incorporated and we are considering the appointment of auditor. Mr Smith, manager of the Fashion House, Chelsea Road branch of the HSBC Bank, has recommended that we approach your firm to enquire whether you would be willing to accept the appointment.

We shall be employing a full-time experienced bookkeeper and the accounts will be kept on an IBM personal computer using a bookkeeping package. We would ask our auditor to undertake the audit and subsequently settle the taxation problems that may arise.

Could you please indicate the fee that you would expect to charge for the service (assuming that you are willing to undertake it) and could you please recommend to us the accounting period we should adopt. Would you recommend 31 June year end, or 31 March, or perhaps some other date?

I await hearing from you with interest.

Yours sincerely

Template 93

To solicitors asking for a quotation

Dear

I am contemplating the possibility of my company making an offer to acquire the entire share capital of an enterprise based in the London. The total purchase moneys involved will be in the order of 10.5 million.

I have already negotiated the necessary financial arrangements enable me to carry out this transaction, and now would like to give to lawyers to proceed. My accountants, Earnest & Mill Partners, have recommended that I ask your firm to act for me.

Can you give me an estimate of the probable costs that I am likely to incur, including all appropriate disbursements? If you feel that in a matter of this nature your charges cannot be predicted in advance could you please give me some general idea, and also let me know the basis upon which your charges will be calculated. If they are based upon an hourly charging rate, could you let me know the amount of that charge? If you need further information to enable you to give an indication of the possible costs involved, please let me know.

Yours faithfully

Template 94

To solicitors making a complaint

Dear

I am writing to you as the senior partner of Elis & Ellis Partners.

Your Mr Manson has been conducting on my behalf a claim that I have been making against Brass Candlesticks Limited. I gave him the instructions in January 1986 and have from time to time since then seen him to give him such further information, as he required.

Now, after two and a half years, learn that he has not issued this in writing, and I am told that, as six years have elapsed since the cause of my complaint arose, I am out of time and have little chance of success in any litigation.

I have, at Mr Matt request, paid your firm on account of the costs involved £15.000. I am sure that I need not explain my feelings. I would like to have an explanation from you of the reasons for the failure to protect my interest and to know from you what action you propose to take to recompense me not only for the loss. I have suffered but also for the frustration, time and expense which this whole matter has involved for me.

Yours sincerely

Template 95

Authorizing a bank to disclose information

Dear

You will be hearing from Anderson Partners & Co chartered and accountants, who will be asking you to provide them with details of my account number 098 098776.

This letter gives you my permission and authority to disclose to them such information as they may request of the operation of the account from 1 January 1999 to date. You should not disclose details before that date, neither should you disclose details of my private account number 098 098776.

Yours sincerely

Template 96

To a bank following agreement for a facility

Dear

I would like to thank you for the help that you agreed to give me morning.

Just to confirm the arrangement, it was agreed that you would allow my account to be overdrawn to the extent of £340,000. This arrangement will continue for a period of three months, after which it will be reviewed. I will be charged interest at the rate of 3 per cent above the bank's base rate, and will pay an arrangement fee £145.000

Relying upon this arrangement, I have today issued a payment for £45,000 in favor of Brass Candlesticks Limited for the first consignment of goods which l have now ordered. I hope that with the help you have given me this will be the start of a very profitable venture.

Yours sincerely

Template 97

Creating a service tenancy

Dear

We have written to you a letter setting out the terms upon which you are to be employed as resident manager of our shop at London Market. . It will be necessary for you to reside at the premises so that you can be available to receive deliveries out of normal hours, and can provide security supervision of the premises during bank holidays and Sundays.

Your employment will include the right to occupy the premises above the shop at No 5, The London High Street. Your occupancy will be on the following terms.

1. You will pay a weekly rent (exclusive of rates) of £34.000

2. You will be responsible for the rates chargeable on the property and for the expense of all gas, water and electricity consumed on the premises.

3. You will be responsible for all interior decoration and the repair of glass in the windows and maintenance of the garden ground at the rear which you will keep clean and free from weeds.

4. We will be responsible for all repairs to the roof and main structure (except for repairs made necessary by any misuse of the property caused by you, or anyone on the property with your permission} and for external decoration.

5   You will not permit anyone, other than members of your immediate family, to reside permanently on the premises.

6   The whole purpose of your occupancy of these premises is to enable you to fulfill your terms of employment, which include the obligation to receive goods and deliveries outside of normal trading hours and to safeguard the security of the shop premises during all times when it is not open for business.

7   This right of occupancy will cease immediately at the end of your employment (however the employment may end) and you will then vacate and give vacant possession of the property.

In acknowledgement of your acceptance of these terms will you please sign and return to me the copy of this letter, which we enclose.

Yours sincerely

Template 98

Requesting permission to change use

Dear

We are in need of additional office accommodation at these premises, and have spoken to the local planning officer to ascertain his view on a possible change of the use of the upper part of the premises to offices. He gives us to believe that there would be no planning objection raised.

Would you please take this letter as a formal application under the terms of our lease for permission, subject to formal planning permission being granted, to change the use of the upper floor from residential use to office use. We will undertake, at our own expense to apply for planning permission for the appropriate change of use.

We await hearing from you.

Yours faithfully

Template 99

Requesting permission to carry out improvements

Dear

We wish to create additional office accommodation on these premises and we enclose herewith plans and a specification of the work we propose.

We believe that this will constitute an improvement to the property, and we would ask for your consent to our carrying out the work.

We will obtain all necessary building and other consents from the local authority, and will have the work carried out entirely at our own expense. We will ensure that no damage is caused to the building and will make good immediately any damage, which does occur.

Please may we hear from you.

Yours faithfully

Template 100

Real-estate opening negotiations for a new lease

Dear

Further to our letter of 21 February, we have now instructed Mr Tom Smith of the firm of Lloyds and Partners to represent us in negotiations for a new lease of these premises. He will be in touch with you in due course. Meantime, we will be continuing to pay our rent at the present rate.

Yours faithfully

LEGAL DOCUMENTS TEMPLATES

Please Note: this LETTER are not real advise and are not to be taken as advice in any way shape of form, are just a guide for letter draft structure.

1. Legal Research Letter
2. Legal Sample Advise Sale Agreement Letter
3. Share Purchase Agreement Sample Advise
4. Advice Dispute
5. Letter Before Claim
6. Draft Particulars of Claim
7. Draft Defence From
8. Draft Email Instruction
9. Points to note advise on expert
10. Draft Attendance Note
11. Real Estate Contract Purchase Propriety
12. Bank Bonds Investment Draft Advise
13. Experts' Without Prejudice Meeting Statement
14. Claimant's Part 36 Offer Letter
15. Defendant's Brief to Counsel
16. Meeting documentation Minutes of a meeting of the board of director

17 Notice of the General Meeting

18 Procedure for Conversion of a Shelf Company on Full Notice

19 Agreement for the Sale of Goods

20 Drafting a Will

21 Company Directors Situation Advise Letter

22 Memorandum Purchase Plant

23 Dispute Letter Answer

24 Banking and Finance

25 Legal Research Landlord Tenant Dispute Memorandum

26 Reply's to Client Share Purchase Agreement

Template 1

Legal Research Letter

Dear

Here are my conclusions in respect of Lara concerns about Mona Choi's directorship and employment in Marry Furniture Ltd (the "Company"). My understanding of the factual situation is set out in the attached report.

Review of Research

To achieve Monica's proposal that Mona is removed from the board, there are two options: either Mona can resign, or James, Monica and Delyth can vote together as shareholders to remove Mona from the board.

To achieve Monica's desire to keep Mona as an employee pending trial, she may not need to take any action, although Mona's employment contract may provide for termination of her employment on her dismissal as a director. However, James may have implied authority, as managing director, to dismiss Mona from her job without Monica's approval. James' authority can be removed by a board decision and Monica can pass such a resolution using her casting vote. In the event that James does not attend any board meeting where his powers of dismissal are to be restricted, Monica may need to be ready to ask Mona to support the appointment of Delyth as a director so that the meeting is quorate and the resolution can be passed. Therefore, if

Monica is concerned that James may act alone to dismiss Mona from her job straight away, Monica would be able to prevent this.

To ensure Mona has no involvement in financial matters and does not contact clients in her continued employment, Monica could follow the same process of obtaining a board resolution to take away Mona's responsibilities which involve finance or contact with the public, subject to any advice of the employment team on varying the service contract.

Monica needs to know about the consequences of a custodial sentence on Mona's employment. If Mona is subject to a custodial sentence (as opposed to remanded in custody pending trial), it is likely that her employment will terminate and that any dismissal will be fair and lawful.

Advice

Whilst a resignation could preserve Mona's personal dignity and would be quicker than holding a shareholders' meeting, Mona may resist resigning. In order to reduce the likelihood of this happening, we could prepare a formal notice to the Company proposing Mona's removal (signed by James, Delyth and Monica) in order to make it clear that if Mona refuses to resign she will be forcibly removed if the matter has to go to a vote. Faced with the prospect of being removed against her will, Mona may then relent and tender her resignation. This would avoid the need for further formal meetings, and would mean Monica can assure her personal clients (or their parents) that the Company acted robustly in response to the allegations, and was poised to secure Mona's forcible removal had she not agreed to resign.

Monica should hold a board meeting to remove Mona's responsibility for contact with customers and financial matters. That is a crucial role for the Company, which cannot be left vacant, so Monica will need to do this herself. The board will then need to either approve a service contract for Monica or else decide how to allocate Mona's responsibilities.

Monica wants to prevent Mona losing her job unless she is sentenced to a custodial sentence. As James may have implied authority to dismiss Mona, Monica should be prepared to call a board meeting to withdraw any implied authority. This should be on a date when Delyth can attend so that Monica and Mona can appoint her if James does not turn up. Monica should send us Mona's employment contract for us to check whether it contains a clause automatically terminating her employment in the event of her removal from the board.

Taking these steps to prevent James from dismissing Mona will be complicated, and could result in creating unnecessary divisions between family members. It is also possible that Delyth will not necessarily want to be a director (even though she can resign at the end of the meeting). I therefore recommend that Monica asks James to agree to have his managing director's powers limited so that it is absolutely clear that he cannot dismiss Mona from her job. Monica could explain to him that this would avoid the need to find a replacement for the whole of Mona's work. Monica could also point out that imposition of a custodial sentence will likely result in termination of Mona's employment in any event, and any such termination resulting from a custodial sentence is likely to be fair and lawful, so is a lower risk strategy than instant dismissal.

To maintain the good relationship with Mona, Monica should explain to Mona in advance why they propose dealing with things in this way. Monica should confirm it in writing, for clarity. I recommend that we draft this letter to go from Monica to ensure that it is accurate. A formal letter from us directly to Mona appears inappropriate in the family circumstances.

In terms of practical steps, I suggest that we do the following:

- Prepare a Form TM01 for Monica to date and file immediately after the meeting; and
- Show Monica the kind of formal wording used in a resignation letter to ensure that it sets out the specific date for termination required by Model Article 18(f).

I suggest we do not actually draft a full resignation letter, as that may appear unnecessarily aggressive. If you or Monica need any further assistance do give me a call, especially if you need me to plan how to set up and run the shareholders' meeting in the event that Mona has to be forced off the board.

Kind regards

Template 2

Share Purchase Agreement Sample Advise

Dear

Share Purchase Agreement dated 12 May 2025

Thank you for your instructions to review your sale of Mona LMB Limited ("LMB") to Paradise Hotels Limited (Paradise ") under the above Share Purchase Agreement. I have had the opportunity to read all of the documentation which you sent to me, including all of the accounting information which you provided to Paradise Hotels Limited and the letter before claim which you recently received from Mike Moris LLP.

Allegation to be investigated

The allegation made against Mona Estate PLC is that it failed to disclose a downturn in the profits of De Halve Moris, LMB' sole hotel in Holland, and that this constituted a material adverse change in the turnover, financial position or prospects of LMB. Such downturn is alleged to have taken place between 30 April 2015 and the completion date of the sale, 24 June 2015.

Profit Forecast for LMB as at 30 April 2015

One of the documents provided to Paradise Hotels Limited on the date the parties signed the Share Purchase Agreement was a Profit Forecast dated 30 April 2015 ("the April Profit Forecast")

The forecast for De Halve Moris for the quarter ending 24 June 2015 was:

- Turnover 190,500.00
- Profit 53,250.00

The management accounts of LMB for the quarter ending 24 June 2015 show that the actual performance of De Halve Larry was as follows:

- Turnover 95,250.00
- Loss 34,750.00

The difference in profits was therefore 88,000.00. I am not sure how Paradise Hotels Limited calculated their alleged loss of 400,000.

Upon further investigation, I have discovered that there was a general decline in hotel trade in Holland during May and June 2015, resulting from unprecedented rainfall which caused major flooding in the region. This clearly had an adverse effect upon the trade at De Halve Larry.

The Disclosure Letter dated 24 June 2050

The disclosure letter says nothing about De Halve Moris or its decline in profits during May and June 2015. On the face of it, therefore, there was a failure to disclose facts relating to the financial position of the Dutch operation of LMB.

Material adverse change?

The overall turnover of LMB for its financial year ending 31 December 2015 was 73.23 million. The turnover of De Halve Moris during that period was £742,857.

The-loss in profits at De Halve Moris for the quarter ending 24 June 2015 of 88,000 is insignificant in that context and would not, in my opinion, have affected the value of LMB as at the date of the sale. It does not represent a "material adverse change".

I trust that my conclusion provides some comfort to you. Incidentally, I did see that .there is something in the Share Purchase Agreement about notice of a claim, and I wondered whether that is something that you had looked at. This is outside of my remit and so I leave that to you and your lawyers.

Please let me know if I can be of any further assistance.

Yours sincerely

Solicitor

Template 3

Draft Advice Dispute

Dispute with Construction Limited

I spoke with our expert, Moris Smith on 20 August 2018. Mr Smith has now considered your architect's designs for the glass roof. Unfortunately, his conclusion may now have an adverse impact on your case against Smithmon Construction Limited ("Smithmon"). Mr Smith has indicated that he is amenable to omitting this from his final report, but for the reasons detailed below I do not consider this to be appropriate.

Impact on your claim against Smithmon

Mr Smith has concluded that the design of the roof was flawed; he says that its metal structure was far too heavy and was not sufficiently supported. He thinks that the cracks in the walls could have been caused by the structure pulling inwards and downwards and that there is a small possibility that the roof collapsed completely of its own accord, rather than through the fault of Smithmon. If this information comes to the attention of the court, you may not succeed in demonstrating that the excavating and pile-driving caused the damage to the roof and this would mean that your nuisance claim would fail.

The consequences of Mr O'Leary omitting his conclusion

If we allow Mr Smith to omit his conclusion about the glass roof from his report, then he will be in breach of his obligations to the court:

The court rules state that Mr Smith has a duty' to be independent and uninfluenced by the pressures of litigation and to be unbiased. These duties are owed to the court and not to you as the party instructing him. He also has a duty to consider all material facts including those which might detract from his opinion; this therefore includes the glass roof designs.

Mr Smith has to make a statement at the end of his report that he has complied with his duties to the court and that he believes that the contents of his report are true. Clearly if he omits the information about the glass roof, he has not complied with his duties and he will potentially be liable for contempt of court due to his breach of his statement. This could result in a fine or even imprisonment.

If I allow Mr Smith to omit his conclusion from his report, then I myself will be in breach of my professional duties as a solicitor. I am not permitted to knowingly allow someone else to mislead the court.

Possible steps which Smithmon could take before the trial

Copies of the plans and specifications for the glass roof were provided to Smithmon during the disclosure process. Smithmon ' expert is likely to see these and he may come to the same view as Mr Smith. This could lead to Smithmon taking one or all of the following steps:

Smithmon ' solicitor may ask Mr Smith questions about the roof design in order to clarify his report. Mr Smith is obliged to answer these questions; if he tries to avoid the issue then Smithmon may become suspicious about the nature of our instructions to him.

Any suspicion about our instructions may lead Smithmon' solicitor to make an application to the court for disclosure of our instructions to Mr Smith. Whilst the court will not routinely order the disclosure of the instructions given to an expert, it may order that the instructions be disclosed if it has reasonable grounds to believe that the substance of the instructions set out in the report are inaccurate or incomplete. It could become apparent that we requested Mr Smith to omit the information from his report. This might result in your claim being struck out or an adverse costs order against you.

Mr Smith will have to meet with Smithmon' expert in. order to identify areas of agreement and disagreement between them. Again, if Mr Smith tries to avoid the issue then Smithmon may become suspicious about the nature of our instructions to him. In his report, Mr Smith is obliged to set out the substance of all facts and instructions which are material to the opinions expressed in his report or on which those opinions are based.

Smithmon could also apply to disbar Mr Smith's evidence completely on the basis that he does not understand his duty to the court. Without any expert evidence, there is little chance of your claim succeeding.

Possible ways which Smithmon could take at the trial

Even if Smithmon does not take any immediate action, they may wait until the trial to raise the issue. They could cross-examine Mr Smith upon the glass roof in the witness box at trial; Mr Smith is obliged to tell the truth and it could become clear that he had omitted information from his report. This could seriously impact on the credibility of his evidence.

Smithmon may also at that point apply for disclosure of our instructions to Mr Smith and/or for permission to cross-examine him on our instructions. This could, again, lead to your claim being struck out or to an adverse costs order against you or to an order disbarring Mr Smith's evidence.

Advice

For all of the above reasons, we must insist that Mr Smith includes his about the glass roof in his final report.

However, we could obtain an alternative Sava on the glass roof from another expert; if this expert's opinion is more favourable than Mr Smith, then we could serve this report instead of Mr Smith's report. This would involve further costs and we would not be able to recover the costs of instructing Mr Smith from Smithmon even if your claim was to succeed.

Alternatively, we could start negotiations to try to settle the claim out of court.

Once you have had a chance to consider the contents of this letter, please me with your instructions.

Yours sincerely

Template 4

Letter Before Claim

Dear

Incident at Letter Before Claim

We are instructed by Mr W Fox and Mrs R Fox of Moon Lodge, Steep Lane, in connection with a claim for damages following an incident which occurred at their home on 1 August 2049.

The facts

Our clients advise us that at approximately 11 pm on 1 August 2049 you drove your motor car Land Cruiser 4x4, 4.5 litre turbo model, registration MRD 13 ('the Car'), on their drive understand you were about to take up a short-term let in part of the premises. The Car into the recently completed extension of our clients' property causing serious damage to the garden, building, furnishings and fittings.

Legal basis of claim

By entering our clients' premises it became your responsibility to ensure that you drove with the degree of care and skill that would be expected from a competent driver.

Factual basis of claim

We are instructed that you drove up the drive at excessive speed and without properly controlling the Car.

You were seen to swerve repeatedly on and off the driveway. The tyre tracks at the property confirm this, It is clear that you failed to apply your Car's brakes sufficiently or at all and that you failed to steer, manage, control or stop the Car so as to avoid the collision. You thereby breached your obligation to drive on our clients' driveway with the degree of care and skill that would be expected from a competent driver. As a result you drove into our client's extension and this will now have to be demolished, rebuilt and refitted.

Responsibility

We have advised our clients that your actions on 1 August 2050 were negligent and that they are entitled to be compensated by you.

Responsibility

We have advised our clients that your actions on 1 August 2050 were negligent and that they are entitled to be compensated by you.

Calculation of damage to the extension at 'Moon Lodge'

Putting right damage to garden & drive xx
Demolishing and rebuilding extension xx
Kitchen refit   xxx
Bedroom refit xxx
TOTAL

Documents relied on

The above figures are based on current available estimates copies of which are enclosed. In addition to the above losses our clients have been put to considerable expense in making safe the extension.

Calculation of loss in making safe the extension Moon Lodge

Weather-proofing the extension
Installing a temporary alarm system for the parts of 'Moon Lodge Accessible from the extension
Making safe the electrical supply to and in the extension
Sealing off the plumbing supply to the extension
TOTAL

Documents relied on

We enclose copies of receipted invoices for the above matters.

Acknowledgment and response

As we are arranging for this letter to be hand delivered to you today, please acknowledge safe receipt of this letter promptly and by no later than 5 September 2049.

Please provide a full written response by 19 September 2049 or such later time as we may agree with you.

Practice Direction on Pre-Action Conduct

We advise you to notify your insurers of this claim, if you have not already done so and take independent legal advice. Should you choose not to instruct solicitors, we enclose a copy of a Practice Direction issued by the courts and we draw your attention to the power of the courts to impose sanctions under paragraph 16.

Alternative Dispute Resolution

At this stage we are not aware that you have any grounds to dispute this claim. If we receive a full written response as requested then our clients will then be in a better position to consider if any alternative dispute resolution method is appropriate to any issue you raise.

Court proceedings

Please note that if you fail to acknowledge and/or respond as requested above we are instructed to start court proceedings against you without further notification. The court proceedings will include a claim for damages as detailed in this letter, interest on those damages and legal costs incurred by our client.

Lisa PLC Insurance Plc

Following the incident you informed our clients that you were insured with this company. We enclose a copy of a letter that we have sent to that company giving formal notification of the possible commencement of court proceedings.

Yours faithfully

Template 4

Draft Particulars of Claim

BETWEEN:

Claimant
Defendant

Particulars Of Claim

1. At all material times the Defendant, a company incorporated in England and Wales, was the sole shareholder and seller of LMB Limited ("the Company").

2. On 7 April 2015 the Defendant, represented by its director Paul Rafferty, telephoned the Claimant's Managing Director, Janette Davies. Mr Rafferty invited the Claimant to take part in a bid for purchase of the Company at an offer price starting in the region of 150,000,000.

3. Between 7 April 2015 and 12 May 2015 the Claimant negotiated with the Defendant with a view to purchasing the entire share capital of the Company. On 12 May 2015, the Claimant and Defendant entered into a Share Purchase Agreement ("the SPA"), a copy of which is attached.

4. On 12 May 2015, the Claimant and Defendant entered into a Share Agreement ("the SPA"), a copy of which is attached.

5. The SPA provided as follows:

   5.1 "Accounts Date" was defined as 30 April 2015, the "Completion Date" was defined as 24 June 2015, "Disclosure Letter" was defined as the letter from the Defendant to the Claimant of the same date as the SPA, and "Warranties" were defined as the warranties set out in Schedule 2 (clause 1);

   5.2 The Seller would sell and the Buyer would buy, with effect from Completion Date, the Sale Shares with full title guarantee (clause 2);

   5.3 At the Completion Date, the Claimant would pay to the Defendant ,v the Completion Date, the Claimant would pay to the Detenaar the Defendant would comply with its obligations under Schedule 1 (clause 4), namely transfer the entire share capital in the Company to the Claimant;

   5.4 The Defendant warranted that, except as disclosed in the Disclosure Letter, the Warranties were true, accurate and not misleading on the Completion Date (clause 5.1).

   5.5 By clause 3(b) of Schedule 2 ("Warranty 3(b)") the Defendant that "Since the Accounts Date…there has been no material adverse change in the turnover, financial position or prospects of the Company".

   6   On the Completion Date, the Claimant transferred the Purchase Price to the Defendant's account at HCBS Bank and

the Defendant transferred the entire share capital in the Company to the Claimant.

7   The Defendant breached Warranty 3(b).

Particulars of Breach of Contract

There was a rapid decline in the trade of the Dutch operation of the Company between 30 April 2015 and 24 June 2015. This was not disclosed to the. Claimant before the Completion Date.

8   As a result of the Defendant's breach of Warranty 3(b), the Claimant proceeded to Completion and paid the Purchase Price as set out in paragraph 6.

9   By reason of the Defendant's breach of contract the Claimant has suffered loss and damage.

Particulars of Loss and Damage

The Claimant's loss is the decline in profit of the Company's Dutch operation between the April 2015 Profit Forecast and the Completion Date, a sum of 400,000.

10   Further, the Claimant claims interest pursuant to Section 35A of the Senior Courts Act 1981 on all sums found due to it at such rate and for such period as the Court thinks fit.

AND THE CLAIMANT CLAIMS:

(1) Damages.

(2) Interest under Section 35A of the Senior Courts Act 1981.

Claimant Signature

Dated

STATEMENT OF TRUTH

I believe that the facts stated in these Particulars of Claim are true. I am duly authorised to sign this statement of truth on behalf of the Claimant.

Signed:
Director

The Claimant's solicitors are London where they will accept service of proceedings on behalf of the Claimant.

To the Court and the Defendant

Template 6

Draft Defence From

IN THE HIGH COURT OF JUSTICE
QUEEN'S BENCH DIVISION '
BETWEEN

Claimant

And

Defendant

1. References to paragraph numbers in this Defence are references to paragraphs in the Particulars of Claim. This Defence adopts the definitions used in the Particulars of Claim.

2. Paragraphs 1 to 6 are admitted.

3. The SPA also provided at clause 6.1 that:

"The Seller shall not be liable for a Claim unless notice in writing of the Claim, summarising the nature of the Claim (in so far as it is known to the Buyer) and, as far as is reasonably practicable, the amount claimed, has been given on behalf of the Buyer to the Seller on or before the first anniversary of Completion Date. ,'

"Claim" is defined in clause 1 of the SPA as "a claim for breach of any of Warranties'

4. The Claimant first notified the Defendant of its claim in a letter from the Claimant's solicitor to the Defendant dated 7 December 2050. The Claimant was obliged, under clause 6.1 of the SPA, to notify the Defendant of its claim by 24 June 2050. It failed to do so. Accordingly, the Defendant is not liable to the Claimant for any losses arising from any breach of warranty.

5. The remainder of this Defence is subject to the above contention that the Claimant failed to comply with the contractual notice period and is therefore prevented from bringing this claim against the Defendant.

6. As to paragraph 7:

    6.1 It is admitted that there was a decline in the Dutch operation of the Company between 30 April 2015 and 24 June 2015. This was due to unprecedented rainfall and flooding in the region between May and June 2015.

    6.2 It is admitted that this decline was not disclosed to the Claimant by the Defendant prior to the Completion Date;

    6.3 The Dutch operation of the Company was a small part of the operation of the Company. It comprised one hotel named De Halve Larry in Tilburg whereas the Company owned 31 hotels in total. The turnover De Halve on Larry during the financial year ending 31 December was less than 2% of the Company's overall turnover of 73.23 million.

6.4 The decline in the profits of De Halve Larry was insignificant in the context of the Company's overall turnover. Accordingly, it is denied that the decline constituted a material adverse change in the turnover, financial position or prospects of the Company.

7. The decline did not affect value of the Company and it is accordingly denied that it would have made any difference to the Purchase Price had it been disclosed to the Claimant prior to the Completion Date.

8. The Defendant denies that the Claimant js entitled to the relief claimed or other relief.

Dated: Signed

STATEMENT OF TRUTH

The Defendant believes that the facts stated in this Defence are true. I am duly authorised by the Defendant to make this statement. '

Signed:

The Defendant's solicitors are

Where they will accept service of proceedings on behalf of the Defendant.

To the Claimant and the Court

Template 7

Draft Email Instruction

Dear

I would like your assistance with this matter in which I act for Antonia Giordano. She has brought proceedings for nuisance against Smithmon Construction Limited ("Smithmon ") arising from an incident at her restaurant in Newcastle-upon-Tyne on 14 July 2017. She alleges that. Smithmon unlawfully interfered with her enjoyment of her land by causing structural damage to her restaurant whilst carrying out building works on a site next door. You will find full details on file in a proof of evidence, which I took from the client.

Antonia consulted the firm very soon after the incident. We are authorised by her insurers to act on both their behalf and Antonia's behalf in bringing a claim against Smithmon. Part of my early advice was to obtain a surveyor's report before any remedial work was undertaken. This was independent from the assessments made by the 'nsurer's claims assessors. I instructed Marisa Savaa chartered civil and structural engineer, with experience in foundation design, subsidence and structural instability. You will find his initial report on file. This has not yet been disclosed to Smithmon .

In view of Mr Sava's conclusions, I formed the view that Antonia had good prospects of success. It took 6 months for the remedial works to be completed and so Antonia has a significant claim for loss of profits. After following the requisite pre-action steps, she issued proceedings against Smithmon. Smithmon served a defence which denies that its works caused any damage.

At a recent Case Management Conference, the court' gave directions for standard disclosure and exchange of witness statements. Both parties were given permission to evidence from an expert in structural engineering.

As part of the disclosure process, I obtained from Antonia's architect a copy of the design and specification for the glass roof. Copies were given to Smithmon and to Marisa Sava

As part of the disclosure process, I obtained from Antonia's architect a copy of the design and specification for the glass roof. Copies were given to Smithmon and to Marisa Sava.

This morning, Mr Sava telephoned me. Please see my note of my conversation with him. Please could you consider about the implications of what Mr Sava has said in so far as the claim against Smithmon is concerned and draft a letter of advice in my name to send to the client? You do not need to concern yourself with the wider implications of what Mr Sava said (including the possibility of a claim against the architects of the glass roof) as I will deal with these separateley.

Many thanks

Template 8

Points to note advise on expert

Dear

Dispute with Limited

I spoke with our expert, Marisa Sava on 20 August 2050. Mr Sava has now considered your architect's designs for the glass roof. Unfortunately, his may now have an adverse impact on your case against Moon Construction Limited ("Moon"). Mr Sava has indicated that he is amenable to omitting this from his final report, but for the reasons detailed below I do not consider this to be appropriate.

Impact on your claim against Moon Ltd

Mr Sava has concluded that the design of the roof was flawed; he says that its metal structure was far too heavy and was not sufficiently supported. He thinks that the cracks in the walls could have been caused by the structure pulling inwards and downwards and that there is a small possibility that the roof collapsed completely of its own accord, rather than through the fault of Moon. If this information comes to the attention of the court, you may not succeed in demonstrating that the excavating and pile-driving caused the damage to the roof and this would mean that your nuisance claim would fail.

The consequences of Mr Sava omitting his conclusion

If we allow Mr Sava to omit his conclusion about the glass roof from his report, then he will be in breach of his obligations to the court:

The court rules state that Mr Sava has a duty to be independent and uninfluenced by the pressures of litigation and to be unbiased. These duties are owed to the court and not to you as the party instructing him. He also has a duty to consider all material facts including those which might detract from his opinion; this therefore includes the glass roof designs.

Mr Sava has to make a statement at the end of his report that he has complied with his duties to the court and that he believes that the contents of his are true. Clearly if he omits the information about the glass roof, he has not complied with his duties and he will potentially be liable for contempt of court due to his breach of his statement. This could result in a fine or even imprisonment.

Yours truly

Template 9

Attendance Note

Attendance Note:

Date:

Interview: 45 Minutes

Client:

Address:

Tel No:

Purchase Instructions

Matter:

Sellers:

Sellers' Solicitors:

Estate Agents:

Price:

Deposit:

Fixtures & Fittings:

Tenure: Freehold

Mortgage: Client has made an application to the Cheltenham &for an advance of 1,25,000 (ordinary repayment commercial mortgage

Survey: Client has arranged for a full structural survey to be carried out this week. Although he has no immediate plans to do so, if the business expands, he might wish to extend the property and so wishes to be certain that it is sound.

Completion Date: Client would like to complete as soon as possible.

Other Matters: Seller have agreed not to charge VAT on the purchase price Estimate of costs on purchase and mortgage – 4,750 + VAT

Template 10

Real Estate Contract Purchase Propriety

DATE

CONTRACT FOR THE SALE OF FREEHOLD LAND WITH VACANT POSSESSION

At

      2 Old Church, London Chelsea SW345NM

Between

Buyer

And

Seller

Contents

1. Interpretation
2. Sale and purchase
3. Conditions
4. Risk and insurance
5. Deposit
6. Deducing title

7. Vacant possession

8. Title guarantee

9. Matters affecting the Property

10. VAT

11. Completion

12. Buyer's acknowledgement of condition

13. . Entire agreement

14. Joint and several liability

15. Notices

16. Third party rights

17. Governing law

18. Jurisdiction

Schedule

Documents of title referred to in clause 5

THIS CONTRACT is dated

PARTIES

Buyer: Name and Address

Seller: Name and Address

AGREED TERMS

1. INTERPRETATION

The following definitions and rules of interpretation apply in this contract.

   1.1 Definitions:

   Buyer's Conveyance: Name and Address

   Competition Date

   Contract Rate: 4% per annum above the Law Society's interest rate from time to time in force.

   Deposit: 125,000 (exclusive of VAT).

   Part 1 Conditions: the conditions in Part 1 of the Standard Commercial Property Conditions (Second Edition) and Condition means any one of them.

   Part 2 Conditions: the conditions in Part 2 of the Standard Commercial Conditions (Second Edition) and Condition means any one of them.

   Property: the freehold property Seller propriety and address

   Purchase Price: 1,50,000 (exclusive of VAT).

   Property: the freehold property at address

   Purchase Price: 1,50,000 (exclusive of VAT)

Seller's Conveyancer:

VAT: value added tax chargeable under the Value Added Tax Act 1994 and any similar replacement tax and any similar additional tax.

1.2 A person includes a natural person, corporate or unincorporated body (whether or not having separate legal personality).

1.3 Unless otherwise specified, a reference to a statute or statutory provision is a reference to it as amended, extended or re-enacted from time to time and shall include all subordinate legislation made from time to time under that statute or statutory provision and all orders, notices, codes of practice and guidance made under it.

1.4 A reference to laws in general is a reference to all local, national and directly applicable supra-national laws as amended, extended or re-enacted from time to time and shall include all subordinate laws made from time to time under them and all orders, notices, codes of practice and guidance made under them.

1.5 A reference to writing or written includes Email communication but not email.

1.6 Except where a contrary intention appears, a reference to a clause or Schedule is a reference to a clause of or Schedule to this contract

1.7 Unless the context otherwise requires, references to clauses and Schedules are to the clauses and Schedules of this contract and references to paragraphs are to paragraphs of the relevant Schedule.1.8 Clause, Schedule and paragraph headings shall not affect the interpretation of this contract.

1.8 1.9 The Schedule forms part of this contract and shall have effect as if set out in full in the body of this contract. Any reference to this contract includes the Schedule.

1.9 1.10 Unless the context otherwise requires, words in the singular shall include the plural and in the plural shall include the singular.

2. SALE AND PURCHASE

2.1 The Seller will sell and the Buyer will buy the Property for the Purchase Price on the terms of this contract.

2.2 The Buyer cannot require the Seller to:

2.3 (a) transfer the Property or any part of it to any person other than the Buyer; or

(b) transfer the Property in more than one parcel or by more than one transfer; or

(c) apportion the Purchase Price between different parts of the Property.

3. CONDITIONS

   3.1 The Part 1 Conditions are incorporated in this contract so far as they:

   (a) apply to a sale by private treaty

   (b) relate to freehold property;

   (c) are not inconsistent with the other clauses in this contract; and

   (d) have not been modified or excluded by any of the other clauses in this contract.

3.2 The Part 2 Conditions are not incorporated into this contract.

4. RISK AND INSURANCE

   4.1 With effect from exchange of this contract, the Property is at the Buyer's risk and the Seller is under no obligation to the Buyer to insure the Property.

   4.2 4.2 No damage to or destruction of the Property nor any deterioration in its condition, however caused, will entitle the Buyer either to any reduction of the Purchase Price or to refuse to complete or to delay completion.

5. DEPOSIT

   5.1 On the date of this contract, the Buyer will pay the Deposit to the Seller's Conveyancer as agent for the Seller.

5.2 The Deposit must be paid by direct credit.

6. DEDUCING TITLE

The Seller's title to the Property has been deduced to the Buyer's Conveyancer before the date of this contract.

The Buyer is deemed to have full knowledge of the title and is not entitled to raise any objection, enquiry or requisition in relation to it (save for matters arising after the date of this contract to which Condition 6.2 shall apply).

7. VACANT POSSESSION

The Property will be sold with vacant possession on completion.

8. TITLE GUARANTEE

The Seller will transfer the Property with full title guarantee.

9. MATTERS AFFECTING THE PROPERTY

The Seller will sell the Property free from encumbrances other than:

(a) any matters contained or referred to in the entries or records made in registers }maintained by Land Registry as at the date of this contract under title xxxx

(b) any matters discoverable by inspection of the Property before the date of this contract;

(c) any matters which the Seller does not and could not reasonably know about;

(d) any matters disclosed or which would have been disclosed by the searches and which a prudent buyer would have made before entering into this contract;

e) public requirements; and

(f) any matters which are unregistered interests which override registered dispositions under Schedule 3 to the Land Registration Act 2002 OR unregistered interests which override first registration under Schedule 1 to the Land Registration Act 2002.

11 VAT

11.1 Each amount stated to be payable by the Buyer to the Seller under or pursuant to this Contract, the Buyer will on receipt of a valid VAT invoice, pay the Seller an amount equal to that VAT as additional consideration on completion.

11.2 If any VAT is chargeable on any supply made by the Seller' under or pursuant to this contract, the Buyer will on receipt of a valid VAT invoice, pay the Seller an amount equal to that VAT as additional consideration on completion.

12 COMPLETION

12.1 Completion will take place on the Completion Date.

Date:
The Schedule

Official copies of the entries in the register of Title number xxxx as at [today's date].

This contract has been entered into on the date stated at the beginning of it.

Signed by Seller

Signed by as the Buyer

Template 11

Bank Bonds Investment Draft Advise

Dear

Thank you for your email addressed to Jo Smith asked for advice on the above matter. Jason has asked me to reply to you on her behalf.

Your colleagues are quite right to warn you that it may be quite difficult for Competent to recover its investment in this situation. There are two key reasons for this: first, the fact that the Bonds are currently in global form, and second, the Bonds have been issued using a fiscal agency structure rather than a trustee structure. I will deal with each of these points in turn.

Global form of note

Traditional bearer bonds are security printed documents on the face of which issuer's debt obligation is printed, and are fully negotiable by virtue of mercantile custom. The practical effect of this is that, like a bank note, the legal title to a bearer is held by whoever has it in their possession, and the owner has the right to enforce the bond against the issuer. However, because of the high cost of producing definitive bonds and the risk that they may be stolen, most bonds, like the Bonds, are generally held in permanent global form by a depositary bank on behalf of the clearing systems on which they are traded. Since bonds held in this form retain their bearer status, the legal owner of the Bonds is Enterprise Bank plc as depositary. Competent has equitable rights in the permanent global bond which represents the Bonds.

Such equitable ownership is not, on its own, enough for Competent to bring proceedings against Lisa Homes plc ("Lisa"). Often, the terms and conditions of bonds held in global form provide that the issuer must provide the investor with definitive bearer bonds following an event of default, and so we would need to check terms of the Bonds to ascertain whether Competent is entitled to definitive Bonds on these grounds. The risk is that even if you are so entitled, Lisa may refuse to provide you with definitive bonds.

Alternatively, Lisa may have executed a deed of covenant in Competing's favour when you invested in the Bonds. As this would be a direct contract between Competent and Lisa, Competent would be entitled to sue for a breach of the terms and conditions of the Bonds even without definitive Bonds. It would be a good idea to check to see if such a deed poll was ever executed.

Fiscal agent structure

I am not surprised that the fiscal agent is proving unhelpful. A fiscal agent represents the issuer rather than the bondholders and is under no obligation to look after interests of the bondholders, unlike a trustee which acts in the best interests of the as a whole and can therefore enter into negotiations with the issuer on behalf of all investors. Consequently Competent will need to take action on its own account to recover its investment – this could be a slow and expensive process and Lisa may have less of a sense of urgency in responding to the demands individual bondholders than it would when dealing with a professional trustee.

I hope that you find this helpful. If you would like us to advise you further, do please let us know. As mentioned previously, we would need to see the relating to the Bonds, specifically the terms and conditions and any deed poll.

Kind regards

Template 12

Experts' Without Prejudice Meeting Statement

Claimant Name V Defendant
Case NO

NOTE OF 'WITHOUT PREJUDICE' MEETING BETWEEN MR AND MR ON 6 NOVEMBER 2024IN ACCORDANCE WITH THE ORDER FOR O'DONNELL ON 6 JUNE 2050

To: the court

Date:

The meeting took place at the offices of xxx am. It was followed by a short site visit to the Claimants' property at xxx.

Agreed issue

1. The sum of 8,000 claimed in respect of emergency weather proofing work following the accident was reasonable in all the circumstances given the inclement weather in August 20xx.

2. A sum of 2,75 is agreed in respect of the installation of a temporary security system at the property pending full repairs.

3. 1,500 is reasonable for the associated electrical and plumbing work.

4. There was no structural damage to the main fabric of Bliss Lodge arising from There was no structural damage to the

main fabric of Bliss Lodge arising from where the extension abuts the house pre-dates the accident and is in any event not a for concern.

5   There is structural damage to the extension's joists. These will need to be stripped out re-fixed. As a result the extension's roof will need to be removed and rebuilt.

6   The extension's foundations are only marginally damaged and can be made good minor.

7   The cost of refitting the kitchen is agreed at 38.775. It is agreed that the majority of the units will need to be replaced because of water damage.

Disputed Issues

1   Mr for the Claimants maintains that the load-bearing walls of the extension are fundamentally damaged and need to be demolished and rebuilt. This effectively means that the whole extension has to be demolished.

The extension has to be demolished to be rebuilt. There is no requirement to demolish the whole extension and the extent of any rebuilding work can be limited to the removal and repair of the roof and joists referred to in paragraph 5 above and the repairing situ of the one damaged wall.

In terms of cost (all figures exclude VAT), the figures are as follows:

Demolition work   x

Rebuild walls x

Clear site x

    2   The cost of removing the roof, repairing the joists and replacing the roofs disputed:

    3   Mr   x

    4   Mr   x

The extent of repairs required to the bedroom and the associated costs are not agreed:

Mr. Strip out, replacer and wallpaper and make good windows and paintwork £xxx

Mr. X Minor repairs to lower half of walls in bedroom including re-wallpaper where necessary £xxxx

Name	Name
(for the Claimants)	(for the Defendant)

Template 13

Claimant's Part 36 Offer Letter

Dear Sirs

Claimant V Defendant Names

PART 36 OFFER: WITHOUT PREJUDICE SAVE AS TO COST

We refer to previous correspondence in this matter.

Our clients are confident that should this matter proceed to trial they will be successful in establishing liability and recovering the full amount claimed from your client. However, in a final attempt to settle the matter we have our clients' instruction to make your client an offer of settlement. For the purposes of CPR, Rule 36.5(1)(b) we confirm that it is our intention that this offer is made pursuant to and should have the consequences set out in Part 36.

In accordance with CPR, Rule 36.5(1)(d) and (e), the offer on the part of our clients is to accept the sum of 175,000 in relation to the whole of their claim for damages, after taking into account your client's counterclaim. For clarity we would confirm that the offer is inclusive of interest.

In accordance with CPR, Rule 36.5(1)© the relevant period is 21 days from the date of service. As we are sending this to you today by first-class post we calculate that the offer will be deemed to be served on 17 November 2017. Please acknowledge and confirm.

Yours faithfully

Template 14

Defendant's Brief to Counsel

IN THE HIGH COURT OF F JUSTICE
QUEEN'S BENCH DIVISION
DISTRICT REGISTRY
BETWEEN

Claimants
And
Defendant

BRIEF TO COUNSEL TO APPEAR ON BEHALF OF THE DEFENDANT AT THE TRIAL OF THE ACTION ON 17 APRIL 2060

Counsel has the following copy documents:

(1) Bundle of correspondence between the parties and solicitors;

(2) Statements of case;

(3) Directions questionnaires and pre-

(4) Trial check lists; Orders made during the action;

(5) Claimants' Part 36 offer letter;

(6) Case summary from case management conference;

(7) Documents obtained from the Claimant on inspection;

(8) The Defendant's documents in Part 1 of his .list;

(9) Exchanged witness statements;

(10) Civil Evidence Act Hearsay Notice;

(11) Exchanged expert reports;

(12) Replies from experts to parties' questions;

(13) Experts' 'without prejudice' statement filed at court;

(14) Case summary from pre-trial review hearing;

(15) Directions for trial;

(16) Proposed index for trial bundle;

(17) Proposed index for core bundle;

(18) Previous instructions to counsel and advice.

BACKGROUND

1. We act for the Defendant in this action* Counsel will be familiar with the main issues having advised on evidence after disclosure. The action is fixed for trial on 17 April 2050 at 10 am at District Registry.

FACTS

2. Counsel is referred to the case summaries prepared in advance of the case management conference and pre-trial review. The facts are briefly as follows.

3. On 1 August 2049 the Defendant drove his brand new car, a 4x4 Land Cruiser to the Claimants' property xxx, where he was due to take up a two month tenancy in that property's converted stable block. The Claimants had given him directions. He arrived at about 11 pm. This was observed by the Claimants' neighbour, x. According to his wife, Mr , the Claimants' builders had earlier that day dropped a pane of glass on the Claimants' driveway. It is the Defendant's case some broken glass was left on the drive. The Defendant drove over the glass which caused his two offside tyres to burst. The car went out of his control. The drive was relatively steep and the Defendant's car careered into Bliss Lodge itself, severely damaging the Claimants' newly built extension.

Issues liability

4. The issues in the action turn mainly on whether:

    (a) the Defendant can be shown to have driven negligently; and

    (b) (b) the Claimants breached their duty, as occupiers, to the Defendant under the Occupiers' Liability Act 1957, in failing to clear away the broken glass and debris and/or warn the Defendant adequately of its presence. It is clear from Mrs statement for the Defendant that the Claimants were aware of the glass on and around the drive and there are no issues arising about the liability of the builders.

5. There is a dispute on the facts about the precise location of the pile of glass and debris The Claimants maintain that it was to the side of the drive and that the Defendant, in driving too fast down the drive, drove slightly off the drive and over the glass. Their position is that if he had not been driving negligently he would not have strayed off the drive and would not have hit the glass. This is supported by their expert, Mr xxx.

6. Clearly if the Claimants succeed on these points, the counterclaim on the Act is likely to fail at least in part. The Defendant will then face at least partial liability for the damage to Bliss Lodge. The evidence on these points is dealt with in more detail bet bellow.

Evidence on liability

7. Counsel is referred to the reports of the accident reconstruction experts, Mr for the Claimants and Mr for the Defendant and to the witness statements of Mr and Mrs. The witness statements are self-explanatory.

8. Neither expert's report is favourable to the Defendant in terms of the speed at which he was allegedly driving before the accident.

9. The experts' reports are inconclusive on the question of whether the broken glass was originally on or beside the drive. Therefore, this remains a disputed fact and will have to be resolved by non-expert evidence only (see above). Mr says that there is evidence of tyre tracks on the grass and he thinks it

likely that they were made before the car hit the glass. This opinion is based on the car's subsequent erratic route. However, Mr says he is unable to tell whether the car went over the grass or glass first. He may well be vulnerable in cross-examination. Both experts are of the view that the car hit the house at something approaching 35 to 40 mph. It appears from the reports that there was glass both on and next to the drive at the time of the inspections, possibly as a result of the accident.

10. Subject to the above comments we have advised the Defendant that there is a risk of a Part 36 offer in order to try to protect his position as to cost possibility of a Part 36 offer in order to try to protect his position as to costs. Nevertheless, he is determined to defend the action and pursue his counterclaim*would Counsel telephone upon receipt of these instructions to discuss. A pre-trial conference can be arranged should counsel considerate necessary.

Claimant's Part 36 Offer

11. Counsel will note that the Claimants made a Part 36 offer where the relevant period expired on 8 December 2024to settle the claim for 175,000 inclusive of interest and taking the Defendant's counterclaim into account. We have advised the Defendant of the potential additional interest, additional costs and additional sum payable under CPR Rule 36.17(4)(a)-(d) should the Claimants obtain a judgment at least as favourable as that at trial.

Issues –quantum

12. The quantum of the counterclaim is agreed, subject to liability, at 72,160.63 (see the case summary).

13. 13. The Claimants' quantum is not agreed. Full details of the issues which are still disputed appear in the without prejudice meeting statement filed by the parties' respective experts on 6 November 2017. There are no issues of remoteness of damage arising and the dispute on quantum relates almost wholly to the scope of demolition and repair work required to the Claimants 'extension. The difference amounts to approximately 72,000.

Trial

14. Duncan Murray of Instructing Solicitors will be attending the trial. We will make the necessary arrangements to ensure that Colonel Trudge attends. Mrs Trudge will not be attending trial. Mrs Trudge is in Australia caring for her ailing sister. A Civil Evidence Act Hearsay Notice was served when her witness statement was exchanged and the Claimants' solicitors have not objected to her absence.

15. Counsel is asked to liaise with Duncan Murray as to the final content of the Trial and Core Bundles.

16. Please let us know if Counsel requires any further information.

Counsel is briefed to appear at the trial of the action on 17 April 2049 at District Registry at 10 am.

Client Name

Template 15

Meeting documentation Minutes of a meeting of the board of directors

Lotus LIMITED

(Company Number)

Minutes of a meeting of the board of directors of HOME DESIGHN & CO Limited (the 'Company') held at 68-70 Sydney Street Chelsea , London WCIR 4NY on   at

PRESENT

Lorena Sun (until the end of item 3.5)

MerryFix (until the end of item 3.5)
Chairperson (until the end of item 3.3)

Tom Smith(with effect from the end of item

IN ATTENDANCE3

Susanne Frith (until the end of item 3.1)
Lisa Young (until the end of item 3.1)
MerryWhite (with effect from the end of item)
MerryMoon(with effect from the end of item 3.5)

Tom Smith
Gorge Moore

1. NOTICE AND QUORUM

1.1 The Chairperson reported that notice of the meeting had been duly served and that a quorum was present.

1.2 1.2 Each director present confirmed that they had no direct or indirect interest in any way in the business to be considered at the meeting (as set out below) which they were required by section 177 of the Companies Act 2006 and the Company's articles of association to disclose.

2. BACKGROUND

The Chairperson reported the date on which the Company had been incorporated and that the Company had been incorporated with registered number 03404723. The certificate of incorporation and a copy of the memorandum and articles of association were produced to the meeting. There was produced to the meeting a copy of the prescribed form (Form IN01) stating the details of the first directors and registered office of the Company. The Chairperson reported that the subscribers to the memorandum of association were Jennifer Harrower and Merry Moon in respect of one ordinary share of 1 each in the share capital of the Company.

3. CHANGE OF DIRECTORS AND COMPANY SECRETARY

3.1 IT WAS RESOLVED that July Home and Lisa Young, having consented to act, be and are hereby appointed to act as directors of the Company with immediate effect.

3.2 Anna Frith reported that she held a directorship of Moon Holdings plc. IT WAS RESOLVED to authorise this directorship and any potential or actual conflict that may arise in connection with it and Margaret Fletcher's position Company, in accordance with section 175 of the Companies Act 2006. It was noted that, pursuant to article 14(1) of the Company's articles of association, Lisa Fith did not vote or count as part of a quorum on this resolution and that, nevertheless, there was a quorum for this item of business transacted by the meeting.

3.3 Merry Moon agreed to stand down as Chairperson and IT WAS RESOLVED that Anna Frith be appointed Chairperson with immediate effect.

3.4 IT WAS RESOLVED that Tim Bradford, having consented to act, be and is hereby appointed to act as the new Company Secretary of the Company with effect from the resignation of Merry Moon from that role.

3.5 There were produced to the meeting LETTER of resignation as directors signed Jennifer Harrower and Merry Moon, and as Company Secretary signed by Merry Moon, to take effect immediately and IT WAS RESOLVED to accept the same.

4. TRANSFER OF SHARES

4.1 There were produced to the meeting duly executed transfers of the subscriber shares as

Transferor   Transferee   No. of shares

4.2 Payment in cash in full satisfaction of the nominal amount of each of these shares received. IT WAS RESOLVED that the transfers be and are hereby approved and that the Company Secretary be and is hereby instructed to: l

- 4.2.1 register such transfers in the Company's register of members;

- 4.2.2 4.2.2 insert a statement in the Company's register of members that the Company now has only one member

- 4.2.3 update the Company's register of people with significant control;

- 4.2.4 cancel the current share certificates of the transferors; and

- 4.2.5 issue share certificates in the name of the transferees named above in due

5 GENERAL MEETING

5.1 There was produced to the meeting a notice convening a general meeting of the Company to be held on short notice, subject to obtaining consent, proposing the following resolutions (the 'Notice'):

Special resolution

That the name of the Company be changed to Digital Direct Limited.

    5.2 IT WAS RESOLVED that:

    5.3 the Notice be and is hereby approved and that a copy of the Notice be to the sole shareholder and the Company's directors forthwith; and

    5.4 the general meeting be convened to ba held forthwith, the consent sole member having been sought to the meeting being held and the resolution set out in the notice being proposed and passed at the general meeting as a special resolution notwithstanding that the general meeting had been called on short notice.

6. ADJOURNMENT

6.1 The meeting was adjourned so that the general meeting could be held.

6.2 The meeting was reconvened, when the Chairperson reported that the general meeting had been held with consent to short notice being obtained from the safe shareholder and that the special resolution proposed in the Notice had been passed.

7. FURTHER RESOLUTIONS IT WAS FURTHER RESOLVED TO:

    7.1 appoint Deloitte LLP as auditors of the Company with immediate effect to hold office until the end of the next period for appointing auditors under section 485(2) of the Companies Act 2006 and to pay Deloitte LLP the ordinary professional charges for their services as auditors;

7.2 change the Company's registered office from 68-70 Red Lion Street, WCIR 4NY to Robin House, Dorchester Road, Northern Industrial Area, Bracknell, Berks RG8 7TR; and

7.3 Change the Company's accounting reference date to 31 March.

8. POST-MEETING MATTERS

8.1 The Chairperson instructed the Company Secretary to:

8.2 Update the registers of directors and secretaries and minute books for directors' and shareholders' meetings.

8.3 Arrange for the following forms and documents to be filed at Companies House:

   a) Forms AP01 (appointment of additional directors) and Form AP03 (appointment of secretary) and Forms TM01 and TM02 (terminating appointment as director and secretary);

   b) B) Form AD01 (change of registered office address);

   c) Form AA01 (change of accounting reference date);

d) Copy of the special resolution passed at the general meeting changing the Company's name to Frith Direct Limited;

e) Form NM01 and a payment for 10 in respect of the change of name filing fee; and

f) Form PSC02 (relevant legal entity with significant control) and

g) Forms PSC07 (ceasing to be an individual with significant control);

8.1.3 arrange for the Company's name to be displayed at its registered office and on all business correspondence.

9. CLOSE

There was no further business and the Chairperson declared the meeting closed.

Chairperson

Date

_____

Template 16

Notice of the General Meeting

NOTICE OF GENERAL MEETING

SMITH LTD (the "Company")

(Company Number: 03404723)

NOTICE IS HEREBY GIVEN that a General Meeting of the Company will be held at 68-70 Red Lion Street, London WC1R 4NY on [date of SGS] at {'time am/pm] for the purpose of considering and, if thought fit, passing the following resolution which will be prop as a special resolution:

THAT the name of the Company be changed to Ritchisons Direct Limited.

By Order of the Board

Name

Company Secretary

Dated:

Registered office:

Note:

As a member of the Company, you are entitled to appoint a proxy to exercise all or any of your rights to attend, speak and vote at the General Meeting. A proxy does not need to be a member of the Company but must attend the General Meeting to represent you.

Template 17

Consent of the Short Notice

CONSENT TO SHORT NOTICE

SMITH LTD (the "Company")

(Company Number)

The sole member of the Company having a right to attend and vote at the General Meeting of the Company to be held forthwith and holding all of the issued shares in the Company giving that right, HEREBY CONSENTS to the convening and holding of the meeting in the attached notice, and to the proposing and passing thereat of the special convened by less than the statutory notice period.

Dated: [date of today]

Sign

Template 18

Procedure for Conversion of a Shelf Company on Full Notice (15 days)

('Smith Ltd")

Definitions:

'MA' Model Articles for private companies

's.' section in CA 2006

Board Meeting 1

1. Who calls? any director could do so MA 9(1)).
2. Notice period – reasonable according to what is usual for the company
3. Quorum – 2 (MA 11(2)), therefore both serving directors must be present.
4. Agenda

    4.1 Report on the formation of the company.

    4.2 Proposed board resolutions to:

    a) appoint Anna Frith and Tom Smith as directors (MA 17(1)(b))(both appointments to take effect immediately) and Tim Bradford as company secretary (with effect from Merry Moon's resignation as company secretary (see item 4.2(b) below)). Merry

Johns to stand down as Chairperson and Anna Frith to take the position of Chairperson (MA 12(1)):

b) accept LETTER of resignation from Jennifer Harrower, as a director, and Merry Moon. As a director and company secretary (both resignations to take effect immediately) (MA 18(f));

c) receive and approve the transfers of subscriber shares (s.771 and MA 26)and to instruct the company secretary to enter the new shareholder Robert Holdings PLC('RHP') in the register of members immediately (s.112(2) and s.113(2)) and add a statement in the register of members that the company has only one member (s.123(2));

d) approve the form of notice of GM. The contents of the notice will include:

1. date, time and place of meeting (s.311);

2. precise wording of special resolution (s.283(6)) [and ordinary resolutions as good practice]; and

3. a statement that a member may appoint a proxy (s.325(1));

e) call a GM (s.302) to pass a special resolution to change the company name (s.77(1));

  f) direct the company secretary to give notice of the GM in accordance s.308 and send it to:

1. every member of the Company (s.310(l)(a)); and

2. every director of the Company (s.310(l)(b)):, and

  g) direct the company secretary to deal with the post meeting matters listed below.

5. Voting – Board must agree by majority decision on the agenda items set out above (MA 7(1)).

  5. Close board meeting.

  6. Close board meeting.

  7. Post meeting

   a) Company secretary to file the following with the Registrar of Companies:

   1. forms notifying appointment of directors to the Registrar of Companies within 14 days (s.167(1)) – Form APO1;

   2. forms notifying termination of directors' appointment to the Registrar of Companies within 14 days (s.167(1)) – Form TMO1

   3. a form notifying appointment of secretary to the Registrar of Companies within 14 days (s.276C1)) – Form AP03;

4. a form notifying termination of secretary's appointment to the Registrar of Companies within 14 days (s.276C1)) – Form TM02; and

5. forms notifying a relevant legal entity with significant control and individuals ceasing to have significant control to the Registrar of Companies within 14 days (s.790VA) – Forms PSC02 and PSC07.

b) Company secretary to:

1. update the register of people with significant control (s.790M) to reflect RHP's shareholding (within 14 days);

2. issue a new share certificate to RHP (s.776) and cancel the old share ; certificates;

3. write up minutes of the board meeting (s.248(1)); and

4. update the company's register of directors and secretaries (s.162 and s.275)

GM

1. Notice period for a GM is at least 14 clear days (s.307(1) and

2. Quorum – in this case one (s.318(1) for single member companies). Now that the shares have been transferred, RHP is the sole member of the company. Need to see a copy of the board minutes of RHP authorising Anna Frith

to act as its corporate representative at the general meeting (s.323(1))

3. 3. Agenda – to propose a special resolution to change the name of the company from 'HOME DESIGHN & CO 156 Limited' to7Ritchisons Direct Limited'.

4. Voting – Special resolution passed by not less than 75% of those voting (s.283(1)and s.283(4)). (Must vote on a show of hands unless a poll is demanded – MA 42.)

5. Close GM.

Board Meeting II

1. Who calls? Any director (MA 9(1)).

2. Notice Quorum Voting – same as Board Meeting must be present as the serving directors

3. Agenda

   3.1 Report that the special resolution was passed at the GM.

   3.2 Propose board resolutions to:

   1. change the registered office (s.87(1));

   2. change the company's accounting reference date (s.392(1));

   3. appoint Deloitte LLP as company auditors (s.485(3)); and

4. direct the company secretary to deal with the post meeting matters detailed below.

4. Close board meeting.

Post-Meeting Matters

1. Filings at Companies House

Company secretary to fife the following with the Registrar of Companies:

a) Copy of special resolution within 15 days (s.30(1));
b) Notice of change of name as soon as possible (s.78(1)) – Form NM01 and
c) Notice of change of registered office as soon as possible (s.87) – Form AD01; and
d) Notice of change of accounting reference date as soon as possible (s.392) – Form AA01.

2. Minutes

Minutes of the board meeting and GM must be drawn up and entered into the company's minutes book (s.248(1) and s.355(1) respectively).

3. Other

The company will also have to comply with s.82 (requirement to disclose the company name in specified locations) and if the company has a seal, produce a new seal to comply with s.45.

Template 19

Agreement for the Sale of Goods

AGREEMENT FOR THE SALE OF GOODS

THIS AGREEMENT is made the _ day of

BETWEEN:

1. ------- of _____of_____ (the "Buyer"); and

2. ------|------ of _____| (the "Seller").

Template 19

Drafting a Will

NOW IT IS HEREBY AGREED as follows:

1. _---, receipt of which the Seller hereby the Seller hereby sells and transfers to the Buyer and his/her successors and assigns absolutely, the following goods (the "Goods"):

2. The Seller warrants and represents that he/she has good title to the Goods, full authority to sell and transfer the Goods and that the Goods are sold free and clear of all liens, encumbrances, liabilities and adverse claims, of every nature and description.

3. The Seller further warrants that he/she shall fully defend, protect, indemnify and harmless the Buyer and his/her lawful successors and assigns from any and all adverse claims, that may be made by any party for possession of the Goods.

IN WITNFSS OF WHITCH have signed this agreement the day and vear first above

Signed by or on behalf of the Buyer   Signed by or on behalf of the Seller

In the presence of (witness) in the presence of (witness)

Name

Address

Occupation

Template 20

Draft a Valid Will

Sample Last Will and Testament

LAST WILL AND TESTAMENT OF

Merry Smith

I, Merry Smith, an adult residing at 5 Cherry Lane, London , London , being of sound mind, declare this to be my Last Will and Testament. I revoke all wills and codicils previously made by me.

ARTICLE I

I appoint Barry Feinstein as my Personal Representative to administer this Will, and ask that he be permitted to serve without Court supervision and without posting bond. If Barry Feinstein is unwilling or unable to serve, then I appoint Charles Reid to serve as my Personal Representative, and ask that he be permitted to serve without Court supervision and without posting bond.

ARTICLE II

I direct my Personal Representative to pay out of my residuary estate all of the expenses of my last illness, administration expenses, all legally enforceable creditor claims, all Federal estate taxes, state inheritance taxes, and all other governmental charges imposed by reason of my death without seeking reimbursement from or charging any person for any part of the taxes and charges paid, and if necessary, reasonable funeral expenses, including the cost of any suitable marker for my grave, without the necessity of an order of court approving said expenses.

ARTICLE III

I devise, bequeath, and give my baseball card collection to my son, James Smith.

I devise, bequeath, and give my books and bookshelves to my sister, Samantha Jones.

I devise, bequeath, and give my jewellery to my wife, Nancy Smith.

ARTICLE IV

I devise, bequeath, and give all the rest and remainder of my residuary estate as follows:

1. 50% to Nancy Smith.
2. 30% to James Smith.
3. 20% to Samantha Jones.

ARTICLE V

Should any beneficiary not survive me by 30 days, his or her share shall be distributed to his or her then surviving children in equal shares.

(Signature)

MerrySmith

SELF-PROVING AFFIDAVIT

The instrument, consisting of this and two (2) typewritten pages was signed and acknowledged by Testator as his Last Will and Testament in our presence, and we, at his request, and in his presence, and in the presence of each other, have subscribed our names as witnesses.

Under penalties for perjury, we, the undersigned Testator and witnesses declare:

1 That the Testator executed this instrument as his Will;

2 That in the presence of witnesses, the Testator signed or acknowledge his signature already made, or directed another to sign for him in his presence;

3 That the Testator executed the Will as his free and voluntary act for the purposes expressed in it;

4 That each of the witnesses, in the presence of the Testator and of each other, signed the Will as witness;

5 That the Testator was of sound mind; and

6 That, to the best of his knowledge, the Testator was at the time eighteen (18) or more years of age.

All of which is attested to this 20th day of February 2013.

(Signature)
MERRYSMITH, Testator
(Signature)
Witness
(Signature)
Witness

REMEMBER to IS A MUST: Date & Signature & 2 Witness that is not a beneficiary to make the will valid and for beneficiary to be able to inherit the will.

Can a Witness To a Will be a Beneficiary?

The rules governing the signing of wills appear straightforward in so far as the will MUST be signed, dated and witnessed by two witnesses, however we unfortunately see wills that sadly fail as these golden rules are often overlooked. The starting point are the witnesses. They must not be the beneficiaries under the will, if they are the gifts to the witnesses fail. Unusually, the will itself remains valid, this means that what is known as a partial intestacy can arise, resulting in the failed gifts (to the witnesses) being subject to the intestacy rules unless the will includes a specific provision for this.

Common other problems we regularly see in wills are as follows:

the will is not signed in the correct place by the testator ie. Immediately above the witnesses

there is no date

the signature on the will is frail

the original will is lost and only a copy can be found

Template 21

Sample Codicil or The Last Will and Testament

CODICIL IT IS THE LAST WILL AND TESTAMENT OF

_____

(your name)

I, _____, an adult residing at
_____

(address)_____(city), _____
(state), being of sound

mind, declare this Codicil to my Last Will and Testament ("Will") dated _____,

_____, effective as of today, _____,
_____.

ITEM I

Article _____ of my Will shall be modified to read:

_____
_____

_____
_____

_____
_____

_____
_____.

ITEM II

Article _____ of my Will shall be stricken in its entirety.

ITEM III

Article _____ shall be added to my Will, and shall read:

_____
_____

_____
_____

_____
_____

YOUR NAME, Testator/Testatrix

_____

Witness

_____

Witness

REMEMEBR To add: Date & Signature & x 2 Witness that is not a beneficiary!

Can a Witness To a Will be a Beneficiary?

The rules governing the signing of wills appear straightforward in so far as the will MUST be signed, dated and witnessed by two witnesses, however we unfortunately see wills that sadly fail as these golden rules are often overlooked. The starting point are the witnesses. They must not be the beneficiaries under the will, if they are the gifts to the witnesses fail. Unusually, the will itself remains valid, this means that what is known as a partial intestacy can arise, resulting in the failed gifts (to the witnesses) being subject to the intestacy rules unless the will includes a specific provision for this.

Common other problems we regularly see in wills are as follows :

the will is not signed in the correct place by the testator ie. immediately above the witnesses

there is no date

the signature on the will is frail

the original will is lost and only a copy can be found

Template 22

Company Situation Advise Letter

Dear

Fashion House Limited (FHL)

I am writing to confirm the information that you gave to me at our meeting and to summarise the main points that we discussed.

Background

You told me that your sister, Lucy, is a director and owner of FHL. Lucy's co-director/owner is recovering from injuries sustained in a car accident and, consequently, Lucy has been running FASHION HOUSE single-handedly for the last eighteen months. You became involved with FASHION HOUSE when Lucy approached you for advice a year ago.

From the outset you were concerned about Fashion House situation. You noted that customers had cancelled orders, record-keeping was poor, and the accounts had not been filed. You concluded that Lucy was out of her depth in the day-to-day operation of Fashion House business. You agreed to meet with Lucy regularly for the purpose of giving her advice on the running of the company. You also prepared a business plan for FHL, but you do not know whether Lucy acted in accordance with that plan.

You said that Fashion House financial situation has continued to deteriorate over recent months, to the extent that FASHION HOUSE is now facing liquidation. Your concerns are whether your involvement in FASHION HOUSE might result in you having to pay or contribute towards

Our ref: VB.CAL/JW 763420 [DATE]

FH's debts, and/or prejudice your position as managing director of Exotic Destinations Limited.

Your involvement with FHL

You can only be made accountable for Fashion House affairs if there is a legal connection between you and the company. On the face of it, there is no such connection: you have not been formally appointed as a director, and you do not own any shares in FHL. However, there is a possibility that your actions could be construed as giving rise to such a legal connection in the form of you being held to be a shadow director of FHL.

For you to be a shadow director, it would have to be shown that FASHION HOUSE acted in accordance with your instructions so that you were, in effect, directing the affairs of FHL. Determining whether or not you are a shadow director requires an objective consideration of all the facts. Whilst the meetings with Lucy and the business plan point towards you being a shadow director, in order to assess this fully, I need more information from Lucy on the extent to which she followed your suggestions and recommendations.

Establishing whether you are a shadow director of FASHION HOUSE is the key question. If you are not a shadow director, then you are not accountable for the affairs of FHL. However, if you are found to be a shadow director, there are some possible adverse consequences.

Liability for Fashion House debts

Even as a shadow director you would not ordinarily incur any personal liability for Fashion House debts. However, one situation where you could be ordered to contribute to those debts, is if you were found to have engaged in wrongful trading. A number of requirements would have to be satisfied before such a finding could be made. Firstly, FASHION HOUSE must have gone into insolvent liquidation; this now seems likely as, since our meeting, Lucy has told you that one of Fashion House creditors has started the liquidation process. Secondly, you must have allowed FASHION HOUSE to go on trading despite the fact that you knew, or ought to have known, that FASHION HOUSE could not avoid insolvent liquidation. Thirdly, you must have failed to do everything that you could to minimise the loss to FH's creditors.

In order to advise you on the likelihood of a finding of wrongful trading, I will need more detail on the precise financial position of FASHION HOUSE, if and when the inevitability of insolvent liquidation should have been apparent, and the steps taken to protect the creditors.

Potential for Disqualification

If you are found to be a shadow director of a company in liquidation, your actions would inevitably be subject to scrutiny. If you were found to have been culpable in the insolvency or any other failings of

FASHION HOUSE, you could have a disqualification order made against you. The effect of disqualification is that you would not be able to be involved in the management of any company, including Exotic Destinations Ltd. The length of disqualification is in the discretion of the court, but a period of between two and five years is usually applied, unless the circumstances are considered to be serious.

Again, I will need to see more information in order to assess whether there is any real possibility of you being disqualified.

Summary

The key question is whether the facts support the conclusion that you are a shadow director of FHL. This is turn depends on whether FHL, through Lucy, acted in accordance with your advice. Only if the evidence supports this finding will the possible adverse consequences become relevant. Those consequences are a personal contribution towards the debts of FHL, in the event that you are found to have engaged in wrongful trading, and disqualification if you are shown to be culpable in the failings of FHL.

I appreciate that the consequences are potentially serious. However, I must stress that at present they are only possibilities. I will need to see much more evidence before I can make a realistic assessment of the risks, if any, that you face.

Next steps

As a first step, we need to establish the extent to which Lucy acted on your advice. Could you therefore let me have a copy of the business plan which you made for FHL, together with any notes that you made of your recommendations and/or meetings with Lucy. Could you also speak to Lucy in order to gauge how she responded to your advice. It would also be helpful if Lucy could provide copies of Fashion House most recent accounts, and any information relating to any other indicators of impending insolvency, such as creditors demanding payment, excessive purchases on credit etc.

Please forward this information to me as soon as possible. Once I have considered it, I will contact you to arrange another appointment to discuss the matter further.

In the meantime, please do not hesitate to telephone me if you have any questions.

Yours sincerely

Partner

Template 23

Memorandum Purchase Plant

MEMORANDUM

[You]

MLR/45/MP

[Date of today]

London Digital Ltd Relocation and purchase of plant

Further to your memorandum of [date], set out below are the key elements of the company procedure required for Lisa Frith to carry out the proposed transactions, and the likely taxation consequences of the sale of the factory. References to "CA06" are to the Companies Act 2006, and to "MA" are to the Model Articles.

Initial board meeting

General issues

This may be called under MA9. A quorum of two of the four directors is required - MA11. The meeting should be minuted, and the minutes kept for at least ten years - CA06 s.248. It is likely to be preferable to deal with any final approval of all four transactions at a second Board

Meeting, as they are form part of a series of transactions which are not intended to happen independently.

There are the following items of business:

The proposed sale of the freehold factory to LDL

This matter falls within the powers of the directors under MA3. It is a matter in which Richard Jarvis has an interest. He is therefore required, under CA06 s.177, to declare the nature and extent of his interest to the other directors - unless the directors are aware of his interest in which case he does not need to declare it. He should however do so as a matter of good practice. By virtue of Special Article 2.1, he can count in the quorum and vote in relation to the matter notwithstanding his interest, so long as he has made a compliant declaration. Article 2.2 allows him to retain the benefit of any such transaction - though CA06 s.180(1) has similar effect in any event.

The proposed sale is a substantial property transaction within CA06 s.190 (see below) and therefore requires the approval of members. The directors may resolve to enter into this transaction conditionally upon approval being obtained, or may wait until the approval of members has been given.

Entry into new lease of premises on the other side of the Hadley Industrial Estate.

This matter falls within the powers of the directors under MA3. It can be dealt with at the second board meeting for the reasons given above.

Acquisition of a new composites moulding machinery.

This matter falls within the powers of the directors under MA3. It, too, can be dealt with at the second board meeting for the same reasons.

Allotment of shares

The power to allot shares is one vested in the directors, but requires the authority of shareholders before it can be exercised (see below), and a special resolution to issue shares on a non-pre-emptive basis (see below), including the provision by the directors of a written statement under CA06 s.571 (see below). It is a matter in which Richard Jarvis has an interest. He is therefore required, under CA06 s.177, to declare the nature and extent of his interest to the other directors. By virtue of Special Article 2.1, he can count in the quorum and vote in relation to the matter notwithstanding his interest, so long as he has made a compliant declaration.

This is a matter in which Tim Desai has an interest within CA06 s.177. Whilst it is certain that the other directors will be aware of her interest, it is still good practice to formally record her interest. For the same reasons as noted above in relation to Louis Moore, Tim can count in the quorum and vote in relation to the matter notwithstanding her interest.

The actual allotment of shares will, nevertheless, not therefore take place until the second board meeting

Approval of written resolutions

The directors should approve the proposal of the written resolutions referred to below - CA06 s.291(3), and the written statement under CA06 s.571, which should accompany the relevant written resolution. The directors should instruct Tim Desai, as company secretary, to circulate copies of the written resolutions and the written statement to all eligible shareholders.

Written Resolutions

There are three required:

An ordinary resolution to approve the arrangement under which Lisa Frith sells the factory premises to Richard Jarvis (as a person connected with a director).

The requirement for approval arises under CA06 s. 190:

☒ The asset (the freehold) is a "non-cash asset" within the meaning of CA06 s. 1163(1)

☒ The non-cash asset is a "substantial" one, as its value exceeds £100,000 - CA06 s.191(1)

☒ LDL is a connected person: it is a body corporate with which Richard is connected (CA06 s. 252(2)(b)) by virtue of the fact that Richard and the persons connected with him (the members of his family include Felicity - CA06 s.252(2)(a) because she is his spouse - CA06 s.253(2)(a)) are interested in shares comprising at least 20% of the equity share capital of LDL. NB as we do not know the proportions in which Richard and Felicity own LDL, it is necessary to consider Felicity as well as Richard.

An ordinary resolution authorising the directors to allot 20,000 new ordinary shares and specifying a date not more than five years from the date of the resolution on which it will expire.

No general power to allot shares exists under CA06 s.550, as the company has more than one class of share. Under CA06 s.551, authorisation may be given by the articles or by (ordinary) resolution of Lisa Frith. As there is no authorisation contained in the articles, an ordinary resolution of the members is required. The authority should be given for just this particular exercise of the power rather than for its exercise generally, in order to comply with the commitment given to Constance Jeffries not to give the directors wider powers than necessary. The limitation on the authority must comply with the provisions of CA06 s. 551(3).

A special resolution authorising the directors to allot the 20,000 new ordinary shares as if CA06 s. 561 did not apply to the allotment.

The new shares are intended not to be offered pre-emptively to the existing members. There is nothing in the articles which permits the directors to allot otherwise than in accordance with the pre-emption provisions of CA06 s. 561.

A special resolution dis-applying the pre-emption rights which would otherwise exist is required by CA06. This cannot be under CA06 s.569 (because the company has more than one class of share). As the directors will not be acting under a general authorisation (see above) a special resolution under CA06 s.571, rather than under s.570 is required. This requires a written statement complying with the provisions of that section (as to reasons etc).

The written statement must be recommended by the directors, and must set out their reasons for the recommendation, the amount to be paid to the company in respect of the allotments, and the directors' justification of that amount. The written statement must be sent to eligible members before or with the written resolution - CA06 s.571.

General issues relating to the written resolutions

All of the shareholders are eligible members - CA06 s. 289. The circulation date is the date on which Tim sends or submits it to members - CA06 s. 290. The eligible shareholders will be told to sign where indicated (s.291(4) CA 2006) and the date by which the resolution must be passed if it is not to lapse. This date is the end of the statutory 28 day period (the 'lapse date' - CA 2006 s.297(1)(b) (since Lisa Frith's articles are silent on the point). The resolutions will be passed as soon as shareholders representing the required percentage of voting shares have signed and returned them. Assuming all shareholders meet the deadline for returning them, the resolutions will be passed.

Second board meeting

A second board meeting is required.

The same issues as to calling, quorum, minuting etc. apply to this meeting. The directors will resolve to:

- Allot 10,000 ordinary shares of £1 each at a premium of £4 per share to Tim

Desai and Rachel Farmer upon receipt of the subscription monies, now that appropriate authority to allot has been given, and the pre-emption rights disapplied, and authorise the issue of new share certificates in respect of these allotments. The same issues as at the first board meeting relating to Tim Desai's interests apply here.

☒ Enter into the proposed sale of the freehold factory to LDL, now that the entry into this transaction has been approved by shareholders. The same issues as at the first board meeting relating to Richard Jarvis's interests apply here.

- Enter into the new lease of premises on the other side of the Hadley Industrial Estate.
- Enter into the contract to acquire the new composites moulding machinery.
- Authorise the appropriate directors to execute the relevant documentation to
- enter into these transactions on behalf of Lisa Frith.
- Instruct Tim Desai, as secretary of Lisa Frith, to carry out the appropriate

company administration. This will include the following matters:

o Filing of the resolutions under CA06 ss. 551 and 571 - these are both resolutions to which Chapter 3 of Part 3 of CA06 applies, and copies of them must be forwarded to the registrar within fifteen days after they are

passed;

o Filing of Form SH01 (return of allotment of shares and statement of

capital) (CA 2006, s.555(3)), within one month

o the issue of share certificates in respect of the allotments o updating Lisa Frith's register of members.

Corporation tax

Set out below is a calculation based upon the assumptions stated in your memorandum. References to "TCGA" are to the Taxation of Chargeable Gains Act 1992.

Stage 1: Identify the chargeable disposal

The chargeable disposal is the sale of the factory premises Stage 2: Calculate chargeable gains

Proceeds of disposal

Less: Acquisition cost Gain (before indexation) Less: Indexation allowance: (845,000 x 0.33)

£570,000 £945,000 £825,000

£165,000 £110,000

s.155 (respectively, freehold land (Head A) and fixed plant and machinery (Head

B)).

- The acquisition of the new plant is intended to take place in the period beginning

12 months before and ending 3 years after the disposal of the old factory (TCGA

s.152(3)). This condition is satisfied.

- It must be established that the factory was used throughout its period of

ownership for the purposes of the trade - though this seems highly likely (TCGA

s.152(1)).

- The acquisition of the new assets will be made for the purpose of their use in

the trade (TCGA s.152(5)). This, too, seems highly likely.

☒ The full value of the consideration will be re-invested (the sale realises less than

the cost of the new plant) (TCGA s.152(1)).

☒ A claim must be made for the relief to apply. (TCGA s.152(1) - "on making a claim".

Where the new asset is a depreciating asset, the effect of TCGA s.152 is modified by TCGA s.154.

- For the purposes of TCGA s.154, an asset is a depreciating asset if it is a

wasting asset, as defined in TCGA s.44.

- TCGA s.44 provides that a "wasting asset" means an asset with a predictable

life not exceeding 50 years, and that plant and machinery shall in every case be

regarded as having a predictable life of less than 50 years.

As the plant is therefore a depreciating asset, the held-over gain is not carried

forward, but instead it is treated as not accruing until the earliest of:

Gain (after indexation)

*correct at the time of writing.

[Note to students: you would be expected to research the applicable rate. It is acceptable to make approximations for the purposes of the current advice - for example, to say, "if the sale goes ahead within such and such a time"; or "June 2050 are the most recent figures".]

This gain will be added into Lisa Frith's taxable profits. Lisa Frith's accounting period coincides with the corporation tax year, so the profit will fall within the 2050/17 Financial Year. The rate of corporation tax for this year is 20% for all companies, regardless of size. This would therefore give rise to an increased corporation tax liability of £22,000.

Roll-over relief may be available under TCGA s.152. There are a number of conditions which need to be satisfied before the relief is available:

- The "old asset" and the "new asset" are both within the class described in TCGA
    - the disposal of the plant
    - the plant ceases to be used for the purposes of the trade; or o 10 years beginning with the acquisition of the plant.

If the client's intention is to use the plant in the trade for the duration of its working life, then the gain will be treated as accruing in the 2026/27 Financial Year. Whilst, therefore, it appears that the relief under TCGA s.152 is available, the gain will not be deferred indefinitely.

Please let me know if you require any further information.

Yours sincerely

Template 24

Dispute Letter Answer

Dear

Dispute with Limited

Our reference: 678968.01/HK Date: [date]

I spoke with our expert, Marisa Sava on 20 August 2018. Mr Sava has now considered your architect's designs for the glass roof. Unfortunately, his conclusion may now have an adverse impact on your case against WMC Construction Limited ("WMC"). Mr Sava has indicated that he is amenable to omitting this from his final report, but for the reasons detailed below I do not consider this to be appropriate.

Impact on your claim against WMC

Mr Sava has concluded that the design of the roof was flawed; he says that its metal structure was far too heavy and was not sufficiently supported. He thinks that the cracks in the walls could have been caused by the structure pulling inwards and downwards and that there is a small possibility that the roof collapsed completely of its own accord, rather than through the fault of WMC. If this information comes to the attention of the court, you may not succeed in demonstrating that the excavating and pile-driving caused the damage to the roof and this would mean that your nuisance claim would fail.

The consequences of Mr Sava omitting his conclusion

If we allow Mr Sava to omit his conclusion about the glass roof from his report, then he will be in breach of his obligations to the court:

- The court rules state that Mr Sava has a duty to be independent and uninfluenced by the pressures of litigation and to be unbiased. These duties are owed to the court and not to you as the party instructing him. He also has a duty to consider all material facts including those which might detract from his opinion; this therefore includes the glass roof designs.

- Mr Sava has to make a statement at the end of his report that he has complied with his duties to the court and that he believes that the contents of his report are true. Clearly if he omits the information about the glass roof, he has not complied with his duties and he will potentially be liable for contempt of court due to his breach of his statement. This could result in a fine or even imprisonment.

If I allow Mr Sava to omit his conclusion from his report, then I myself will be in breach of my professional duties as a solicitor. I am not permitted to knowingly allow someone else to mislead the court.

Possible steps which WMC could take before the trial

Copies of the plans and specifications for the glass roof were provided to WMC during the disclosure process. WMC' expert is likely to see these and he may come to the same view as Mr Sava. This could lead to WMC taking one or all of the following steps:

- WMC' solicitor may ask Mr Sava questions about the roof design in order to clarify his report. Mr Sava is obliged to answer these questions;

if he tries to avoid the issue then WMC may become suspicious about the nature of our instructions to him.

Any suspicion about our instructions may lead WMC' solicitor to make an application to the court for disclosure of our instructions to Mr Sava. Whilst the court will not routinely order the disclosure of the instructions given to an expert, it may order that the instructions be disclosed if it has reasonable grounds to believe that the substance of the instructions set out in the report are inaccurate or incomplete. It could become apparent that we requested Mr Sava to omit the information from his report. This might result in your claim being struck out or an adverse costs order against you.

- Mr Sava will have to meet with WMC' expert in order to identify areas of agreement and disagreement between them. Again, if Mr Sava tries to avoid the issue then WMC may become suspicious about the nature of our instructions to him. In his report, Mr Sava is obliged to set out the substance of all facts and instructions which are material to the opinions expressed in his report or on which those opinions are based.

WMC could also apply to disbar Mr Sava's evidence completely on the basis that he does not understand his duty to the court. Without any expert evidence, there is little chance of your claim succeeding.

Possible steps which WMC could take at the trial

Even if WMC does not take any immediate action, they may wait until the trial to raise the issue. They could cross-examine Mr Sava upon the glass roof in the witness box at trial; Mr Sava is obliged to tell the truth and it could become clear that he had omitted information from his report. This could seriously impact on the credibility of his evidence.

WMC may also at that point apply for disclosure of our instructions to Mr Sava and/or for permission to cross-examine him on our instructions. This could, again, lead to your claim being struck out or to an adverse costs order against you or to an order disbarring Mr Sava's evidence.

Advice

For all of the above reasons, we must insist that Mr Sava includes his conclusion about the glass roof in his final report.

However, we could obtain an alternative opinion on the glass roof from another expert; if this expert's opinion is more favourable than Mr Sava, then we could serve this report instead of Mr Sava's report. This would involve further costs and we would not be able to recover the costs of instructing Mr Sava from WMC even if your claim was to succeed.

Alternatively, we could start negotiations to try to settle the claim out of court.

Once you have had a chance to consider the contents of this letter, please telephone me with your instructions.

Yours sincerely

Template 25

Reply's to Client Share Purchase Agreement

Dear

Share Purchase Agreement dated 9 June 2026

Thank you for your instructions to review your sale of LMB Limited ("LMB") to Paradise Hotels Limited ("Paradise ") under the above Share Purchase Agreement. I have had the opportunity to read all of the documentation which you sent to me, including all of the accounting information which you provided to Paradise Hotels Limited and the letter before claim which you recently received from Govans LLP .

Allegation to be investigated

The allegation made against EEE PLC is that it failed to disclose a downturn in the profits of Anna Frith, LMB' sole hotel in Paris, and that this constituted a material adverse change in the turnover, financial position or prospects of LMB. Such downturn is alleged to have taken place between 27 April 2050 and the completion date of the sale, 21 June 2050.

Profit Forecast for LMB as at 27 April 2025

One of the documents provided to Paradise Hotels Limited on the date when the parties signed the Share Purchase Agreement was a Profit Forecast dated 27 April 2050 ("the April Profit Forecast").

The forecast for Anna Frith for the quarter ending 21 June 2050 was:

- Turnover £1890,500.00
- Profit £876,250.00

The management accounts of LMB for the quarter ending 21 June 2050 show that the actual performance of Anna Frith was as follows:

- Turnover £678,250.00
- Loss £567,750.00

The difference in profits was therefore £88,000.00. I am not sure how Paradise Hotels Limited calculated their alleged loss of £400,000.

Upon further investigation, I have discovered that there was a general decline in hotel trade in Holland during May and June 2050, resulting from unprecedented rainfall which caused major flooding in the region. This clearly had an adverse effect upon the trade at Anna Frith.

The Disclosure Letter dated 1 June 2056

The disclosure letter says nothing about Anna Frith or its decline in profits during May and June 2050. On the face of it, therefore, there was a failure to disclose facts relating to the financial position of the Dutch operation of LMB.

Material adverse change?

The overall turnover of LMB for its financial year ending 31 December 2050 was £93.23 million. The turnover of Anna Frith during that period was £842,857. This represents less than 2% of LMB' overall turnover.

The loss in profits at Anna Frith for the quarter ending 21 June 2050 of £88,000 is insignificant in that context and would not, in my opinion, have affected the value of LMB as at the date of the sale. It does not represent a "material adverse change".

I trust that my conclusion provides some comfort to you. Incidentally, I did see that there is something in the Share Purchase Agreement about notice of a claim, and I wondered whether that is something that you had looked at. This is outside of my remit and so I leave that to you and your lawyers.

Please let me know if I can be of any further assistance.

Yours sincerely

Template 26

Banking and Finance

MEMORANDUM

Re: Facilities Agreement

You have asked me to prepare a memorandum identifying those provisions in the London City Facility Agreement which require amendment to reflect the terms of the extract Term Sheet or are generally unfavourable to NBS and the syndicate.

1. Parties: the three parties, Digital PMC ("Digital"), Moris PLC ("Moris"), and Cloud PLC ("CLOUD") need to be added as both borrowers and as guarantors. Moris and CLOUD will be borrowing under the revolving credit facility in addition to Digital, and all three parties will be cross- guaranteeing the obligations of each other.

2. Clause1-DefinitionsandInterpretation

   - Definition of "Availability Period": requires amendment to reflect the fact that two facilities are being made available by the lenders. Appropriate wording for the availability period for the new revolving credit facility needs should be included (starting at the date of the agreement and ending up to and including one month before the termination date), and the availability period for the new term facility needs changing from 90 days to 30 days.

- Definitions of "Commitment", "Facility" and "Total Commitments:" these need amending to reflect the fact that two facilities are being made available.

Suggestions are to:

o Change the definition of "Facility" to "Facility A" and to cross-reference to clause 2.1. A new definition of "Facility B" should be inserted to cover the revolving credit facility and refer to a new clause 2.2 (see below)

o Include new definitions of:

- "Facility" (to mean Facility A or Facility B);
- "Facility A Commitments" and "Facility B Commitments" (ie: the Commitment of each Lender under each separate facility); and
- "Total Facility A Commitments" (£89,000,000) and "Total Facility B Commitments" (£45,000,000)

You have been asked to draft a memorandum which will be used as the basis for a meeting with the client. Accordingly, your answer should be in memorandum format, and use language and style which is consistent with a professional communication.

- Definition of "Loan": amendment required so that the term will mean a Facility A Loan or a Facility B Loan (and definitions for these two terms will also be required).

- Definition of "Margin": amendment required to reflect the figure in the term sheet with respect to the term facility (i.e. 0.5%). A new limb to the definition is required to be included to refer to the different interest rate being applied to the revolving credit facility.

- Definition of "Obligors": this must be amended to refer to each Borrower and each Guarantor. The definition is important as it will be used throughout the Digital Facilities Agreement to create legal obligations in favour of the lenders.

- Definition of "Material Adverse Effect": this is one of the most negotiated definitions in a facilities agreement. The lenders will want this definition to be drafted as widely and as subjectively as possible whereas borrowers want the definition to be construed as narrowly and as objectively as possible. Consequently, the "Borrower" should be amended to refer to "any Obligor" on the basis that there is more than one borrower, and each company is acting in the capacity as both a borrower and a guarantor.

- Definition of "Total Commitments": requires amendment to refer to the total of the "Total Facility A Commitments" and "Total Facility B Commitments." The figure of £67,000,000 should be replaced with £56,000,000.

- New definitions will also need to be included to reflect that the new facilities are being secured (e.g. definitions of "Security Trustee" (i.e. NBS) and "Security Documents").

Consequential amendments to other definitions such as "Finance Parties" and "Finance Documents" will also be required.

3. Clause 2: The Facility

- Clause 2.1 requires amendment to reflect that there are two facilities. Extra limbs will need to be added to make clear that the revolving credit facility is being made available to Moriss, Digital and CLOUD, and the term facility is being made available to Digital only.

4. Clause 8: Prepayment and Cancellation

This clause requires a number of amendments to reflect the two facilities. In addition, other changes are recommended as the clause as currently drafted is overly favourable to the borrower. The following amendments are suggested:

- The current drafting of clause 8.4 should be amended to specifically deal with Facility A (the term facility), with a separate new provision added to deal with the prepayment requirements for Facility B (the revolving credit facility).

- The borrower to which a Facility A or Facility B loan applies (as applicable) should be required to provide the Agent with longer notice of its intention to prepay. One Business Day is not sufficient.

- Prepayment amounts are currently required in amounts/multiples of £67,000. This may be administratively burdensome for the Agent and a higher minimum prepayment amount of, say, £670,000, would be more appropriate.

- Clause 8.4 must be amended to accord with the Term Sheet, that is, prepayment should reduce the remaining instalments in inverse order of maturity, not "rateably". This reduces the length of the overall loan facility and therefore the time that the banks are exposed to the credit risk of the Group.

- Clause 8.7 should be amended to provide that the relevant borrower pays Break Costs if it prepays on any date other than the first day of an Interest Period. This is to cover the syndicate's own costs of borrowing on the interbank market. The lender may also consider charging a prepayment fee.

5. Clause 9.1: Calculation of Interest

This clause must include a reference to mandatory costs to conform to the term sheet. A definition of "Mandatory Costs" will be required in the facilities agreement if not already provided.

6. Clause 19: Representations

- NBS should insist that every Obligor be made to make the representations, not just Digital as currently drafted. Representations are an important means of getting the borrowing group to disclose any issues which could present a risk to the lenders before the facilities are utilised, and of ensuring that its position does not deteriorate over the life of the facilities.

- The Obligors should be required to regularly repeat the representations (or at least specific ones which is in line with market practice). Representations are usually repeated on the date of each utilisation request, each utilisation and on each interest payment date.

7. Clause 22.2: Compliance with Laws

This undertaking should be made by all the Obligors. From the lenders' perspective it would be better to amend this undertaking so that it would be breached if the Agent (or Majority Lenders) considers that the failure to comply with any law is reasonably likely to have a Material Adverse Effect. This favours the lenders as the test becomes subjective rather than objective and the hurdle is lowered i.e. 'reasonably likely to' rather than 'would'.

Template 27

Legal Research Landlord Tenant Dispute Memorandum

MEMORANDUM

PLC

Landlord and tenant dispute [Today's date]

We act for London More Ltd. ("the Company"), a property investment company. Mr Tom Smith is the sole shareholder and director of the Company. The Company has recently received a letter before action from one of its tenants, Mr Graig Frith ("the Claimant"). The Company owns a long lease of Flat 3, 61 Lion Yard St, Cambridge. The lease states that the demise extended to the internal surfaces of the walls, ceiling and floor and included the right to use the common parts to access the flat. The Company granted a sub-tenancy of the flat to the Claimant by means of a 12 month assured short hold tenancy which commenced on 1st June 2024. The potential claim relates to an incident on 5th August 2024 when the Claimant fell on uneven paving on the path leading to the front door of the house. As a result of the fall the Claimant sustained injuries including a broken arm. The Claimant is claiming damages against the Company on the basis that it failed to keep the path in repair, and therefore had breached covenants implied into the sub-tenancy. The Claimant also says that as the Company has breached these covenants he will be terminating the tenancy early and leaving the premises on 31st December 2024.

The Company denies the claim, Mr Smith states that the Company cannot be held liable for the path outside the building as the Company does not own the entire building. Mr Smith had not visited the premises since the Claimant moved in, nor had the Company been notified of any disrepair to the path. I think there was a recent ruling on a similar case in the Supreme Court but cannot recollect what the decision was. As the Company denies breaching any covenants Mr Smith feels that there is no right to terminate the tenancy early.

Please could you research both issues?

Mr Smith also requires our advice on a separate issue. The Company also owns a building which is divided into office units. One of the tenants has recently sought to exercise its break option in a lease of one of the units. The break option required 6 months' notice and was conditional on the tenant giving vacant possession. The tenant gave notice on 1st April 2024and vacated the premises on 1st October 2017. During the tenancy, the tenant had carried out alterations, including the installation of internal partitioning. Those alterations were authorised by a licence for alterations. The licence also required the tenant to reinstate the premises to their original condition at the end of the term or upon sooner determination of the licence. However after the tenant vacated the unit, the Company discovered that they had left the partitioning and some other items (kitchen units and floor coverings) in the premises. The Company wrote to the tenant asking them to remove the partitioning and other items. The tenant responded stating that the items were annexed to the premises and had become fixtures, which they were not obliged to remove. Mr Smith would like to know the Company's legal position here, whether the partitioning and other items are fixtures and whether leaving them breaches the requirement to give vacant possession and therefore invalidates the break clause?

I am meeting with Mr Smith tomorrow afternoon to have a preliminary discussion on both matters.

Chapter 3

Social Letter

1. Event Invitation Social letter
2. Event Invitation
3. Making other straightforward requests
4. Making not-so-straightforward requests
5. An alternative to complaining: Requesting information
6. Announcing a graduation
7. Announcing a move
8. Announcing an engagement
9. Announcing a marriage
10. Announcing a birth
11. Announcing an adoption
12. Announcing a divorce
13. Sending holiday greetings
14. Accepting an invitation
15. Congratulating on a graduation
16. Congratulating on a promotion, award, or other achievement
17. Congratulating on an engagement or a marriage
18. Thanking for a gift or other kindness
19. Sending get-well wishes for an illness or accident
20. Declining an invitation
21. Delivering bad news with apology

22 Event Conference Invitation
23 Requesting information
24 Soliciting participation in an activity
25 Persuading someone to accept a leadership position
26 Confirming others' participation in an activity
27 Agreeing to participate in an activity
28 Polite refusal to a request to serve or contribute
29 Thanking others for their contributions or time
30 Acknowledging a refusal to serve or contribute
31 Refusing a leadership role
32 Resigning a leadership role
33 Personal greeting
34 Explaining delayed reply
35 A visitor from abroad
36 Apology for poor service
37 Apology for cancelling an appointment
38 Regretting an oversight
39 Conveying unwelcome news
40 LETTER of thanks
41 Formal letter of congratulation on a promotion

Template 1

Event Invitation Social letter

Dear

Andrew K. Levinson and I will be married on Saturday, May 16, 2004. We would be honoured if you could attend.

The ceremony will begin at 4 p.m. at the United Hebrew Congregation at 1338 North Main Street. A dinner reception will follow.

We hope you can join us to help celebrate this happy occasion.

Yours truly

Please respond by May 9, 2099

Template 2

Event Invitation

Dear

Alex and I were wondering if you, Eric, and the kids were free the weekend of September 12? The fall foliage should be beautiful then, and we'd love to have you spend the weekend us down here in our "wilderness."

I think Alex would like to take the guys fishing, and I'd be happy taking a long drive through the country and finding a nice to picnic, weather permitting.

I do hope you can join us for the weekend. Let us know.

Love from us all

Template 3

Making other straightforward requests

Dear

I can't tell you how relieved I am that Granddad made it through another bout with heart trouble. Let's pray he won 't have any more.

We had agreed to share expenses on the flower arrangement I had sent to his room, and here are the details on that. The entire cost, including delivery, was £42.87. Jim has agreed to chip in some too, so your share is only £14.29.

You can get this. To me however it's most convenient; a check by mail would be fine. Thanks!

Love

Template 4

Making other straightforward requests

Dear

Hey, buddy, I need that drill back from you sometime in the next week. Amanda and I will be in and out running errands most of the weekend; if you come by and we're not there, leave it in the garage, okay? (Call me if you've forgotten the trick to get in.)

Thanks, Say, how do those new doors look?

Template 5

Making not-so-straightforward requests

Dear

I can't tell you how relieved I am that Granddad made it through another bout with heart trouble. Let's pray he won't have any more. Would you mind sharing expenses on the flower arrangement I had sent to his room? I didn't have a chance to ask you about this ahead of time, but I took the liberty of signing the card "Love from your grandkids."

The entire cost, including delivery, was £42.87. Jim has agreed to chip in some too, so your share would be only £14.29. If you can't or would rather not chip in, let me know either way, okay? Jim and / can handle it alone if you need us to.

Send me a check or call me as soon as You can. Thanks!

Love,

Template 6

Making not-so-straightforward requests

Dear

Do you think I could get that drill back I loaned you last month Amanda and I are considering our own home-remodelling project, and I just remembered that I loaned you my drill. We want to install bigger windows in the kitchen-if that is, we can find some we like. (We've been shopping for the last three weeks solid!)I don't imagine we'll make any final decisions until next weekend, so if you can get the drill back to me by, say, next Sunday, I'd appreciate it!

Thanks, Say, how do those new doors look?

Template 7

An alternative to complaining: Requesting information

Dear

Jill and I need your help with an on going frustration we've been experiencing. Could we talk about landscaping decisions either of our families make that affect the space between our houses?

Please don't misunderstand. We have enjoyed the evergreens you planted in the "no man's land" between our houses. They're very attractive and give both of our homes additional privacy. We were thinking, however, of planting wildflowers there before the trees went in. Because we've always had difficulty knowing that uneven area, we thought wildflowers would make it easier to maintain.

You and May have been wonderful neighbours, and we hate to even bring this landscape issue up; I know, however, that issues can fester and grow between people when they don't talk about them. We value our relationship with you both too much to let that happen.

Can we talk further about this and other landscaping issues affecting both of our houses? I 'll try to catch up with you sometime this weekend to get your thoughts on this issue.

Thanks for your understanding

Template 8

Announcing a graduation

Dear

I am pleased to announce that on May 9, 2004, was graduated From Purdue University with a degree in nursing. I 'Il be starting work in critical care at the Veteran's Hospital in just a few weeks.

Thank you for your interest over the years in my education and other endeavours. I've always valued your guidance and support

Sincerely

Template 9

Announcing a move

Dear

Hey, we've moved! Kelly's work has taken us north to Minneapolis, Minnesota. After much debate, Kelly accepted a great job at Best Bet's headquarters here. It was a good move for both of us (I have family here), and we're looking forward to everything Minneapolis has to offer, except perhaps sub zero winter temperatures.

Please make note of our new address and phone number.

18377 Lakeview Boulevard

London

SW13PS

Take care of yourselves, and consider visiting us soon, okay?

Love from both of us

Template 10

Announcing an engagement

Dear

I wanted you to be one of the first to know some happy news.

Lisa More and I are engaged to be married!

Lisa and I have known each other for just over a year, and he's like no one I've ever met before* We haven't set a date yet, bur we're thinking maybe ready fall.

We'll keep you posted.

I can't wait for you to meet Lisa!

Love

Template 11

Announcing a marriage

Dear

I'm delighted to let you know that Janet and I were married in her hometown of Houston, Texas, on Saturday, February 7, 2004.

The ceremony was small and informal, just our style. Will be settling in Amarillo, near my family and most of our friends. Janet will continue to be known as Janet Tomlinson.

We're both very happy and look forward to our new life together!

Love to you both

Template 12

Announcing a birth

Dear

Brian and I are happy to announce the birth of our first child, a daughter, Amanda Elizabeth. Mandy, as we'll call her, was born on April 30 at 2:35 and weighed 7 pounds, 9 ounces.

We're all well and gradually adjusting to this new family of three.

All the best to your family,

Template 13

Announcing an adoption

October 28, 2037

Dear Mr. and Mrs Frith

Please allow us to share some good news. We're parents for second time! On October 10, 2004, we adopted our second child, Joseph Patrick He was just one week old when we brought him home.

His older sister, Katie, isn't quite sure what to make of Joseph yet, but she already seems quite fond of him.

We're as happy as we can possibly be!

Kind regards

Template 12

Announcing a divorce

Dear

Eric and I were unfortunately divorced last month, and /now living at a new address:

86 East Street

London SW39PM

The children will be living with me here. I've also gone back to using my maiden name, "Weisberg."

I know I speak for Eric when I say we have both valued your

Friendship over the years and hope we can keep in touch.

Love

Template 13

Sending holiday greetings

Dear

Holiday greetings from our family to yours!

This year has been a busy one for the James's Christen, as you know, started college at Tennessee State this fail; Steven and I have missed her horribly and have had a bit of a difficult time adjusting to the proverbial "empty nest." What do we do with our time now? Our older daughter, Amy, has been a real support to us during this time. She and her husband, Tom, who live just 30 minutes away, celebrated their second wedding anniversary with a new baby-our grandbaby! Born April 10, Amanda Erin came into the world intense red hair and Amy's blue eyes, Big brother Trevor seems crazy about his little sister.

The twins are also well: John's still in California working as a computer technician and claims he has the best job in the world. Alan and his wife, Debbie, prefer the country life and have started a small organic farm on the outskirts of Indianapolis. Their 2-year-old daughter, Emily, continues to be a great joy to both her parents and Steven and me, who spoil her terribly.

Steven still enjoys his work with the university, and I've I been considering part-time secretarial work to occupy my time. I'm still very involved as a volunteer with the public schools, which I'd like to continue, but I'm also feeling an urge to reorient myself to the business world. With Christen at school, I'm beginning to consider some exciting new prospects for my working life. Steven, bless him, supports any I .a I have, no matter how fleeting.

And our health has never been better, I'm happy to report. Steven has me jogging (okay, waking) with him in the mornings, and we've both managed to lose a little weight.

That's largely what's been happening at our house very much like to hear what's been happening at yours.

Happy Holidays!

Please drop us a line when it's convenient, and please accept our warmest wishes for a happy holiday season and year ahead. Elizabeth and Steven

Template 14

Accepting an invitation

Dear

What wonderful news! Jerold and / would be pleased to join you and your fiancé' for your marriage ceremony and dinner you and your fiancé for Count on two of us.

We're looking forward to it!

Kind regards,

Template 2

Accepting an invitation

August 22, 2057

Dear

We'd be delighted to join you for a weekend in the "wilderness!"

Tom has a Girl Scout outing that weekend, so she unfortunately won't be joining us. She's quite content, though, spend the rest of the weekend, after her outing, at a girlfriend b house.

Tom and the boys are certainly up for fishing. I say we let them deal with the hooks and worms while you and I take ourselves on a picnic. It'll be fun to catch up. I'll call you next weekend to discuss the details.

Looking forward to it!

Template 15

Congratulating on a graduation

Dear

I understand from Tim Jeffries that you have graduated from Silvgold College. What an accomplishment. 'Congratulations.

Way back when you helped my husband and me with those occasional odd jobs, I knew that your dedication to excellence would help you succeed with whatever you chose 'o do. Jim and I wish you the very best as you begin your life as a working professional

Best regards

Template 2

Congratulating on a graduation

Dear

Hey, congratulations. I'm ready proud of you, April, for obtaining your nursing degree from Purdue. As a Purdue grad my self I know something of how hard you worked to get that degree. You should be quite proud of yourself.

Best of luck to you,

Template 16

Congratulating on a promotion, award, or other achievement

Dear

I was thrilled to read in this week's paper that you're being honoured for your work with the homeless. Your selfless dedication to such an important cause donating countless hours participating in everything from home construction to home financing to life-skills support, is indeed construction to home financing to life-skills support, is indeed admirable.

Congratulations on receiving an honour you so clearly deserve!

Regards

Template 2

Congratulating on a promotion, award, or other achievement

Dear

Congratulations on your new job!

We ran into Jane at the grocery store CEO, which mentioned your great news. The job sounds like a real challenge-one I feel certain you will find rewarding. (You always did enjoy a good challenge!)

I wish you a smooth transition into life at Tomlin Electronics and much success in the years to come!

Blessings to you

Template 17

Congratulating on an engagement or a marriage

Dear

We noticed your engagement announcement in Sunday newspaper. What wonderful news!

As you know, your mother and father have been dear friends of ours for years, and we were delighted to learn of this latest cause for celebration in your family.

Our very best regards to you and your fiancé.

Very sincerity yours

Template 2

Congratulating on an engagement or a marriage

Dear

I hear congratulations are in order., I was so happy to hear that the two of you were married last month. I can't think of a better-suited couple (except for perhaps Ellie and me).

Best wishes for a long, happy life together.

Yours sincerely

Template 18

Thanking for a gift or other kindness

Dear

I really enjoyed dinner at your place last Saturday night. You have lots of interesting friends! Jamey and I, in fact, have talked have lots of interesting friends! Jamey and I, in fact, have talked about getting together for lunch sometime. We seem to have a lot in common.

Thanks so much for including me. You've really helped to make my adjustment to a new town a little easier.

Yours sincerely

Template 2

Thanking for a gift or other kindness

Dear

Your generous £100 gift was so thoughtful. As you suggested, Jim and I do need a lot of things to set up our new household, and your gift will certainly come in handy, (We're thinking it will give us a good start on some pots and pans.')

Give us a good start on some pots and pans!) "Okay, I know what you're thinking: "What's Edie going to do cook!

Once we have a functioning kitchen, we would very much like the two of you to join us for a nice me meal. I promise to let Jim do the cooking.

Yours sincerely

Template 19

Sending get-well wishes for an illness or accident

Dear

I was so sorry to hear about Uncle Rob's recent hospitalization. Mother told me that he would need solid bed rest for several weeks. I bet he's going crazy having to stay put. Aunt Syl, I happen to have a little time on my hands lately, so if you 'll accept this, I'd like to come by next week to help out in any way I can. (I'll even do some cooking, if you can stand it.)

Would that be all right? I 'll call you before / come by. You and Uncle Rob have always looked out for me, and I'd very much like the opportunity to return the favour.

I love you both,

Template 2

Sending get-well wishes for an illness or accident

Dear

I was shocked to hear from Jean 7'homas about your last week. But I'm thn7led you'll fully recover in time Jean mentioned that I might be allowed to visit you in a few days, so plan on seeing me one day next week after work.

Please know that I am thinking of you and praying for your speedy and complete recovery.

I miss you here

Template 20

Declining an invitation

Dear

What wonderful news! I know you and Andrew have dated for quite some time, and I'm thrilled to see the two of you taking quite some time, and I'm thrilled to see the two of you taking that Mr. Jolson and I have been planning a once-in-a-lifetime to Europe for months.

Unfortunately, our trip means we will be of the country on May 16. We're so sorry we wont be able to attend you special event. Please accept our wishes for a wonderful day and a long life together.

The enclosed check is to help with anything you need, as you will begin your life together.

Kind regards

Template 2

Declining an invitation

Dear

How tempting was your offer to spend the weekend watching the leaves turn! I could sure use a nice "wilderness" geta way.

That weekend is a particularly busy one for us. I've volunteered to chaperone an outing with Edie's Girl Scout troop, and it's Eric's weekend for the Resins. Looks like will have to take a rain check.

Maybe we can plan for another weekend or even have you visit us up here. We can't offer much in the way of trees, but I'd sure enjoy seeing you guys. I 'Il call you after our busy weekend, okay?

Love to you all

Template 21

Delivering bad news with apology

Dear

I know you're wondering why I haven 'I returned your drill. It's a bit of a long story, but if you 'll bear with me, I 'll explain.

I used the drill to install the new doors, which really look fantastic, by the way. Then another project came up: installing shelves in our garage. Elaine has begged me for shelves to help contain some of the clatter out there, so I took the opportunity to contain some of the clutter out there, so I took the opportunity take on that project too.

Well, that project went fine, and I used the new shelves right away, to temporarily store your drill alongside my own electric equipment which I had been storing in the basement.

To make a long story short, the garage door was inadvertently   [left open one afternoon about two weeks ago, and well, buddy, I 'm afraid your dn7l was stolen along with about £500 of my own equipment.

I'm really sorry we were so careless. And I also apologize for not calling you when it happened; / didn't realize until I got your not calling you when it happened; I didn't realize until I will replace your drill, of course; I just haven't had the chance to get out to get one. Now that I know you need you need it immediately, I 'll get it to you by the end of the week.

Thanks for your understanding

Template 22

Event Conference Invitation

Institute of Secretaries

London House, West Street, London SW1

Telephone 020 8987

2432Email communication 020 8987 2556

Dear

2090 SECRETARIES CONFERENCE, 8/9 OCTOBER 2090

As a valued member of the Institute of Secretaries, I have pleasure in inviting you to attend our special conference to be held at the Savoy Hotel, London on Tuesday/Wednesday 8/9 October 2004.

This intensive, practical conference for professional secretaries aims to:

- Increase your managerial and office productivity
- bring you up to date with the latest technology and techniques
- enable networking with other secretaries

The seminar is power-packed with a distinguished panel of professional speakers who will give expert advice on many useful topics. A Software me is enclosed giving full details of this seminar which I know you will not want to / miss.

If you would like to join us please complete the enclosed registration form and return it to me before 30 June with your fee of 50 per person.

I look forward to seeing you again at this exciting conference.

Yours sincerely

Conference Secretary

Encs

Template 23

Requesting information

Dear

I'm writing to you for information on getting involved with the United Church Federation's anti-violence activities.

Your organization is becoming quite well-known for its nondenominational approach to bringing the power of prayer to sites of violent crime. I would very much like to be a part of such an effort.

Could you please tell me how I might become a participant in your Immediate Action Prayer Chain? I can be reached at 123-6758.

Thank you for your leadership of such powerful action against violence in our community. I look forward to hearing from you so that I may join you in your work.

Sincerely

Template 24

Soliciting participation in an activity

Dear

Please consider taking an active part in bettering our environment by participating in a new neighbourhood, recycling Software.

Recycling your steel and aluminium cans, plastic bottles and milk jugs, and newspapers is easy and goes a long way to protecting our environment. Recycling reduces landfill waste, air pollution caused by incinerator fumes, and even poor ground water quality.

If you're willing to give recycling a try, you need to do nothing. Within the next week you will receive a storage tub and complete guidelines on how the Software works. Our neighbourhood association will cover your cost for the first six months of service. After that (should you decide to continue with the Software), the cost is minimal: typically £3 to £5 per month.

If you prefer not to participate in the Software, please call our neighbourhood association office (555-2312), and someone will gladly pick up your storage tub.

Thanks for considering recycling. We on the recycling, committee feel certain you'll find it one of the easiest ways you can help us all to protect our environment.

Yours sincerely

Template 24

Persuading someone to accept a leadership position

Dear

Would you consider heading up a Crime Watch effort on our block?

Several neighbours including Joan Kern, Tim Allison, Merry Merrick, and I thought you would be perfect in this role; and we'd be thrilled to help by hosting meetings, providing refreshments, or doing whatever needs to be done.

You would be our neighbourhood's primary contact with our You would be our neighbourhood's primary contact with our Police Department representative, Officer Rap St. John. In a brief conversation I had with him, Officer St. Merry told me that getting a Crime Watch group going doesn't take much effort: planning quarterly meetings, leading those meetings, and keeping neighbours in touch with one another seems to be the gist of it.

We thought you would be perfect for the role because everyone knows you, you're a devoted neighbour to so many of us, and your home office keeps you around the neighbourhood a little more often than the rest of us.

Would you be willing to consider taking on this role? I'll call you next week-after you've had some time to think about it-to find out what you're you're thinking, and you're also welcome to call Office St. Joan directly for more information's about what would be involved. He's at the 48th Precinct, phone 549-5454.

We've all talked about the need for this in the past; we all agree it's important. Will you help us make it a reality?

We'd all owe you one!

Yours sincerely

Template 25

Confirming others' participation in an activity

Dear

The time has come to get our new soup kitchen off the ground! If you're receiving this letter, you've expressed an interest in the past in helping out with this important community outreach project. Well, it's time!

Just how you can get involved, and how much time you give, is completely up to you. Here are a few possibilities:

- Help prepare food (two-hour shifts).
- Help serve food (two-hour shifts),' Help to pick up supplies or food (one- to three-hour.
- Help in set-up or clean-up (one- and two-hour shifts).
- Help in promoting the kitchen (time varies by activity).

The kitchen is scheduled to serve its first weekly meal on May 3. Please call or sign up at the church to volunteer your time beginning Monday, March 29. (Church office phone is 655-8287.) Many activities need to happen prior to May 1,the sooner you can volunteer with something, the better our opening should be!

Thank you, again, for expressing interest in helping to get our new kitchen rolling!

In gratitude

Template 26

Agreeing to participate in an activity

Dear

I received your notice about the East Creek clean-up on June 27, and I'd be happy to participate. I do have a few questions I'd like to ask, however.

I have an 8 a.m. commitment to work out with a friend. I have an 8 a.m. commitment to work out with a friend. Could 1 join the group shortly after 9 a.m.?

. Should I bring garbage bags, shovels, and so on, or do you expect to have plenty?

Could you give me a quick call with this information sometime before the clean-up? I'd appreciate it. My home number is 555-6574. (Leave a message during the day if you'd like.)

I'll see you at the clean-up!

Yours sincerely

Template 27

Refusing a request to serve or contribute

Dear

I'm afraid I won't be able to help out with the soup kitchen as I had hoped.

Since I first expressed interest in helping out with the kitchen, my time has become significantly more limited. In January, I decided to return to school part-time; getting back into a routine of studying, attending classes at night, and continuing to work full-time is proving more difficult than I had expected.

If my schedule lightens up at all, I promise to call you. I really would like to help out with a cause I believe can make a real difference to the community. Best of luck in getting the soup kitchen off the ground!

Yours truly

Template 28

Thanking others for their contributions or time

Dear

Well, our first meeting was a hit! I can't believe how many people showed up, and we have you to thank for such a great turnout.

Your idea to deliver "personal invitation" postcards was brilliant. Thanks for all the work you did to design a card, print cards up, and deliver them.

The real benefit to getting in our neighbours to show up, of course, is the ability we have now to spread the work around! I plan to make some calls later this month to make sure we don't lose our momentum, so let me know what role you'd like to take from here, okay?

Thanks, again, for helping to get things off to such a great start!

Sincerely

Template 29

Acknowledging a refusal to serve or contribute

Dear

Thanks for your note explaining your inability right now to help out with the soup kitchen.

I wish you could be involved, of course, but I do understand, and I sincerely appreciate your letting me know so I can better plan for the volunteers we need.

You're always welcome, of course, to become more involved. We will continue to need volunteers well into the future, so please let me know if your schedule allows you to participate.

Yours sincerely

Template 30

Refusing a leadership role

Dear

Thank you for having the confidence in me to suggest that I Lead a North Side recruitment effort for the United Church lead a North Side recruitment effort for the United Church Federation's anti-violence activities. As you know from my regular involvement in the United Church Federation's work, your mission is one I firmly believe in and would like to support in any way I can.

I worry, however, that orchestrating a recruitment effort will take my time and effort away from the prayer work itself. To be completely honest with both you and myself, I'm drawn more to the work and also feel I would not be particularly good at heading up such an effort.

I worry, however, that orchestrating a recruitment effort will take my time and effort away from the prayer work itself. To be completely honest with both you and myself, I'm drawn more to the work and also feel I would not be particularly good at heading up such an effort.

So while I'll be happy to participate in the recruitment effort if I can, I do not feel I should head it up.

Thanks for your understanding of my decision. I do have someone else in mind who I feel would be both willing and better-suited to lead the recruitment effort. J'Il call you within the week to share my thoughts with you.

Warmest regards

Template 31

Resigning a leadership role

Dear All

Thanks, everyone, for your willingness to make our block a little safer with Crime Watch.

My role as coordinator over the last six months has been exhausting but completely rewarding. Thank you for helping exhausting but completely rewarding. Thank you for helping me to get such an important effort rolling for our block.

With the birth of my second child just three months away, I feel the time has come for me to pass the role of coordinator along to someone else. A new-born and a toddler are all I feel I'll be able to manage by March, and I'm afraid Crime Watch might receive short shrift if I continue as coordinator.

So effective January 31, I'll be resigning as your Crime Watch coordinator.

Please, if you're willing to discuss taking on this role January 31, or would simply like more information about what it involves, please call me (654-8214) before our January meeting.

So many people have devoted just as much time as I have in getting Crime Watch going on our block that I feel certain we can keep the momentum going. If you're moved to consider taking on the coordinator role, please do. I can assure you you'll get all the help you need to be successful.

Sincerely yours

Template 32

Personal greeting

Dear

I am sorry not to have replied sooner to your letter of 25 October regarding the book English d Commercial Correspondence. My Export Director is in Lebanon and Syria on business; as I am dealing with his work as we did as my own I am afraid my correspondence has fallen behind.

Whether this book should be published in hardback or paperback is a decision I must leave to my Editorial Director, Tracie James, to whom I have passed on your letter. No doubt she will be writing to you very soon.

I hope you are keeping well.

With best wishes

Yours sincerely

Template 33

Explaining delayed reply

Dear

I am sorry we cannot send you immediately the collection and price list ! requested in your letter of 13 March as we are presently out of stock.

Supplies are expected from our printers in 2 weeks' time; as soon as they are

Received, we will send a copy to you.

Yours sincerely

Template 34

A visitor from abroad

Dear

I was pleased to receive your letter of 24 April and to learn that your colleague, Mr Merry Gelling, is making plans to visit England in July. We shall be pleased to welcome him and to do all we can to make his visit enjoyable and successful.

I understand this will be Mr Gelling's first visit to England, and am sure h will wish to see some of our principal places of interest. Suitable Software is something we can discuss when he arrives. I would be pleased to introduce him to several firms with which he may like to do business.

When the date of Mr Gelling's visit is settled please let me know his arrival I will arrange to meet him at the airport and drive him to his hotel He be assured of a warm welcome.

Sincerely

Template 35

Apology for poor service

Dear

You for your letter of 12 June regarding the poor service you received

When you visited our store recently.

The incident was most unlike our usual high standards of service and courtesy. The member of staff who was rude to you has been reprimanded; he also expresses his regret.

I am enclosing a gift voucher for 20 which you may use at any Omega store. If I be of any further assistance to you please do not hesitate to contact me.

With my apologies once again.

Yours sincerely

Template 36

Apology for cancelling an appointment

Dear

I am so sorry that I had to cancel our meeting yesterday at such short notice. As my secretary explained to you I am afraid an urgent matter came up which I had to deal with immediately.

I understand our appointment has been rearranged for next Tuesday 12 May at 11.30.

Perhaps we can extend our meeting over lunch.

Yours sincerely

Template 37

Regretting an oversight

Dear

I was very concerned when I received your letter of yesterday stating that the central heating system in your home has not been completed by the date promised.

On referring to our earlier correspondence I find that I had mistaken the date for completion. The fault is entirely mine and I deeply regret that it should have occurred.

I realise the inconvenience which my oversight must be causing you and will do everything possible to avoid any further delay.

I have already given instructions for this work to take first priority; our engineers will be placed on overtime to complete the work. These arrangements should ensure that the work is completed by next weekend.

My apologies once again for the inconvenience caused.

Yours sincerely

Template 38

Conveying unwelcome news

Dear

It was good of you to let me see your manuscript on English for Business I Collected. I read it with interest and was impressed by the careful and thorough way in which you have treated the subject, I particularity like the clear and concise style of writing,

Had we not recently published Practical English by Freda Leonard, a book that

Covers very similar ground, I would have been happy to accept your manuscript

For publication then the circumstances, I am unable to do so and am returning your manuscript with this letter.

I am sorry to have to disappoint you.

Yours sincerely

Template 39

LETTER of thanks

Dear

Thank you for your letter of 30 March returning the draft of the collection we propose to send to our customers.

I am very grateful for the trouble you have taken to examine the draft and comment on it in such detail. Your suggestions will be very helpful.

I realise the value of time to a busy person like you and this makes me all the appreciative of the time you have so generously given.

Yours sincerely

Template 40

Formal letter of congratulation on a promotion

Dear

I would like to convey my warm congratulations on your appointment to the   Board of Fashion Industries Ltd.

Fellow directors and I are delighted that the many years of service you have given to your company should at last have been rewarded in this way.

We all join in sending you our very best wishes for the future.

Yours sincerely

Perfect Phrases for Business LETTER

Effective orientation office

1. How do new employees find out how things workaround here?
2. If you were new here and a little lost, which employee would you talk to?
3. Everyone is so busy that I haven't gotten a detailed orientation* Are there resources I can use to get my bearings?
4. Looking for someone to take me under his or her wing
5. I have a list of information that was provided to me. Do you see any gaps or things I ought to know that aren't listed?
6. When you need help figuring out how things work, what person do you talk to? Sometimes I feel lost.
7. I don't know, but I'II find out
8. That's a new one for me, Do you have suggestions about how l can find the answer for you?
9. I haven't encountered that yet. Would you like for find out for you? I'II be glad to look that up for you. Where should look first?
10. That's a new one for me. ls there someone with experience I can ask?
11. How would you do this if you were l?

12. I'm trying to learn how you do it here. Can you steer me in right direction?

13. Before ! out a lot of time into this, will you take a look to sure I'm on the right track?

14. My bad. My lesson,

15. This what I would call a learning experience.

16. I'd like to establish some basic communication guidelines so our messages will be more efficient and things run more smoothly.

17. I've found that when my managers and l agree on how we're going to communicate, things flow better.

18. We all have different ideas of what good communication l like to get us on the same page about what It Is for us.

19. If something I say isn't clear, please Insist I clarify.

20. I'm sensitive, but I do want to know if something I say or do Isn't right, Promise you'll tell me?

Perfect Lines, To Establish Mission

1. What would a perfect world look like where everyone benefited from what we do?
2. Fill in the blank: Imagine a world where ...
3. Why are we important?
4. What makes us unique?
5. What's our greatest contribution to the (world, company)?
6. What values feed our mission and vision?
7. What values do we share?
8. Matters most: quality, service, or profit?
9. What do you like about our products (services)?
10. What would make you like our products ?
11. What makes work worth doing for you?
12. Two people you admire and two qualities each embody.
13. What values would you be willing to die for?
14. What does it mean to work here?
15. Do you want it to mean?
16. What qualities do you believe should drive our business?
17. This initiative aligns with our mission because
18. I admire your commitment to our (mission, vision, values).

19. Milestone shows a deep commitment to (mission, vision, values).

20. Let's use our (mission, vision, values) to decide this.

Delegation

1. There is an opportunity here for you to …

2. This project needs to be done right. That's why I'm bringing it to you.

3. I'm asking you to do this because I know I can trust you.

4. I know how busy you are. However, I will have a request.

5. I need your help.

6. What this project means to you is … .

7. I'll make sure my manager knows you made a difference when I really needed you.

8. I need (item) by (date) because .

9. I have written out instructions. Let's go over them together.

10. The deadline is (date), the quality specifications are (specs), and the budget is (budget).

11. Of these three, the priority in this project is (priority)

12. An example of what it will look like is (example).

13. What questions do you have off the bat?

14. Did leave out?

15. What would you like reviewed?

16. Let me make sure my instructions are clear. What is your understanding of what I told you?

17. What questions remain?

18. Ideas do you have about (aspect of job)?

19. Do you see a better way of doing this?

20. What do you see as a challenge here?

21. Hey, I like the way you (observation).

22. The way, great job on (item).

23. Don't know how you do that, but I'm sure glad you do!

24. Are you getting the help you need?

25. Is there anything you want me to know?

Investigate a Complaint

1. I need to talk with you about something you may have seen or heard.

2. You have been identified as a witness for something that happened.

3. What did you see or hear? When and where did this take place? Did you tell anyone about it?

4. Did (the employee who complained) say anything what happened?

5. Did (the accused employee) say anything about the incident?

6. Have you witnessed other incidents between (the employee who complained) and (the accused employee)?
7. Have you heard these issues discussed in the workplace?
8. When, and by whom?
9. Have you ever had problems with (the employee who complained) or (the accused employee)?
10. Did you and the (complaining, accused) employee (the area of work the complaint is about, for example, invoices, weapons, taking equipment home)?
11. Did you see an incident between (the accused employee) and (the employee who complained) last week?
12. What have you heard that leads you to that conclusion?
13. Anyone else there when that happened?
14. Did anyone else receive documentation?
15. I've heard differently. Do you think the allegations I have are invented? Why?
16. Why do you think others remember it differently?
17. I expect this discussion to be kept confidential.
18. Reflect on what goals you want to target for the next review period.
19. I would like to meet with you for a performance evaluation (date, time). In the meeting I will review your performance over the past (time frame). I invite you to review my performance as your manager.

Make Your Manager Look Good if are good!

1. Whatever he does, you can be sure he will give it 100 percent.
2. Will love working with her! She's the best!
3. He's my mentor, and I couldn't have a better one!
4. You're going to be so pleased with this proposal. [Manager's name] spent a lot of time on getting all the Information you will need.
5. I couldn't have a better manager.
6. I have learned so much, working with him.
7. I really like working with her. She's amazing.
8. I've been working with Manager's name] for [time span now, and I keep discovering more to like and admire. For example, she's very innovative.
9. You aware that the person you're criticizing so harshly Is my employer, and we're a team?
10. That's not the usual practice in this office, Let me take the Information and see what happened so we can correct lt.
11. I hear what you're saying, and I'm sorry for the hassle. I'll apologize for the department.
12. I'm glad you're sharing this, is how we Improve.
13. I'm sorry that happened. The best way to approach her ls (to approach}.
14. I am a professional, and I do expect to be treated as one.
15. I respect your professionalism, and I ask you to respect mine,

PROFESSIONAL ENGLISH WRITING

Email Vocabulary:

The following list has synonyms, which project more or variety to your business writing.

Need – require
Buy – purchase, procure
Very – particularly
Give me – provide me with
Just – merely
Help – assist
Sell – supply

REPORTING

People said it was.
People mentioned that it was…
People stated that it was….
People regarded it was…
People claimed that it was…
Considered it was to be…
People rated ….as being.*.
By contrast , it was cited that…
The bar chart indicates a survey on ..on factors.
Whereas… there are contrasting results…

DESCRIBING THE PROCEDURE

The procedure for… is as follows.
In order to …the following process takes place.
First of all…

Then...
After that...
At the next stage . . .
This is done by...
Finally...
This completes the procedure.

OTHER USEFUL PHRASES TO REPORT

In all cases there was an increase in..*
By far.. ,,
This figure had more than doubled...
Second greatest volume of..
An increase of approximately...
Showed significant rises were...
At the lower end of the scale...
The chart confirms the increased popularity of..
The trend was reversed...
The trend confirmed...
Ate was at its highest but then it started to decrease.

USEFUL PHRASES FOR REPORTS AND PROPOSALS

If you consider... you could be convinced by an favour of.,.,
But you have to think about another aspect of the problem...
I do not feel this is a direct cause of...
Of course it goes without saying that...
Of course it goes without saying that...
There has been a growing body of opinion that..
There has been a growing body of opinion that..
The situation can be addressed by adopting the methods mentioned above.,.
While I admit that.... I would argue that...
One approach would be...
A second possibility would be to...

Obviously,...However,
This suggests that..
In addition,..
To sum up...
In fact..
I tend to disagree..
Overall,...
I am unconvinced by..
Overall,.
In the final analysis.,.
Ultimately
To conclude
In conclusion...
On the other hand.,.
There is no doubt that...
This could involve...

EXPRESSING VIEWS

I would argue that*..
I firmly believe that...
It seems to me that..
I tend to think that...
People argue that...
Some people think ...
Many people feel that...
In my experience...
It is undoubtedly true that..
It is certainly true that....

REFUTING AN ARGUMENT

I am unconvinced that...
I don not believe that..

It I hard to accept that…
It is unjustifiable to say that…
There is little evidence to support that…

PROVIDING SUPPORT

For example,..
For instance,…
Indeed,. . .
In fact,. . .
Course,. …
It can be generally observed that…
Statistics demonstrate…
Statistics demonstrate…
If this is/were the case…Firstly,. . .
Naturally,. . –
In my experience…
Let me illustrate…

DEFINING/EXPLAINING

I would argue that.
By this I mean…
In other words..
This is to say…
To be more precise..
Here I am referring to…

USE SPARINGLY

First/second, etc…
In addition….
Moreover..
Furthermore,…
Nevertheless/nonetheless…

On the hand…
Besides…
Consequently…
In contrast…
In comparison. .

USE MODERATELY

While…
Meanwhile…
Although…
In spite of…/ Despite the fact that…
Though…
As a result…
However…
Since. . .
Similarly. ,
Thus…
In turn

OTHER USEFUL PHRASES

My response to this argument depend on what is meant by…
There is surely a difference between…. And….
I intend to illustrate how some of these differences are significant to the argument put forward.,
However, whilst I agree that… I am less convinced that…
I certainly believe that…
One of the main arguments in favour of….is
In other words…
Admittedly, in some ways…
Surely,. .
Arguably..
Either way…

In any case...
The most important point is that...
Another point is that.
Of crucial importance , in my opinion, is...
The most important point is that
Another point is that...
Of crucial importance ,in my opinion, is...
There is , however, another possible way of defining.
Therefore...
Is no doubt that...
One approach would be..
However, it is possible to tackle this serious issue in a number ways.
A second possibility would be to...
..this could involve...
Supporters of...argue that...On the other hand it cannot be denied that...
Opponents of... point out that ... and argue that...
People feel that this is unacceptable because...

INTRODUCING A FALSE ARGUMENT

It could be argued that...
Some people would argue that...
There is also the idea implicit in the statement that...
It is often suggested that...

DEMOLISHING A FALSE ARGUMENT

This is partly true, but...
To a certain limited extant, there is some truth in this...
However, the implication that... is oversimplification.
This argument has certain specific logic, but...

PROPOSING A CORRECT ARGUMENT

It is clear that....
The real situation...
Obviously...
On the contrary...
It is therefore quite wrong to suggest

MEETINGS TERMINOLOGY

Ad boc: from Latin, meaning 'for the purpose of', as for example when a sub-is set up specially to organise a works outing.
Adjourn: to hold a meeting over until a later date.
Adopt minutes: minutes are 'adopted' when accepted by members and signed up by the Chair.
Acceptance: every offer has to be accepted to create a contract.
Appropriation: the act of allocating to a contract the specific are to be transferred.
Advisory: providing advice or suggestion, not taking action.
Agenda: a schedule of items drawn up for discussion at a meeting.
AGM: Annual General Meeting: all members are usually attend.
Apologies: excuses given in advance for inability to attend meeting.
Articles of Association: rules required by Company law which govern a com-pany's activities.
Attendance list: in some committees a list is passed round to be signed as a record of attendance.
Bye-Iaws: rules regulating an organisation's activities.
Casting vote: by convention, some committee chairmen may use a 'casting vote' to reach a decision, if votes are equally divided.
Chairwoman: leader or person give authority to conduct a meeting.
Chairwoman agenda: based upon the committee agenda, but containing notes.
Common law: the inherent law that was applied in common to the rules and customs that existed. It became an expression to be used to distinguish between those rules and the rules of equity, and from there

it has become extended to distinguish between the unwritten laws and the Acts passed by Parliament.

Consideration: some right, interest, profit or benefit given, or some forbearance, detriment, loss or responsibility given, suffered, or undertaken. Every contract must either be supported by consideration or be made under seal.

Committee: a group of people usually elected or appointed who meet to con-duct agreed business and report to a senior body.

Convene: to call a meeting.

Decision: resolution minutes are sometimes called 'decision minutes'.

Executive: having the power to act upon taken decisions.

Extraordinary meeting: a meeting called for all members to discuss a serious issue affecting all is called an Extraordinary General Meeting; otherwise a non-routine meeting called for a specific purpose.

Ex officio: given powers or rights by reason of office.

Appendix

USEFUL WEBSITES

Everyone who writes needs to use a dictionary or thesaurus from time to time or at least they should. If you rry doing a search on any search engine for 'dictionary' you will see that there are actually hundreds and hundreds of different sites.

Here are my tips for some interesting and useful online dictionaries and language resources on the Internet:

www.xrefer.com

Xrefer's free site contains encyclopaedias, dictionaries, thesauri and books of quotations from the world's leading publishers. All cross-references, all in one place, providing a single information source.

www.yourdictionary.com/

claims to be the most comprehensive and authoritative portal for language and language-related products and services on the Internet, with than 1800 dictionaries for over 250 languages.

www.oed,com/

English Dictionary

An expensive subscription service, but some background documents and a Word of the Day are free.

www.plainenglish.com

Plain English Campaign

This is an independent pressure group fighting for public information to be in plain English. The site includes useful examples of what is and what is not 'plain English', free guides and much more.

www.worldwidewords.org

Wide Words

This is a fascinating list of English words and phrases, giving not only their but how they came about.

www.foreignword.com

This is a link to hundreds of online dictionaries and translation engines, and thousands of specialised glossaries.

www.thesaurus.com

Roget's Thesaurus

An online version of Roget's Thesaurus of English words and phrases.

www.dictionary.com

An online dictionary and thesaurus.

www.ask.elibrary.com

A comprehensive digital archive for information seekers.

www.nexislexis

Legal and Business LETTER Templates, Tools and Research.

LEGAL IMPLICATIONS OF LETTER

English law has full-fledged from many different seeds. Unlike the majority of the laws in continental Europe, very little of our law is written down. 'Common Law', as we call it, is a fundamental law which is enforced in used to be called the common law courts. It was the recognition by those courts of the principles, customs and rules of conduct which used to observe.

The law of defamation has grown up in this way. When something said about a person, which would tend to make others think badly of him, that is defamation. If it is in a permanent form, such as a letter, it is a libel. If it is spoken, it is a slander. In early days libel was a matter for the Churchly was punished with an award of damages, nevertheless no loss could be shown, Slander was a matter for the common law courts which (except where the slander suggested a criminal would only give damages on proof of loss. So when writing a letter, thought must be given to what is being said lest someone can say they have been libelled. To constitute a libel needs three things. A wrongful statement that tend to disparage someone; 'publication' of that statement to some third party (publication means intentionally communicating the information); and, lastly, the absence of any form of privileged occasion.

When you are asked to give a reference for an ex-employee, there is an obligation on you as described as. . That obligation creates a privilege that entities you to say what you really think, even though it may be defamatory of the ex-employee. The privilege can, though, be lost if you say what you say maliciously. That means that you are something with an improper motive: if, for example, you deliberately trying to cause injury and prevent his being employed. In other cases the privilege is less likely to occur. Being a libel, anyone so defamed can bring an action without having to prove the damage he has suffered. What is more, if the court thinks that the libel was a particularly grave matter, it can award exemplary damages. That means large sums.

COPYRIGHT

When someone has created some work, a piece of writing, a painting, a tune, some fruit of his brain, he is entitled to claim that it is his and to make anyone who uses it pay for the privilege. The LETTER set out in this book, for example, are in origin the subject of a claim for copyright. The right to reproduce the work may be implied from the way in which the work has been made available; these LETTER, or the precedent books in a lawyer's office, have been made available and individually (not as a collection) can be freely used without acknowledgement of their authorship. Not everything is like that. If you write a letter and enclose with it a copy of a plan, the copyright in the plan belongs to the architect who drew it, and he could object and insist that he be paid for the use of his plan.

If you write to someone with a map showing the way to your office, if the map was a copy of an ordnance survey sheet, you need a licence from the Ordnance Survey Department for the eService. Any quotation from a copyright work should acknowledge the source of the work and only be made with permission of the author. These principles just as much to the words of a letter as they do to a book. The difference is that a letter has such a limited number of readers, and the author has no thought of personal gain, so that any possibility of claim being made can, in practice, be ignored.

USE IN LITIGATION

The most important part of the conduct of any proceedings is the process which lawyers call 'discovery'. This is a process which is part of all court proceedings in those parts of the world which use the common law system. Basically that means the whole of what used to be the British Empire and it includes the United States of America, Canada and Australia. Some (especially the United States) have wider ranging powers of discovery than we do here. All insist that all documents, including LETTER, which have any relevance to the case must be disclosed, You must say, not merely those that you have, but also those which have at any time been in your 'possession or power'. You can be made to swear on oath to the completeness of the list that you make. Any letter that is written which may be read out in court must be very thought about. It will be read in context and out of context. The language used will be considered critically and if it bears more than possible meaning, the meaning most unfavourable to you will be possible meaning, the meaning most unfavourable to you whom against trying to 'do it yourself'.

*********THE END ******

Printed in Great Britain
by Amazon